From Roanoke to Raleigh

From Roanoke to Raleigh

Freemasonry in North Carolina, 1730-1800

RIC BERMAN

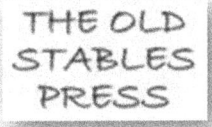

• Oxfordshire •

Copyright © 2018 Ric Berman
The right of Richard Berman to be identified as the author of this work has been asserted in accordance with the Copyright, Designs and Patents Act, 1988.

First published 2018 in Great Britain
The Old Stables Press, Goring Heath, Oxfordshire RG8 7RT
theoldstablespress@gmail.com

All rights reserved. Except for the quotation of short passages for the purposes of criticism and review, no part of this publication may be reproduced, stored in a retrieval system, or transmitted in any form or by any means without the prior permission of the author.

Unless specified otherwise, images and illustrations are copyright © Grand Lodge of A.F. and A.M. of North Carolina or copyright © UGLE Library & Museum of Freemasonry and used with their kind permission. The *Cornerstone Plate* is within the Image Collection, #P0004, of the North Carolina Collection Photographic Archives, The Wilson Library, University of North Carolina at Chapel Hill, and used with their permission.

Cover Image: Portrait of Joseph Montfort, 'Provincial Grand Master of and for America', by Nathaniel Dance-Holland, RA, *c.*1771, reproduced by kind permission of Theo Johns Fine Art Limited.

British Library Cataloguing in Publication Data
A CIP catalogue record for this book is available from the British Library

Library of Congress Cataloguing-in-Publication Data
Berman, Ric
From Roanoke to Raleigh: Freemasonry in North Carolina, 1730-1800/Ric Berman
p. cm.
Includes biographical references.

ISBN: 099575683X
ISBN-13: 9780995756830

Freemasonry - History - 18th century.
America – History - 18th century.
England – History - 18th century.
Ireland – History - 18th century.
I. Title

For Bernard Barker
Emeritus Professor of Education, University of Leicester
and one time
Assistant Master (History)
Haberdashers' Aske's School, Elstree

Other titles by the author

The Foundations of Modern Freemasonry –
The Grand Architects: Political Change and the
Scientific Enlightenment, 1714-1740

Schism: the Battle that Forged Freemasonry

Loyalists & Malcontents:
Freemasonry & Revolution in the Deep South

Loyalists & Malcontents:
Freemasonry & Revolution in South Carolina & Georgia
Revised, Illustrated 2nd edition

The Prestonian Lecture:
Foundations - new light on the formation and early years of
The Grand Lodge of England

Espionage, Diplomacy & the Lodge -
Charles Delafaye and The Secret Department of the Post Office

Contents

Acknowledgments · xii
Abbreviations · xiii
Foreword · xvii
    The Lodge at Savannah · xix
    Solomon's Lodge, Charleston · xxi
    The Beginnings of Freemasonry in North Carolina · · · · · · · · · · · · · xxiii
An Introduction to Carolina · 1
    The Carolina Charter · 1
    The Fundamental Constitutions of Carolina · 4
    Slavery · 5
    Migration · 7
    Governance, Ownership and Control · 8
    It's Always the Economy… · 12
    'To all ingenious and industrious persons … there is a New Plantation' · · · · 20
    Domestic Disunion · 23
Chapter One: Freemasonry in North Carolina · 26
    North Carolina's first two Masonic Governors · · · · · · · · · · · · · · · · · · · 26
Chapter Two: London Calling · 50
    Martin Bladen and the Board of Trade · 50
    Smith and Rice in North Carolina · 62
Chapter Three: Johnston, Dobbs and the Land Grabbers · · · · · · · · · · · · · · · 64
    Gabriel Johnston · 64
    Henry McCulloh · 67
    Eleazer Allen · 82
    Arthur Dobbs · 84
Chapter Four: Benjamin Smith · 93
    The First Provincial Grand Master of North and South Carolina · · · · · · 93
Chapter Five: Freemasonry at Cape Fear · 100
    Cornelius Harnett Jr. and Wilmington Town · · · · · · · · · · · · · · · · · · · 100
    St John's Lodge · 102

Chapter Six: Joseph Montfort · 108
    Joseph Montfort - 'Grand Master of and for America' · · · · · · · · · · · · · 108
    The Lodge at Halifax · 117
    A New English Charter · 120
    Deputed as Provincial Grand Master · 123
    Reflections · 131
Chapter Seven: The Montfort Lodges · 134
    St John's Lodge, New Bern · 135
    St John's Lodge, Kingston · 146
    Dornoch Lodge, Bute County · 156
    Royal Edwin Lodge, Windsor · 159
    Royal William Lodge, Winton · 164
    Unanimity Lodge, Edenton · 167
Chapter Eight: 'Over the Hills and Far Away' · · · · · · · · · · · · · · · · · · 172
    The Irish in Pennsylvania and North Carolina · · · · · · · · · · · · · · · · 172
    The London Irish · 175
    Antients Freemasonry · 176
    Antients Freemasons · 179
    The Antients Grand Lodge · 180
    Freemasonry on the American Frontier · 182
Chapter Nine: Governor Tryon and the Battle of the Alamance · · · · · · · · 186
    The Regulator Movement · 186
    William Tryon · 193
Chapter Ten: Irish, Antients and other early North Carolina Lodges · · · · · · 204
    Old Cone Lodge, Salisbury · 204
    Phalanx Lodge, Charlotte · 216
    The First Lodge in Pitt County · 218
    Union Lodge, later Phoenix Lodge No. 8, Fayetteville · · · · · · · · · · 221
    Blandford-Bute Lodge, Bute County, later Warren County · · · · · · · · 225

Chapter Eleven: Revolution and Beyond · 232
    Towards a new Grand Lodge · 232
    The First Grand Masters · 240
Chapter Twelve: A Masonic Education? · 255
    The University of North Carolina · 255
Afterword · 267
Appendices · 273
Appendix One · 274
    'Moderns' Provincial Grand Masters in North America · · · · · · · · · · · · 274
Appendix Two · 276
    Royal White Hart Lodge, Halifax · 276
Appendix Three · 278
    Trustees of the University of North Carolina, 1789-95 · · · · · · · · · · · · 278
Appendix Four · 281
    American Military Lodges during the War of Independence · · · · · · · · 281
Appendix Five · 283
    Members of the Rose Tavern Lodge · 283
Appendix Six · 285
    The Will of William Herritage · 285
Appendix Seven · 293
    Phoenix Lodge No. 8 · 293
Selected Bibliography · 295

Acknowledgments

The primary sources used to research this work in America were made available principally from the Special Collections at the Wilson and University Libraries at the University of North Carolina at Chapel Hill, and from the archives of the Grand Lodge of North Carolina at Raleigh and its now constituent lodges across North Carolina. Thank you for providing access and for your unstinting assistance. The research in North Carolina was funded in part by Archie K. Davis Fellowships in 2016 and 2017, and my sincere thanks are extended to the Chairman, Secretary, Treasurer and Board of the North Caroliniana Society.

Primary material in relation to Britain and Ireland was obtained from a multitude of sources and I would like to acknowledge the support of the Department of History, Philosophy and Religion at Oxford Brookes University, and the librarians and archivists at the British Library, the Institute of Historical Research, the University Library at the University of Cambridge, the Bodleian Libraries at the University of Oxford, and the Library and Museum of Freemasonry at the United Grand Lodge of England, Great Queen Street, London, where I have the honour to be a trustee.

Many people in the United States and United Kingdom have given their time to support this project and I should give special mention and thanks to the officers of the Grand Lodge of North Carolina and, in particular, Bryant Webster, Gene Cobb, Speed Hallman, Walton Clapp III, Steven Campbell and Jonathan Underwood. It has been a pleasure to get to know you and to break bread together.

Ric Berman
February, 2018
Oxfordshire

Abbreviations

1723 *Constitutions*	James Anderson, *The Constitutions of the Freemasons* (London: John Senex & John Hooke, 1723).
1738 *Constitutions*	James Anderson, *The New Book of Constitutions of the Antient and Honourable Fraternity of Free and Accepted Masons* (London: Cæsar Ward and Richard Chandler, 1738)
AQC	*Ars Quatuor Coronatorum*, the *Transactions* of Quatuor Coronati Lodge, No. 2076, London
BL	British Library
Burney	The Burney Collection of 17th and 18th century newspapers at the British Library
CSRNC	Colonial and State Records of North Carolina
CUP	Cambridge University Press
DNCB	*Dictionary of North Carolina Biography*, 6 volumes, William Powell (ed), (Chapel Hill, NC: UNCP, 1979-1996)
edn	edition
ed(s)	editor(s)
Espionage, Diplomacy & the Lodge	Ric Berman, *Espionage, Diplomacy & the Lodge* (Goring Heath: The Old Stables Press, 2017)
et al.	and all the others
fl.	flourished
Foundations	Ric Berman, *The Foundations of Modern Freemasonry. The Grand Architects: Political Change and the Scientific Enlightenment, 1714–1740* (Brighton: Sussex Academic Press, 2012 & 2014)
FCP	Four Courts Press
FRS	Fellow of the Royal Society
GLNC	Grand Lodge of North Carolina
GM/DGM	Grand Master/Deputy Grand Master

Grand Lodge *Minutes I*	*The Minutes of the Grand Lodge of Freemasons of England, 1723-1739*, QCA (London, 1913), *AQC Masonic Reprint* volume X
Grand Lodge *Minutes II*	*The Minutes of the Grand Lodge of Freemasons of England, 1740-1758*, QCA (London, 1960), *AQC Masonic Reprints* volume XII
HMSO	His/Her Majesty's Stationery Office
Ibid.	from the same source
IHR	Institute of Historical Research
Lane's *Masonic Records*	John Lane, *Masonic Records, 1717–1894*
LL	*London Lives 1690-1800*: www.londonlives.org
LMA	London Metropolitan Archives
Loyalists & Malcontents	Ric Berman, *Loyalists & Malcontents: Freemasonry and Revolution in the Deep South* (Goring Heath: The Old Stables Press, 2015).
MP	Member of Parliament
MS[S]	Manuscript[s]
NA	National Archives
NC	North Carolina
n.s.	new series
ODNB	*Oxford Dictionary of National Biography* (Oxford: OUP); 2004 edition unless stated otherwise.
o.s.	old series
OUP	Oxford University Press
PC	Privy Councillor
PGM	Provincial Grand Master
QC	Quatuor Coronati Lodge, No. 2076, London
QCA	*Quatuor Coronatorum Antigrapha*
Schism	Ric Berman, *Schism: The Battle that Forged Freemasonry* (Brighton: Sussex Academic Press, 2013)

SP	State Papers
SPCK	Society for the Propagation of Christian Knowledge
Strype	John Strype, *A Survey of the Cities of London and Westminster*
UGLE	United Grand Lodge of England
UNC	University of North Carolina
UNCP	University of North Carolina Press
U.S.	United States
USC	University of South Carolina
WM	Worshipful Master (of a lodge)
YUP	Yale University Press

A Map of Virginia, North and South Carolina, and Georgia
Printed for R. Baldwin. Paternoster Row, London, *c.*1755.
Reproduced in the *London Magazine or, Gentleman's monthly intelligencer*, volume XXIV, July 1755

Foreword

In his introduction to *The Beginnings of Freemasonry in North Carolina and Tennessee*[1] Haywood laments the absence of primary source material. Conjecture and romance provide a poor substitute and it is this which explains why his and other accounts begin with the misconception that 'prior to 1735 the Craft was actively at work in North Carolina'.[2] Haywood states that this was 'Solomon Lodge' at Cape Fear, and that the lodge was chartered in 1735 by the grand master of the Grand Lodge of England, Viscount Weymouth.

Hughan and Stillson make a similar case, writing that 'at the same time (1735) that the warrant was granted to the Charleston Solomon's Lodge, a warrant was granted for a lodge of the same name at Wilmington, North Carolina'.[3] They claim that 'by some mistake' Charleston was not entered onto the grand register while Wilmington was.[4] But this is also incorrect. It was the Lodge at Savannah in Georgia that was recorded on the grand register, not Wilmington.

Following Haywood's lead but not that of Parramore who is more sceptical,[5] similar information appears on the website of the Grand Lodge

---

[1] Marshall De Lancey Haywood, *The Beginnings of Freemasonry in North Carolina and Tennessee* (Raleigh, NC: published privately, 1906).

[2] Ibid., p. 2.

[3] William James Hughan & Henry Leonard Stillson, *History of the Ancient and Honorable Fraternity of Free and Accepted Masons, and Concordant Orders* (Boston, MA, & New York, NY: Fraternity Publishing Co., 1893), p. 301; but cf. p. 300 where this is apparently contradicted - 'The earliest knowledge we have of Freemasonry in North Carolina is the warranting of a lodge at Wilmington, on Cape River, in the Province of North Carolina, in March, 1754, being No. 213 on the Register, Grand Lodge of England'.

[4] Ibid.

[5] Thomas C. Parramore, *Launching the Craft: The First Half-Century of Freemasonry in North Carolina* (Raleigh, NC: GLNC, 1975), pp. 2-5.

of North Carolina where a *Historical Table* refers to a lodge formed in the 1730s at Masonboro in New Hanover County.[6]

All of these pronouncements are mistaken. There is no evidence of a lodge at Masonboro or Wilmington in the 1730s. Indeed, Wilmington was not incorporated as a town until 1740 and Masonboro was substantially undeveloped until the late 1750s.[7]

Although the name 'Masonboro' appears on John Collet's map of 1770, it is absent from detailed drawings produced in the 1730s and mid-1750s.[8] Moreover, with regard to the name's origins, the *North Carolina Gazetteer* explains that the area below Wilmington was termed 'Mason Borough' not in the 1730s but in the *latter* part of the eighteenth century 'because members of the order of Masons … built houses there'.[9]

The reference is to Caleb Grainger, a merchant and freemason who owned an estate and summer house near the coast south-east of Wilmington.[10] After his death in 1765, Grainger's estate was sold for the

---

[6] GLNC website accessed 1 February 2018: http://grandlodge-nc.org/center-for-members/historical-list-of-lodges.

[7] The land was then owned by Caleb Grainger (1725-1765). Cf., Donald R. Lennon & Ida Brooks Kellam (eds), *The Wilmington Town Book, 1743-1778* (Raleigh, NC: Division of Archives and History, North Carolina Department of Cultural Resources, 1973).

[8] John Collet, *A Compleat map of North-Carolina from an actual survey* (London: S. Hooper, 1770). Masonboro does not appear on the *Chart of his Majesties Province of North Carolina* (London: William Mount & Thomas Page, 1738), nor on Richard Baldwin's map published in the *London Magazine*, XXIV (1755), p. 312.

[9] William S. Powell & Michael Hill, *The North Carolina Gazetteer*, 2nd edition: *A Dictionary of Tar Heel Places and Their History* (Chapel Hill, NC: UNCP, 2010), p. 334. The same point is made in J. Christy Judah, *The Two Faces of Dixie* (Wilmington, NC: Coastal Books, 2009), p. 112.

[10] Thomas Godfrey Jr. (1736-1763), stayed at Grainger's house at Masonboro in 1759 where he completed *The Prince of Parthia* and composed several poems including *Masonborough*, a tribute to the area.

benefit of his three sons.[11] Part was acquired by William Hooper,[12] another freemason, who subsequently constructed his own summer home on the property.

But perhaps the most definitive argument against the existence of Haywood's Cape Fear lodge is in the records of the Grand Lodge of England, which confirm that only two lodges were warranted in the American South in the 1730s - those at Savannah and Charleston.[13]

THE LODGE AT SAVANNAH

Georgia freemasonry has a tradition that the Lodge at Savannah, later renamed Solomon's Lodge No. 1,[14] obtained its warrant via James Oglethorpe, the co-founder of the colony, who brought it to Georgia on his return from Britain in 1736. This is possible, but it is more plausible that the charter was in the possession of Roger Lacy,[15] a wealthy settler who had been appointed provincial grand master for Georgia by the Grand Lodge of England in 1735, shortly before he sailed for the colony.[16]

---

[11] J. Bryan Grimes, *North Carolina Wills and Inventories* (Raleigh, NC: Trustees of the Public Libraries, 1910), pp. 202-7.

[12] William Hooper (1742-1790), one of North Carolina's three signatories to the Declaration of Independence.

[13] There is also no record of a lodge at Masonboro in the registers of the Grand Lodge of Ireland or the Grand Lodge of Scotland.

[14] The lodge at Savannah was named 'Solomon's Lodge' in 1770. Cf., W.B. Clarke, *Early and Historic Freemasonry of Georgia, 1733/4-1800* (Georgia, GA: published privately, 1924). The lodge is shown as No. 75 in 'A List of Regular Lodges' in Samuel Prichard, *Masonry Dissected* (London, 1760), twentieth edition, p. 24.

[15] Also written as 'Lacey'. Egmont records that Lacy was the first colonist to migrate to the Georgia colony at his own expense: Egmont, *Diary of the Earl of Egmont*, vol. II, p. 193. The comment is probably incorrect but nonetheless provides an indication of Lacy's relatively prominent social and financial position.

[16] *Masonic Year Book, Historical Supplement* (London: UGLE, 1969), 2nd edn, p. 47.

Lacy appears as a member of two London lodges, the King's Arms at St Paul's that met formerly at the Goose and Gridiron, one of the four lodges that founded the Grand Lodge of England,[17] and the Swan Tavern in Long Acre.[18] He was well-known within grand lodge, not least because in December 1730 he was one of five who committed jointly to underwrite the cost of the annual grand feast by volunteering to serve as a grand steward.[19] Lacy was so appointed on 29 January 1731.[20]

In contrast, there is no evidence to indicate that Oglethorpe was a freemason, albeit that he associated with men who were, including James Vernon,[21] one of the most active of the Georgia Trustees.[22] Oglethorpe is not recorded as a member of any English lodge, although this does not preclude him from having been a freemason, nor does he appear as a visitor in the minutes of the Grand Lodge of England or any other lodge, whether in connection with the Georgia colony or otherwise.[23] Equally relevant, Oglethorpe was a prominent Tory, albeit a loyal Tory, at a time when London freemasonry was dominated by Whigs.

---

[17] The lodge's most prominent past master was the mercurial Duke of Wharton. In Lacy's day the master was John Georges and the senior warden Robert Gray. Both were well-connected members of upper-middling London and Fellows of the Royal Society. John Georges (*fl*.1719–1738), was also WM (1723) of the Goose and Gridiron, now Lodge of Antiquity, No. 2; and Robert Gray (*fl*.1728-1731), a director of the Honourable East India Company and a member of Martin Folkes's lodge at the Bedford's Head, Covent Garden.

[18] Grand Lodge *Minutes I*, pp. 32 and 170. Charles Fullwood, the master of the lodge, was in 1728 a member of the Westminster and Middlesex grand jury: *London Gazette*, 12-15 October 1728.

[19] Grand Lodge *Minutes I*, p. 137.

[20] Grand Lodge *Minutes I*, p. 142.

[21] James Vernon (1677-1756). Cf., *Loyalists & Malcontents*, pp. 136-7.

[22] Cf., Berman, 'The Early Years of Georgia Freemasonry', *Heredom*, 24 (2016), 225-54.

[23] Grand Lodge *Minutes I*, esp. p. 235.

SOLOMON'S LODGE, CHARLESTON

Solomon's lodge at Charleston had been working for a year or so before it received its warrant, having been formed in 1734 or 1735 in conjunction with freemasons from Boston Massachusetts. The minutes of St John's Grand Lodge in Boston record that 'sundry Brethren going to South Carolina met with some Masons in Charleston who thereupon went to work, from which sprung Masonry in those parts'.[24] But Charleston did not seek a warrant from St John's.[25] John Hammerton, the master, looked instead to London and the Grand Lodge of England. It was enviably simple for him to do so.

Hammerton was a member of South Carolina's royal council and its secretary and register.[26] But an arguably more significant connection lay in his membership of the Horn Tavern in Westminster, the most important of the four lodges that founded the Grand Lodge of England. At the Horn's social summit were five men with direct blood-links to the crown. Four were grandsons of Charles II: the Duke of Richmond, the master of the lodge and a former grand master; the Duke of Grafton; the Earl Delorraine; and the Earl of Dalkeith, another past grand master.[27] The fifth, James Waldegrave, was the

---

[24] *Proceedings in Masonry: St John's Grand Lodge 1733-1792* (Boston, MA: Grand Lodge of Massachusetts, 1895), pp. 4-5.

[25] 'Warrant shopping' – applications to more than one grand lodge – was not uncommon. It allowed lodges to improve their chance of obtaining a warrant as well as 'trade up'. The latter may explain why Joseph Montfort acquired a charter directly from the Grand Lodge of England despite the Royal White Hart Lodge Halifax already holding a warrant issued by St John's Lodge Wilmington.

[26] Hammerton had been appointed secretary and register in 1731. He was granted the position of receiver-general of the quit-rents for North and South Carolina shortly afterwards.

[27] Charles Lennox, 2nd Duke of Richmond (1701-1750); Charles FitzRoy, 2nd Duke of Grafton (1683-1757); Henry Scott, Earl Delorraine (1676-1730); and Francis Scott, Earl of Dalkeith, 2nd Duke of Buccleuch (1705-1751).

grandson of James II;[28] he was created Earl Waldegrave by George II in 1729 and was afterwards ambassador to Paris, one of Britain's most prestigious diplomatic postings.

The Horn dominated the masonic hierarchy at grand lodge into the 1730s, providing five grand masters between 1719-26 and a deputy grand master in every year bar two from 1720-35. Its members sat as senior and junior grand wardens, and as grand secretary and grand treasurer, and the lodge supplied a majority of the members of the charity committee, the *de facto* standing committee of grand lodge.

Around a third of the Horn's members were MPs, nearly a quarter Fellows of the Royal Society, and a similar number served as magistrates - several as chairman of the bench.[29] The lodge also contained high-ranking military officers, including two generals and ten colonels, while others held senior posts at the departments of state and the exchequer.

George Payne, the deputy grand master who issued the warrant for Solomon's Lodge in late 1735, was the deputy master of the Horn,[30] and it was Payne who subsequently appointed Hammerton provincial grand master of South Carolina.[31] Not coincidentally, Hammerton, like Lacy, had also volunteered to act as a grand steward in December 1730.[32]

---

[28] James Waldegrave (1684-1741).

[29] William Cowper, Nathaniel Blackerby and Leonard Streate each chaired the Westminster and Middlesex magistrates' benches.

[30] Solomon's Lodge Charleston was not listed in the grand register of the Grand Lodge of England until 1760 and in 1762 was given No. 74, vacated by the preceding Bristol Lodge. It was later numbered 49 (1780) and 45 (1792). The lodge made no fee payments to the Grand Lodge of England after 1781 but was retained on the register until 1813. Cf., Lane's *Masonic Records*.

[31] Cf., *Loyalists & Malcontents* for a detailed discussion. They were among eight men who were appointed PGMs in North America from 1730-50. Cf., appendix one for a complete list.

[32] Grand Lodge *Minutes I*, p. 137. Although Hammerton put his name forward he was not selected.

The Beginnings of Freemasonry in North Carolina

Although there is an argument that the absence of evidence of a warrant issued to a lodge in North Carolina before 1754 is no more than an example of inadequate eighteenth-century record-keeping, there are other reasons to suppose that freemasonry did not develop in the province until the late 1740s.

In the first half of the eighteenth century, lodges were generally meeting places for the social and financial elites. In the American South this comprised an upper echelon of planters, merchant-traders, lawyers and public officials - a 'plantocracy' whose members could afford the expense of joining one of the most fashionable fraternal associations of the age. More pointedly, lodges tended to appear only when a social structure had developed and where such men were present in appropriate numbers.

This was the case in Charleston from the mid-1730s. It was less so in Savannah, where the lodge functioned as a 'tippling club' for the colony's wealthier migrants and failed to develop further until the mid-1750s when Georgia's economic growth accelerated.[33]

The hard evidence of lodge charters, private journals, personal correspondence and press reports confirm that freemasonry was active in South Carolina and Georgia from 1734 and 1735. But no such evidence is available for North Carolina until 1754, the year a petition was sent to London from St John's Lodge in Wilmington seeking authorisation from the Grand Lodge

---

[33] *Loyalists & Malcontents*, pp. 134-55 and 163-85. With slavery banned and land grants restricted, Georgia's economy failed to develop and settler wealth eroded. Georgia freemasonry withered as a consequence and the lodge at Savannah was dormant until the 1750s when slavery was legalised and administration transferred from the trustees to the crown. Thereafter the economy rebounded, new merchant and planter elites emerged, and freemasonry revived. In a bare two years, 1756-57, the lodge at Savannah welcomed more than thirty new initiates and by 1760 contained a majority of the royal council, the colony's principal public officers, and its most prominent planters and merchants.

of England.[34] The fee for the lodge warrant, 12 guineas,[35] was settled on 27 June[36] and the lodge was subsequently entered onto the grand register as No. 213.[37]

The date of Wilmington's application does not imply that freemasonry did not exist at Cape Fear before 1754. It more probably implies the opposite. Colonial lodges were generally formed and working before any application for a warrant was made, whether to London or elsewhere. But although there were settlers at Wilmington in the 1730s, it is unlikely that the town had developed sufficiently to support a lodge until the mid or late 1740s.[38]

What was true of Wilmington was true elsewhere. Freemasonry emerges in North Carolina in the mid-eighteenth century in a handful of towns that were social hubs and regional centres for trade and administration. Examples include Halifax and New Bern, each of which grew in tandem with the local economy and flourished on the back of the production of naval stores and lumber, fur and deerskin trading, and the mounting acreage of land under cultivation. A similar dynamic was present in other communities, with lodges formed at Crown Point in Pitt County, Kingston in Lenoir County and Windsor in Bertie County.

---

[34] Before being chartered as a town in 1740, Wilmington was known variously known as New Liverpool, New Town and New Carthage. The name 'Wilmington' was in honour of Spencer Compton, Earl of Wilmington, one of Governor Johnston's patrons. He is discussed below.

[35] A guinea, at the time a coin of c.¼ oz of gold, was equal to twenty-one shillings, that is, £1 1s 0d. Luxury goods, horses and professional services were traditionally priced in guineas.

[36] Lane's *Masonic Records*. Also Grand Lodge *Minutes II*, pp. 79-80.

[37] The lodge appears as such in 1756.

[38] Lawrence Lee, *The Lower Cape Fear in Colonial Days* (Chapel Hill, NC: UNCP, 1965); also H.T. Lefler and A.R. Newsome, *North Carolina: the History of a Southern State* (Chapel Hill, NC: UNCP, 1954). Even in 1765 the taxable white population of Wilmington was only 529. Cf., William L. Saunders (ed), *Colonial Records of North Carolina* (Raleigh, NC: Trustees of the Public Libraries by Order of the General Assembly, 1893), volume VII, 145-7.

North Carolina freemasonry expanded further in the second half of the eighteenth century as Scottish migrants settled the Upper Cape Fear valley and its hinterland, and Scots-Irish migrants the Piedmont, from the Fall Line to the Appalachians. But before we consider the build-out of freemasonry and the influence of successive waves of migrants, it is appropriate to set a context.

An Introduction to Carolina

The Carolina Charter

The French and Spanish explored and endeavoured to settle Carolina in the early sixteenth century. The first serious attempt to do so by England was prompted by Walter Raleigh[1] half a century later in the 1580s.

Roanoke, the colony he co-financed, failed to survive and it was not until the mid-seventeenth century that Nathaniel Batts[2] established a trading post at Salmon Creek in what would become Bertie County, and the Virginia colony subsequently sanctioned an overspill settlement on the Albemarle Sound.[3]

The colonists prospered and more land was acquired from the local first nations. But this did not mark the foundation of a new province. That would occur only in 1663 following the restoration of the monarchy in England and the grant of the Carolina Charter to eight of Charles II's close political allies.

The charter gave its beneficiaries legal title to an expanse of territory that stretched south from Virginia to Spanish Florida and west from the Atlantic to the Pacific.[4] It was worded in terms similar to the licence granted

---

[1] Cf., Rory Rapple, 'Gilbert, Sir Humphrey (1537–1583)', *ODNB*, online edn, Jan 2012, accessed 24 Feb 2017.

[2] Nathaniel Batts (1620?-1679). Cf., *DNCB*.

[3] Alan D. Watson, *Bertie County: A Brief History* (Raleigh, NC: NC Department of Archives and History, 1982), Introduction.

[4] *Charter of Carolina*, 24 March 1663, revised 30 June 1665. The original grant ran south from Virginia's southern border at 36 degrees north, to 31 degrees north, incorporating what is the current state of Georgia. The southern boundary was redrawn in 1665 to 29 degrees north to include the Albemarle settlements. The Lords Proprietors were Edward, Earl of Clarendon; George, Duke of Albemarle; William, Earl of Craven; John, Lord Berkeley; Anthony, Lord Ashley; Sir George Carteret; Sir John Colleton; and Sir William Berkeley.

by Elizabeth I to Sir Humphrey Gilbert[5] and taken-up by Raleigh on Gilbert's death.[6] French and Spanish claims to America were challenged and the first nations denigrated as 'barbarous people [with] no knowledge of Almighty God'. The objective was colonisation and commercial exploitation, with Carolina's new 'true and absolute Lords and Proprietors' enjoined to expand and develop England's dominions and 'by their industry and charge to transport and make an ample colony'. Their reward would be the profits that would flow from land rents and the exploitation of natural resources.

The Lords Proprietors divided Carolina into three loosely defined areas. Albemarle, bordering Virginia, already lightly settled, was named for the Duke of Albemarle; and Clarendon, the middle section, for the Earl of Clarendon. Craven, the third, incorporated everything south of Cape Fear. It was named for William, Earl of Craven, and would later become South Carolina.

In order to reduce their outlay and minimise risk, the Lords Proprietors sought colonists willing to self-fund their passage. In return colonists would be granted land subject to an initial rent-free period and thereafter to a modest annual 'quit-rent'.[7]

The first such arrangement was agreed with John Yeamans, a Barbados planter who headed an investor group willing to underwrite a settlement at Cape Fear and transport prospective colonists.[8] Yeamans was vouched for by Sir John Colleton, whose fellow Proprietors were delighted to accept his proposal, rewarding Yeamans with the title of governor and securing him a baronetcy.

---

[5] Sir Humphrey Gilbert (1537-1583).

[6] Raleigh was Gilbert's half-brother.

[7] An annual land tax by which the tenant is free (quit) of any other rental charge. For its feudal origins, cf., Beverley W. Bond, Jr., 'The Quit-Rent System in the American Colonies', *American Historical Review*, 17.3 (1912), 496-516.

[8] Robert M. Weir, 'Yeamans, Sir John, first baronet (1611–1674)', *ODNB*, online edn, Jan 2008, accessed 21 February 2017.

Yeamans' three-ship expedition sailed from Barbados in 1665 but met with limited success. Two vessels were lost at sea and with only one making land the settlement lacked provisions let alone critical mass. The colony nonetheless survived for almost two years before being abandoned. Yeamans made a second attempt in 1669. One ship was lost and a second delayed, but the third, the *Carolina*, a 200-ton frigate, the largest of the three-vessel fleet, made land in May 1670 near present-day Beaufort. Nonetheless, although a small settlement was constructed, opposition from the local tribes forced its relocation.

The successor settlement was some 270 miles to the south at Albemarle Point on the Ashley River. Additional colonists followed and within the space of ten years there was pressure to move to a larger site. This would be to the east around the deep water bay at the mouth of the Ashley and Cooper rivers.[9] Named for Charles II, Charles Town was renamed Charleston after the War of Independence.[10]

The large majority of Carolina's settlers in the three decades to 1700 came from Barbados and the Caribbean, with the balance principally from other colonies in North America, mainly Massachusetts and Virginia. Only a minority – albeit a growing minority - were from the home nations of England, Scotland, Ireland and Wales, or religious refugees from Europe. The influences that shaped Carolina in its early years were thus derived principally from the Caribbean sugar colonies. They resulted in a plantation-based economy and a political and social structure topped by an inter-married, inter-connected elite whose affluence and influence would dominate the communal landscape for a century.

---

[9] The rivers were named for Anthony Ashley-Cooper, later 1st Earl of Shaftesbury (1621-1683), the Lords Proprietors' *de facto* leader. Cf. Tim Harris, 'Cooper, Anthony Ashley, first earl of Shaftesbury (1621-1683)', *ODNB*, online edn, Jan 2008, accessed 24 February 2017.

[10] The modern spelling is used throughout except in direct quotes.

THE FUNDAMENTAL CONSTITUTIONS OF CAROLINA

The Fundamental Constitutions,[11] a document drafted principally by Lord Ashley's secretary, John Locke,[12] were adopted by the Lords Proprietors in 1669 and although not ratified by Carolina's assembly nor implemented in full, provided the colony with a framework for political governance. They also served a marketing purpose, underlining the availability of land and the Proprietors' commitment to religious toleration.

Excepting Catholicism, Carolina would be a religious sanctuary with churches recognised following a simple declaration by congregants 'that there is a God', 'that God is publicly to be worshipped' and 'that it is the duty of every man … to bear witness to truth'.[13] The *Constitutions* also confirmed that 'no person … shall disturb any religious Assembly' or 'molest or persecute another for his … way of worship'.[14]

The attraction to religious refugees is obvious. St Philip's, an Episcopalian church, opened in Charleston in 1681; a Baptist church followed in 1682; a Presbyterian church in 1685; and a Huguenot church in 1686. Other Protestant denominations established places of worship in the 1690s. A Quaker Meeting House was founded in 1715 and, having previously met in private homes, there were sufficient Sephardic Jews in Charleston in the 1740s to begin the construction of a synagogue.[15]

The Proprietors also offered electoral enfranchisement to free men of age who had a stake of at least 50 acres in the colony.[16] Office-holders required a

---

[11] *The Fundamental Constitutions of Carolina*, 1 March 1669: *CSRNC*, volume 1, pp. 187-206.

[12] J.R. Milton, 'Locke, John (1632-1704)', *ODNB*, online edn, May 2008, accessed 4 October 2017.

[13] *The Fundamental Constitutions of Carolina*, clause 100.

[14] Ibid., clauses 102, 109.

[15] Kahal Kadosh Beth Elohim, founded in 1749.

[16] Clause 85.

larger landholding and greater wealth: 'the sheriff [and] justices shall [hold] five hundred acres apiece freehold within the precinct for which they serve';[17] and 'no man shall be chosen a member of parliament who has less than five hundred acres of freehold within the precinct for which he is chosen'.[18] Jury service was also the preserve of stakeholders: 'in the Precinct Court no man shall be a juryman under fifty acres of freehold; in the County Court or at the Assizes no man shall be a grand-juryman under three hundred acres of freehold';[19] and in the Proprietors' Courts a juryman required five hundred acres.[20]

Regarding governance, the *Constitutions* assured Carolina's electorate that they might 'choose from among themselves an assembly in the nature of a parliament [with] the sole power of making all laws and laying taxes when need requires for the use of the colony and the governors and council see the laws put in execution'.[21] There was also a commitment to legal rights regardless of country of origin,[22] and to equality under the law - 'no cause, whether civil or criminal, of any freeman, shall be tried in any court of judicature without a jury of his peers'.[23]

SLAVERY

Slavery provided the economic foundations for Carolina's development with Yeamans initiating the process by importing some 200 slaves from his Barbados estates. The right to own slaves as property was enshrined in the *Constitutions* which stated that 'every freeman of Carolina shall have absolute

---

[17] Clause 61.
[18] Clause 72.
[19] Clause 68.
[20] Ibid.
[21] *CSRNC*, volume 1, pp. 153-5: 'Advertisement concerning the settlement of the Cape Fear area, 1666'.
[22] Clause 118.
[23] Clause 111.

power and authority over his negro slaves'.[24] Although drawn up by Locke, ironically an opponent of slavery,[25] this aspect of the *Constitutions* was influenced by John Colleton, whose wealth was based in part on extensive Barbadian sugar plantations.[26]

Slavery had been introduced to the Caribbean in the mid-seventeenth century as an alternative to indentured white labour. The practice was promoted by Dutch and Portuguese traders who had been trafficking slaves to Brazil since the 1500s and were looking for new markets. In Barbados the number of slaves increased from 200 or so in the 1640s to more than 40,000 by 1670, over two-thirds of the island's population. By 1700 the proportion had risen to three-quarters.

The rationale was plain. Slaves were cheaper than indentured white labour, had greater immunity to disease, and were more skilled at agriculture. In addition, slave children could be added to the labour force at virtually no cost. And since a child's legal status was determined by that of the mother, sexual exploitation was commonplace and in that context if no other 'justifiable'.[27]

---

[24] Clause 110.

[25] 'Slavery is so vile and miserable an estate of man, and so directly opposite to the generous temper and courage of our nation, that it is hardly to be conceived that an Englishman, much less a Gentleman, should plead for it'. Cf., Locke, *First Treatise of Government* (1690): volume 4 of *The Works of John Locke in Nine Volumes* (London: Rivington, 1824).

[26] Richard S. Dunn, *Sugar and Slaves: The Rise of the Planter Class in the English West Indies, 1624-1713*, (London: Jonathan Cape, 1973). Also, J. E. Buchanan, *The Colleton Family and the Early History of South Carolina and Barbados, 1646-1775* (University of Edinburgh, PhD Thesis, 1989); and 'The Colleton Family in South Carolina', *South Carolina Historical and Genealogical Magazine*, 1.4 (1900), 325-41.

[27] Conversely, sexual intercourse between a male slave and white woman had severely negative repercussions if discovered. Cf., Martha Hodes, *White Women, Black Men: Illicit Sex in the Nineteenth-Century South* (New Haven, CN: YUP, 1997); Thomas A. Foster, 'Sexual Abuse of Black Men Under American Slavery', *Journal of History and Sexuality*, 20.3 (2011): 445-64; and J.M. Alain, 'Sexual Relations Between Elite White Women and Enslaved Men in the Antebellum South: A Socio-Historical Analysis', *Inquiries Journal*, 5.8 (2013).

Within less than three decades Carolina's Low Country mirrored Barbados.[28] The adoption of slavery and a plantation-based economy was a function of financial self-interest and not simply geography. It gave rise to social, legal and political structures that encouraged racism overtly, especially within the white under-class, and led inexorably to concentration of land ownership.

Whether in the Caribbean or Carolina, planters with access to the right connections, capital and credit bought-out their smaller neighbours in a self-reinforcing process with the result that land and wealth - and the influence that each conveyed - became the preserve of a politically-unchallenged minority.

MIGRATION

The number of Carolina settlers from the Caribbean declined towards the end of the seventeenth century and in the following decades the largest proportion of incomers, up to half, had migrated from other American colonies, especially Virginia and Maryland, in search of inexpensive cultivable land. Another third or so were from Britain and Ireland, with the balance drawn from Europe, a combination of Huguenots, Moravians, Lutherans and other refugees fleeing religious persecution and seeking new economic opportunities.[29]

Promotional material commissioned by the Lords Proprietors emphasised the advantages of Carolina's coastal plain and especially Albemarle and Craven counties. Pamphlets and newspapers advertised the benign climate and natural resources,[30] with prospective migrants encouraged with land

---

[28] Cf., Walter B. Edgar, *South Carolina: A History* (Columbia, SC: USC Press, 1998), pp. 36-9.

[29] Ibid. Also *Colonial and Pre-Federal Statistics*, Series Z 1-19, Estimated Population of American Colonies: 1610-1780; and Series Z 20-23, Percent Distribution of the White Population by Nationality: 1790.

[30] Thomas Ashe, *Carolina, or a Description of the present state of that country* (London, 1682), reprinted in Bartholomew R. Carroll, *Historical Collections of South Carolina* (New York, NY: Harper & Bros., 1836), vol. I.

grants of fifty acres per person 'to be held forever, annually paying a penny an acre ... to commence two years after it is surveyed'.[31]

Earlier marketing had offered even better terms: 'every man and woman that transport themselves before the 24 June next being 1667 shall have for himself his wife and each of his children and every man servant he shall bring armed with a firelock or matchlock musket ... 100 acres of land for each of them to him and his heirs forever paying for every 1,000 acres 10*s* per annum to the Lords for an acknowledgement and for every woman servant and slave 50 acres'.[32]

The explanation for the seeming generosity was simple. The value of the Lords Proprietors' stake in Carolina was a function of the number of colonists that could be persuaded to settle. The pamphlets may have failed to mention the perils of disease and the risk of attack from the French and Spanish and their allies among the first nations, but the overall thrust was accurate. Many of Carolina's rivers were navigable and gave access to the interior. The coastal plain and its hinterland were fertile. Charleston offered a secure deep water harbour for the largest ocean-going vessels. And London soon provided financial bounties to promote trade with the mother country.

Inside two generations Craven County was on the road to economic success and Albemarle following suit, with exports of deerskins and naval stores funding land clearance, new infrastructure and agricultural development.

GOVERNANCE, OWNERSHIP AND CONTROL

Carolina's proprietorial government followed the road map laid out in the *Fundamental Constitutions* with a commons house of assembly representing the colony's land owners alongside a governor and council. The council evolved to become an upper house in miniature on the English constitutional model, with council members appointed by the governor and by London, and with

---

[31] Ibid.

[32] *CSRNC*, volume I, pp. 153-5, 'Advertisement, 1666'.

its president, the most senior member, deputising for the governor in his absence.

The powers residing in the governor were a combination of constitutional and executive authority, including the ability to call elections and disband the assembly, as well as control over appointments to administrative and judicial offices. There was also a system of checks and balances, albeit unintended. The governor and his senior officials were not paid by London but funded via a share of the quit-rents or money bills that were passed by the assembly, a criterion that on occasion compromised the intended political dynamic.

The most prominent figure in the assembly was its speaker, elected by the assemblymen from among themselves. There were no political parties as such but rather self-interested factions. Until the early 1730s, North Carolina's assembly was split between rival groups within the northern part of the colony. From the mid-1730s until the 1750s, the divide was predominantly between colonists from the Albemarle Sound region and more recent arrivals at Lower Cape Fear. And from the late 1750s and early 1760s, settlers in the eastern coastal plain were ranked against those in the Piedmont.

The last division was exceptionally bitter and led to the Regulator Movement, and to a virtual civil war in North Carolina from the late 1760s through to the Battle of Alamance in 1771.[33]

The passing of ownership and control of the Carolinas from the Lords Proprietors to the British crown was triggered by the colonists themselves and followed the failure of the Proprietors to plan and fund an adequate defence to repeated assaults on the colony. Queen Anne's War (1702-13), the North American theatre of the War of Spanish Succession, placed the American colonies on the front line against the French and Spanish, with inland trading posts and farming settlements attacked across a ragged frontier that extended from Canada and New England to

---

[33] See chapter nine.

Carolina. But of more consequence was the Yemassee War (1715-17), in which the colony – principally South Carolina - faced a hostile alliance of first nation tribes.[34]

Outlying and inlying farms and settlements were attacked and some 400 colonists killed. Many survivors fled to Charleston where the influx almost overwhelmed the available food supplies and accommodation. Hostilities endured for nearly three years and ended not through military victory but because mutual enmity between the different tribes eventually outweighed their common anti-settler sentiments.

The economic impact of the Yemassee War was considerable and lay at the centre of what developed into a political revolt in favour of crown rule. The colonists were led by Arthur Middleton, a first generation Carolinian born to Barbados migrants. He was one of the colony's principal planters with estates that exceeded 12,000 acres in South Carolina alone.[35] Middleton presided over a convention in Charleston in December 1719 at which a resolution was passed demanding change and approving a direct petition to George I.

Representations over governance were not new. Carolinians had argued for partition of the province in the late seventeenth century and for a deputy governor to be appointed to administer the northern half, a division that was put into effect in 1712 with the creation of North Carolina. But in 1719 the issue was not how to improve administration so much as how to ensure Carolina's survival.

The colonists' concern, shared by London, was that the Lords Proprietors were unwilling and unable to safeguard the province. And with

---

[34] The tribal alliance included the Apalachee, Apalachicola, Catawba, Cheraw, Cherokee, Congaree, Muscogee, Waxhaw, Yemassee and Yuchi.

[35] Alexander Moore, 'Middleton, Arthur (1681-1737)', *ODNB*, online edn, May 2005; Walter B. Edgar & N. Louise Bailey, *Biographical Directory of the South Carolina House of Representatives* (Columbia, SC: USC Press, 1977), volume II, pp. 454-5. Middleton also owned land in Barbados and England.

Britain's ship owners and merchants' financial interests aligned with South Carolina's plantocrats, their joint parliamentary lobbying proved effective. Carolina was becoming one of Britain's more important trading partners and the argument that crown governance was required to secure its defence was accepted.

Crown rule was introduced to South Carolina in 1720 and to North Carolina a decade later. Negotiations over compensation took years to conclude but a virtually immediate corollary was an increase in confidence and a greater availability of land grants. The acreage under cultivation in both colonies was allowed to expand, and the greater output and flow of exports led directly to increased revenues and higher land values. The sister colonies' planters and merchants gained immensely and their higher revenues were expended in greater consumption of British manufactures and invested in the acquisition and clearance of land, new buildings and wharves, and a sharp expansion in the number of black slaves.[36]

The commonality of interest between Carolina's elites and their counterparts in England grew stronger from the 1730s as increased trade led to higher profits on both sides of the Atlantic. But this commercially-golden era would last barely more than a generation.

Economic logic was trumped by mercantilism as London imposed a stream of restrictive regulations and taxes. The resulting shift in the terms of trade proved corrosive, propelling the thirteen colonies towards political resistance and eventual independence.

But the tipping point would not occur until the mid-1760s and 1770s. Until then, the vast majority of the planters, merchants and politicians that sat atop Carolina – South and North - were content with their status as among the most affluent members of Britain's flourishing global Empire.

---

[36] *Colonial and Pre-Federal Statistics*, Series Z 155-64, Slaves Imported Into South Carolina by Origin, 1707-1777.

It's Always the Economy…

Although overlooked by most economic historians, the North Carolina economy thrived in the eighteenth century. One reason for its success was a sustained rise in migration such that by the late 1770s it was the third most populous colony in America behind Virginia and Pennsylvania.[37] Compared to South Carolina, whose population rose from around 5,700 in 1700 to some 180,000 in 1780, including 97,000 slaves, North Carolina grew from 11,000 to more than 270,000, of which 90,000 were slaves.[38]

North Carolina has long been regarded as less economically successful when compared with its sister colony however this view is based largely on trade statistics that are incomplete and inaccurate. The division in output and exports between the two Carolinas is virtually impossible to measure given that much of North Carolina's principal exports - deerskins, animal pelts, naval stores, lumber, rice and tobacco - were shipped from ports in Virginia and South Carolina and attributed to those colonies.

Smaller ships could of course land and take-on goods at North Carolina's ports but larger vessels, assuming that they were willing to navigate the sand bars that ringed the North Carolina coast, were required to on and off-load cargo via smaller boats or flats, a practice that was inconvenient and expensive. Transatlantic trade therefore flowed to and through Virginia and South Carolina, whose harbours could accommodate larger vessels and whose traders and merchants benefited from economies of scale and could offer more competitive prices.

This explains why colonial and pre-federal statistics underestimate the value of North Carolina's trade and development, and why the colony's

---

[37] *Colonial and Pre-Federal Statistics*, Series Z 1-19, Estimated Population of American Colonies: 1610-1780.

[38] Ibid. Cf. also, William Saunders (ed), *Colonial Records of North Carolina* (Raleigh, NC, 1886) volume II, Preface.

exports were frequently attributed to its neighbours.[39] The argument applies not only to lumber products and naval stores, North Carolina's most valuable exports, but to output across the board. This was not unknown at the time. Indeed, Governor Tryon was clear on the problems it caused for North Carolina and complained to the Board of Trade in the 1760s regarding the resulting inequities:

> I must beg leave to observe a practice I am told prevails in the customs of the port of London, it is this, that all vessels clearing or entering at said port to or from either of the two Carolinas are entered in the books as trading to or from Carolina generally without the distinction of North or South Carolina. That this was the case I have been credibly informed at the time the agents of South Carolina and Georgia solicited for the Act of Parliament afterwards granted to those colonies to export rice to certain foreign markets, at which time the imports into the port of London from the two Carolinas were extracted from the custom house books under the title of Carolina and placed to the credit of the exports of South Carolina, which served to swell the importance and flourishing trade of the south government, while a great majority of naval stores were actually shipped from this province. On these considerations and that this province may have the credit of its own exports and produce, not so contemptible as in the estimation of her sister colonies, I humbly hope that the Lords Commissioners of his Majesty's Treasury or the honorable Commissioners of his Majesty's customs will give orders that the trade of North and South Carolina directed to the port of London may for the future be respectively distinguished.[40]

---

[39] *Colonial and Pre-Federal Statistics*, Series Z 213-26: Value of Exports To and Imports From England by American Colonies and States: 1697-1791.

[40] *CSRNC*, volume 7, pp. 693-7: William Tryon to William Petty, Marquis of Lansdowne, 7 March 1768.

The Carolina deerskin trade was huge and supported a network of frontiersmen operating over thousands of miles of trails across the continental interior, as well as brokers, agents and more than a hundred merchants in Charleston alone.[41] Exports averaged around 55,000 pelts annually between 1700 and 1715, rising to a peak of over 160,000 in the 1740s. The trade was so profitable that deerskins remained the second most valuable export attributed to South Carolina until the 1750s,[42] and even then the shift was not triggered by a decline in volume or value but by rising revenues from other exports, including indigo and naval stores. But deerskins were sourced from both South and North Carolina, not South Carolina alone. Indeed, the Moravians' store at Bethabara, a collection point in the northern Piedmont, on its own accounted for more than 6% of total deerskins exports from Charleston in the 1760s.

North Carolina also dominated the trade in naval stores, lumber and forestry products. But with a high proportion shipped through Charleston, George Town and Beaufort, the bulk was declared as originating from 'Carolina' or South Carolina.[43] In a similar vein, North Carolina's tobacco exports were made largely through Virginia and credited to that colony.[44] And the province's agricultural products and livestock, the bulk exported by coastal vessels or driven overland to adjacent colonies, often went under- or unrecorded. As Tryon notes accurately, the impact of misstatements of origin on such a scale was considerable, not least in the political and economic influence accreted by Virginia and South Carolina at North Carolina's expense.[45]

---

[41] W.O. Moore, Jr., 'The Largest Exporters of Deerskins from Charles Town, 1735 - 1775', *South Carolina Historical Magazine*, 74.3 (1973), 144-50.

[42] Rice was the colony's most valuable export.

[43] *Colonial and Pre-Federal Statistics*, Series Z 500-3, 504-9.

[44] *Colonial and Pre-Federal Statistics*, Series Z 441-8; also Z 460-72.

[45] The extent of the omission was vast and can be seen analogously in the trade statistics for Scotland where customs data was differentiated: *Colonial and Pre-Federal Statistics,* Series Z 227-44: Value of Exports To and Imports From Scotland by American Colonies and States: 1740-1791.

South Carolina's economy was based principally on rice, the colony's main cash crop, which was sold in rising volumes to Britain, the Caribbean and across Southern Europe. Output was so substantial that rice accounted for between half and two-thirds of the total value of South Carolina's recorded exports until the 1770s.

Exports had begun modestly at 200-300 tons in the early 1700s but doubled to more than 530 tons by 1710 and rose again to exceed 3,600 tons in the 1720s. From that point rice cultivation took-off, with annual exports recorded at around 9,000 tons by 1730, 15,000 tons by 1740, and around 18,000 tons in the 1750s.[46] Output rose further over the following decades and in the 1770s exports stood at around 35,000 tons per annum.[47]

The price of rice moved in tandem with global demand and supply but averaged £6 - 8 per ton across the period, other than in the 1740s when prices were some 30% lower at around £4 per ton.[48] Estimating rice planters' profits is difficult but the average return on equity allowed an efficient grower to double his capital within five years: a return of around 20% per annum at a time when interest rates were 4%. The result was predictable: the demand for credit expanded alongside a parallel increase in the price of land and the slaves to work it. South Carolina's factors, merchants, lawyers and ship owners benefited hugely, with Charleston becoming the wealthiest town in what was arguably one of the wealthiest colonies in North America.

Nonetheless, although South Carolina produced the majority of America's rice with around 70,000 acres under cultivation, rice was also

---

[46] R.C. Nash, 'South Carolina and the Atlantic Economy in the Late Seventeenth and Eighteenth Centuries', *Economic History Review*, ns, 45.4 (1992), 677-702, esp. 680.

[47] *Colonial and Pre-Federal Statistics*, Series Z 481-5, Rice Exported from Producing Areas: 1680 to 1789, *et al.*

[48] Cf., Kenneth Morgan, 'The Organization of the Colonial American Rice Trade', *William and Mary Quarterly*, 3rd series, 52.3 (1995), 433-52. Also, Peter A. Coclanis, 'Rice Prices in the 1720s and the Evolution of the South Carolina Economy', *Journal of Southern History*, 48.4 (1982), 531-44.

produced in North Carolina, having been introduced in the late 1720s when South Carolina planters acquired land grants across the Lower Cape Fear.[49] Land clearance was commonly carried out by slaves brought from the planters' South Carolina estates and many slaves remained to work the plantations afterwards.

Some historians have argued that rice production in the Lower Cape Fear was trivial, occupying 'only about 500 acres',[50] and was no more than 'an adjunct to the naval stores industry'.[51] But such comments are based in part on statistics from Charleston and London which attribute almost all rice exports to South Carolina alone. Given the mismatch, it is not unreasonable to conclude that the importance of rice cultivation in the Lower Cape Fear, and especially Brunswick County, may have been under-recorded.

Although the Lower Cape Fear region began to produce rice for export only in 1730, North Carolina's assembly included rice as one of the colony's official commodities the following year. The marshes along the Cape Fear River offered a near-perfect environment for rice farming and output rose to a level sufficient to encourage the construction of rice mills at plantations around Brunswick and Wilmington,[52] albeit that most are documented in the late eighteenth century and the beginning of the nineteenth. They include the *Orton* plantation just above Brunswick, later owned by Governor Benjamin Smith; the *Clarendon* plantation five miles below Wilmington; and *Belvedere*, a plantation on the Brunswick River owned successively by Benjamin Smith and Daniel Russell.[53]

---

[49] Georgia also became a major rice exporter from the late-1750s.

[50] James M. Clifton, 'Golden Grains of White: Rice Planting on the Lower Cape Fear, *North Carolina Historical Review*, 50.4 (1973), 365-93.

[51] James M. Clifton, 'The Rice Industry in Colonial America', *Agricultural History*, 55.3 (1981), 266-83.

[52] The Eighth Census of the United States, 1860 (Washington D.C.: Census Office, 1864-6), gives the number of rice mills on the Lower Cape Fear as ten.

[53] Cf., also, *The Farmers' Register* (Edmund Ruffin, 1833), volume I, p. 687.

But notwithstanding the probable value and volume of rice produced in North Carolina, it is nevertheless correct that lumber - pine boards, staves and headings, and naval stores - tar, pitch and turpentine, were the principal drivers behind North Carolina's economic growth in the first half of the eighteenth century.

A bounty to encourage the production of naval stores had been introduced by Britain in 1705,[54] a reaction to the rise in prices that followed the grant of a naval stores monopoly by Sweden to the Stockholm Tar Company and the restrictions imposed during the Swedish-Russian War from 1699-1721. Britain had for years run a *c.*£200,000 annual trade deficit with Denmark and Sweden as a result of imported naval stores. The bounty was designed to encourage an alternative source of supply and to generate profits in America that would expand the demand for imported British goods.

The bounty was in place for two decades until 1725 when it was suspended briefly following overproduction. It was reinstated in 1729 and remained in place until the 1770s. While London may have assumed that New England, New York and Pennsylvania would be the principal beneficiaries, it was North Carolina with its fast-growing longleaf pine forests that reaped the largest financial advantage, with the colony accounting for over half of America's naval stores.[55]

Each ten acres of North Carolina's pine forests could be tapped for around 100 barrels of crude turpentine annually. The vast majority of the

---

[54] The bounty was £4 per ton for tar and pitch; £3 per ton, turpentine and rosin; £6 per ton, hemp; and £1 per ton for masts, yards and bowsprits. The bounty was set a level designed to equalise production costs in America as compared to the Baltic. Cf., Justin Williams, 'English Mercantilism and Carolina Naval Stores, 1705-1776', *Journal of Southern History*, 1.2 (1935), 169-85.

[55] Charles C. Crittenden, *The Commerce of North Carolina, 1763- 1789* (New Haven, CN: YUP, 1936), p. 73. Also, Percival Perry, 'The Naval-Stores Industry in the Old South, 1790-1860', *Journal of Southern History*, 34.4 (1968), 509-26, esp. 510; and Justin Williams, 'English Mercantilism and Carolina Naval Stores, 1705-1776', *Journal of Southern History*, 1.2 (1935), 169-85.

thousands of barrels produced went to Britain, with the balance to the West Indies. Common tar was manufactured from fallen trees which were split and then fired in a kiln. Higher quality green tar was made from a combination of live and dead wood and fetched a premium, but was produced only in modest quantities. Three barrels of tar produced two of pitch, which was manufactured by burning tar in cauldrons or pits.[56]

Processing lumber and naval stores underpinned early economic development in the Lower Cape Fear,[57] with Wilmington acting as an entrepôt for these products as well as cotton and rice. The town also served as a distribution hub for imported and manufactured goods sourced from Philadelphia, Boston, New York, and especially Charleston, which quickly became the main commercial centre for the Southern colonies.[58]

Wilmington's factors and merchants were active in both the export and import trades, and generally paid on commission. They consolidated shipments, arranged coastal and transatlantic transport, and provided credit and barter services, exchanging agricultural produce, naval stores and lumber for imported goods. Traders elsewhere in North Carolina, including Edenton and New Bern, offered similar arrangements.

Although few if any North Carolina merchants had the financial muscle to compete with Charleston's Benjamin Smith, Henry Laurens, John Savage or Gabriel Manigault, many were highly successful nonetheless. Not all were based in the colony's principal ports. Important inland commercial

---

[56] For example, K.H. Ledward (ed), *Journals of the Board of Trade and Plantations: volume 7, January 1735 - December 1741* (London: HMSO, 1930), pp. 61-7.

[57] The first wood mill was established in New Town in 1727; forty years later some fifty mills were in operation processing more than 3 million feet of lumber per year.

[58] Louis Kyriakoudes, 'The Southern City: Merchants and Boosterism in Ante-Bellum Wilmington, North Carolina', *Honors Essays* (Chapel Hill, NC: UNCP, 1985), volume II. Cf., also, John B. Payne, American Coastwise Commerce, 1763-1775 (UNC, unpublished PhD Thesis, 1964).

hubs including Halifax and Cross Creek had developed by the 1760s and attracted merchants sponsored by firms as far away as Scotland.[59] But the majority of traders were home-grown independents, many operating across the region from multiple locations, with a few larger merchant houses such as *Hogg & Clayton* maintaining an office in Charleston.[60]

Economic growth and the wealth it delivered spurred the development of freemasonry in North Carolina in the 1750s and 1760s, and despite the paucity of primary sources, many prominent merchants can be identified within the ranks of North Carolina's masonic lodges. Cornelius Harnett Jr. of St John's Lodge Wilmington is the most obvious example but it would be wrong to disregard several of his masonic colleagues, including William Hooper, Joshua Toomer and the Campbell family. The lodge at New Bern contained at least fifteen merchants including the Williams family, David Barron, Richard Ellis, James Green, the Guion family, Thomas Haslen, John Horner Hill, Alexander McAuslan, Thomas McLin and John Wright Stanley. Edenton's Unanimity Lodge had at least four: John Boggs, Charles Bondfield, John Cooper and William Scott. That at Pitt County included John Simpson, among others. And although the lodge at Halifax comprised a majority of planters, several, including Montfort, McCulloch and Campbell, were also merchant-traders.[61] Merchants and store owners were likewise members of many of the Piedmont's lodges.

A combination of rapid population growth and expanding domestic and international trade spurred North Carolina's commercial development, increasing demand and generating a self-reinforcing cycle of wealth creation. As settlement stretched west into the Piedmont over the second half of the eighteenth century, the colony's output expanded to encompass a broader range of agricultural products, including livestock. And with the Piedmont accessed more easily from the north and south rather than North Carolina's

---

[59] Crittenden, *The Commerce of North Carolina*, p. 97.
[60] Stuart O. Stumpf, 'South Carolina Importers of General Merchandise, 1735-1765', *South Carolina Historical Magazine*, 84.1 (1983), 1-10.
[61] Crittenden, *The Commerce of North Carolina*, p. 97.

eastern seaboard, new trading and business links were forged as produce was despatched to Charleston, Hampton and other ports in South Carolina and Virginia for consignment on vessels sailing for Britain and the Caribbean.[62]

'TO ALL INGENIOUS AND INDUSTRIOUS PERSONS ... THERE IS A NEW PLANTATION'[63]

Bath, one of the first major settlements in North Carolina beyond the Albemarle Sound, is sited around ten miles west of the mouth of the Pamlico and Pungo Rivers. The town was incorporated in 1705, the first in North Carolina to be recognised formally, and was settled initially by French Protestants - Huguenots - fleeing religious persecution. Bath expanded over the following decade and attracted migrants from other colonies, including Maryland and Virginia. It became the *de facto* regional capital and the base for three of the Lords Proprietor's governors - Robert Daniel, Thomas Cary and Charles Eden.[64]

The best known if most notorious resident was probably Edward Teach - 'Blackbeard' - who settled at Plum Point in June 1718.[65] Pardoned and protected by Governor Eden, who had probably been paid to do so, Blackbeard's piracy ended five months later with his death on 22 November 1718 in a skirmish near the Ocracoke Inlet on the Outer Banks. He was

---

[62] Ibid., p. 73. Cf., also, Perry, 'The Naval-Stores Industry in the Old South, 1790-1860'; and Francis Carroll Huntley, 'The Seaborne Trade of Virginia in Mid-Eighteenth Century: Port Hampton', *Virginia Magazine of History and Biography*, 59.3 (1951), 297-308.

[63] W. Noel Sainsbury (ed), *Calendar of State Papers Colonial, America and West Indies: volume 9, 1675-1676 and Addenda 1574-1674* (London: HMSO, 1893), pp. 144-6: Shaftesbury Papers: 'New Plantation at Cape Florida, Carolina'.

[64] Robert Daniel (1646-1718), governor, 1703-05; Thomas Cary (d.1718), governor, 1705-06, 1708-11; and Charles Eden (1673-1722), governor 1713-22. Until 1712, the incumbent was technically deputy governor for the northern part of the province of Carolina.

[65] Edward Teach, 'Blackbeard' (c.1680-1718).

killed by a small naval force led by Lieutenant Robert Maynard under orders from Governor Spotswood of Virginia who had offered a bounty for Blackbeard's capture or death.[66]

Bath's commercial zenith was brief and it was soon overshadowed by ports less restricted by shallow water and sandbars. The town also declined in political importance. Although North Carolina's assembly met at Bath on three occasions, it was later passed over in favour of Edenton and then New Bern, the second town to be incorporated in North Carolina.

New Bern is located where the Trent and Neuse rivers merge. Its founder, Christoph Graffenried,[67] a minor Swiss nobleman, led an influx of several hundred mainly Swiss settlers in 1710 but a majority of the town's early inhabitants were religious refugees from the German Rhineland - the Palatinate.[68]

Thousands of Palatine exiles had arrived in London in the autumn and winter of 1708/09 fleeing religious persecution. Many had been encouraged by pamphlets promoting settlement in the American colonies and hoped or believed that they would be granted free passage. By mid-1709 London housed over 13,000 refugees. Most were accommodated in tents to the east of London at Blackheath and Camberwell, and at Deptford at the Royal Navy's rope yard. And Charles Cox, a brewer, housed another 1,400 at his warehouses at Southwark on the south bank of the Thames.[69]

The government was forced to act. The majority of Palatines were resettled in upper New York to act as a buffer against the French, or dispatched to Ireland to bolster the number of Protestants in the country, but a small minority

---

[66] Cf., George Humphrey Yetter, 'When Blackbeard Scourged the Seas', *Colonial Williamsburg Journal*, 15.1 (1992), 22-8. Blackbeard boarded Maynard's ship and Maynard and Blackbeard ended up in hand-to-hand combat.

[67] Baron von Christoph Graffenried (1661-1743).

[68] The Swiss connection is in the name: New Bern or 'Neuse Bern', a compression of Bern on the Neuse River.

[69] Cf., Berman, *Foundations*, pp. 83-4, 101-2.

was permitted to sail for New Bern, accompanied by John Lawson, North Carolina's surveyor-general.[70] Many died during the transatlantic crossing and others fell ill after arriving in the colony. Nonetheless, with Graffenried's support the colony stabilised and the population reached 400 within a year. And although New Bern was almost destroyed during the Tuscarora War less than four years later, the town was rebuilt and subsequently flourished.

In the late 1720s and 1730s, the focus of settlement shifted further south with a growing number of migrants arriving at Brunswick and New Town,[71] Cape Fear's two ports. The area had been populated initially by incomers from South Carolina but migration from Ireland and Scotland soon became a more important factor in the region's development. Accounts of Cape Fear's commercial potential were relayed back across the Atlantic and encouraged further migration such that within barely more than a decade settlement had pushed ninety miles along the Cape Fear River.

Migration increased further in the 1740s when Governor Gabriel Johnston opened up the interior to Highland Scots following the defeat of James Stuart's supporters at Culloden. Johnston offered incomers 50 acres per person at low prices with an exemption from land tax for up to a decade.[72] The strategy was acceptable to London. Few policies were more effective in preventing a future Jacobite insurrection than the removal of potential insurgents 3,600 miles west across the Atlantic. Scottish migration remained a major influence throughout the eighteenth century, driven by the pull of family connection and decent commercial prospects, and the push of land clearance and famine.[73]

Cross Creek was established in the late 1750s, initially as a trading post at the intersection of two trails: the North-South Road that connected Cross

---

[70] John Lawson (1674-1711), explorer, surveyor and author of *A New Voyage to Carolina* (London, 1709). He was subsequently captured and killed by the Tuscarora.

[71] Wilmington.

[72] Cf., Jenni Calder, *Scots in the USA* (Edinburgh: Luath Press, 2005).

[73] Especially in the 1770s and thereafter.

Creek with Brunswick and Hillsborough, and the Yadkin Road that linked it to Salisbury. A few years later, property lots were sold and a town laid out.

Within less than a decade Cross Creek had developed into a regional commercial centre and the second largest town on the Cape Fear behind Wilmington. The town lay at the heart of a widely-spread farming community producing lumber and naval stores as well as corn, rye, flax and cotton. Part was shipped down-river to Wilmington for processing and export, and part to Charleston. Land clearance brought cattle, hog and sheep farming to the region, and by the late 1760s the town boasted tanneries and forges alongside grain and saw mills and stores and taverns. Its economic success spawned further growth with English and Irish migrants following where the Scots had led.

In 1778 Cross Creek merged with Campbellton, just over a mile away, and in 1783 the combination was renamed Fayetteville in honour of the Marquis de Lafayette, a retitling that masked the region's loyalist sympathies during the war.[74]

Domestic Disunion

Settlement of the North Carolina back-country - the Piedmont - became marked from the early 1750s. The majority of migrants travelled overland south along the Great Wagon Road and the Upper and Fall Line Roads from Pennsylvania, Maryland and Virginia. The incomers were a mix of relocating colonists seeking less expensive cultivable land and new arrivals, mainly from the north of Ireland but also Europe, especially the German states.

Unlike the eastern coastal plain which was predominantly Anglican, the Piedmont was occupied by a heterogeneous mix of Pennsylvania Quakers, Ulster Presbyterians, English Dissenters, and German Moravians and Lutherans.

---

[74] Marquis de Lafayette (1757-1834). Fayette County was established the following year when the general assembly split Cumberland County into Fayette and Moore Counties. The principal loyalists were Highland Scots.

An evangelical religious revival in the 1760s, 'the first Great Awakening', ushered in other denominations, including Methodists and Baptists, both of which put down deep roots across the back-country and along the frontier.

The principal divisions in North Carolina were however not religious but political, social and economic. North Carolina's oldest settled areas around the Albemarle Sound had resented giving up power and sharing control over patronage with those they disparaged as relative newcomers whether at Bath, New Bern or Cape Fear. But in the 1760s, the political mêlée pivoted away from disagreements between the different east coast factions towards a dispute that set the east coast establishment as a whole against the politically under-represented but increasingly heavily populated Piedmont. The east's reluctance to alter the status quo and existing power dynamic, and an unwillingness to approve new counties in the west, the basis of electoral representation, was designed to preserve its dominance and resist a westward shift in political gravity.

The lack of proportionate representation for the Piedmont exacerbated other issues. The east-dominated legislature had authority to appoint office-holders and since patronage was as powerful a political factor in New Bern as in London, eastern placemen dominated the lists of those chosen as sheriffs, court clerks, surveyors, land agents and other public officials across the frontier.

With no connections to those they administered, eastern appointees applied few brakes to their self-interest. The Piedmont's farmers and traders were subject to fines and taxes that appeared to be or were arbitrary. And if they appealed, faced legal costs and court fees that could dwarf the original claim, even if successful. Where payment was not made promptly and in specie, their properties were open to seizure and auction, and could be and were sold at a fraction of intrinsic value. Many of those bidding were easterners, frequently the friends or family of men complicit in the seizure. Misfeasance and corruption were commonplace and western resentment substantial and justified.

Antagonism between east and west was not limited to North Carolina. Similar disputes occurred in other colonies from Massachusetts to Georgia.

Differences over which policies should be adopted to protect the frontier;[75] whether and how the first nations should be accommodated; what taxes should be levied and at which rates; and the all-consuming issue of representation, featured in the legislatures of most if not all the thirteen colonies. But in North Carolina the acrimony between the two sides extended beyond legislative debate. The province was riven by civil war with western settlers taking-up arms in an attempt to control and regulate their own affairs.

The Regulator Movement has been analysed and described in numerous books, articles and theses.[76] Its relevance in this work is that it offers an analogy to what occurred within North Carolina freemasonry, with those in the east looking mainly to the established authority of the Grand Lodge of England, and those in the centre and west guided by Irish and Antients freemasonry, introduced to North Carolina principally by the émigré Irish and London Irish.

---

[75] The reluctance of the Quaker administration in Pennsylvania to protect frontier settlements militarily was a key driver behind settler relocation.

[76] For example, J.J. Hamilton. *Herman Husband: Penman of the Regulation* (PhD thesis, Wake Forest University, NC, 1969); C.J. Stewart, *The Affairs of Boston in the North Carolina Backcountry during the American Revolution* (PhD thesis, University of North Carolina at Greensboro, NC, 2010); J.L. Walker, *The Regulator Movement: Sectional Controversy in North Carolina, 1765-1771* (PhD thesis, Louisiana State University, LA, 1962); J.P. Whittenburg, *Backwoods Revolutionaries: Social Context and Constitutional Theories of the North Carolina Regulators, 1765-1771* (PhD thesis, University of Georgia, GA, 1974). Also, Richard M. Brown, *The South Carolina Regulators: The Story of the First American Vigilante Movement* (Cambridge, MA: Belknap Press, 1963); M. Kars, *Breaking Loose Together: The Regulator Rebellion in Pre-Revolutionary North Carolina* (Chapel Hill, NC: UNCP, 2002); M.L.M. Kay & L.L. Cary, 'Class, Mobility, and Conflict in North Carolina on the Eve of the Revolution' in Jeffrey J. Crow and Larry E. Tise (eds), *The Southern Experience in the American Revolution* (Chapel Hill, NC: UNCP, 1978).

Chapter One

Freemasonry in North Carolina

North Carolina's first two Masonic Governors

Sir Richard Everard

Freemasonry may have had little more than a tangential role in Sir Richard Everard's appointment as governor of North Carolina but his membership of the Rose Tavern Lodge in London's Temple Bar[1] illustrates his social status and provides an insight into how patronage was wielded in the eighteenth century.

The Rose Tavern's members included wealthy merchants, professional men and members of parliament, both Whig and Tory.[2] John Kemp, the master of the lodge, was a City merchant,[3] as was his senior warden, John Pollexfen, a sometime High Sheriff of Devonshire who had inherited an immense estate at Mothecombe in South Devon.

Pollexfen traded from Plymouth[4] and London, where he had a house in Walbrook, a few yards from the Royal Exchange in the heart of the City. The family had long-standing commercial relationships with the American colonies with his late father, a member of the Council of Trade and Plantations, taking a close interest in the defence and security of Carolina.[5] Nicholas

---

[1] The Rose Tavern was located in Cross Key Alley at the corner of Thanet Place, Temple Bar. Strype describes it as 'a well-customed house with good conveniences of rooms and a good garden'.

[2] A complete list of members is given in appendix five.

[3] Kemp traded principally with Hamburg and the Baltic.

[4] Cf., *Daily Post*, 8 February 1738.

[5] Cecil Headlam (ed), *Calendar of State Papers Colonial, America and West Indies: volume 20, 1702* (London: HMSO, 1912), pp. 588-92, 15 September 1702. Cf., also,

Pollexfen, John's cousin, another member of the lodge, had inherited the majority of the family trading business and was also based at Walbrook.

The lodge included five parliamentarians, three of whom were staunch Tories. Sir John Chichester[6] represented Barnstable from 1734-40. His father had also sat for the constituency, most recently from 1713-18. Sir John's name is included in a list of prospective supporters sent in 1721 to the exiled James Stuart, the Pretender; he also corresponded with Jacobite agents during the Atterbury plot of 1722 but was not arrested.[7]

Sir Thomas Twisden, another London merchant, represented Kent as a Tory from 1722-27.[8] The family had purchased the Bradbourne estate in the mid-1650s and sat for the Maidstone and Rochester constituencies in parliament. They were suspected of being Jacobites and rumoured to have visited James Stuart in Paris, but this may have been simply a matter of political insurance.[9]

Henry Pacey,[10] MP for Boston in Lincolnshire from 1722 until his death in 1729, had been Boston's mayor in 1708 and again in 1720. The borough was consistently Tory and Pacey, a loyal corporation man and landowner, held office locally as deputy recorder from 1709-15 and again from 1724-27.

Richard Grassby, 'Pollexfen, John (1636-1715)', *ODNB*, accessed 4 November 2017.

[6] Sir John Chichester (1689-1740), 4th baronet.

[7] *Report from the Committee appointed by the House of Commons to examine Christopher Layer and others* (1723), appendix F. 11. Cf., also Berman, *Espionage, Diplomacy & the Lodge*.

[8] Sir Thomas Twisden (1688-1728), 3rd baronet.

[9] Romney Sedgwick (ed), *The History of Parliament: the House of Commons 1715-1754* (Martlesham: Boydell & Brewer, 1970). Cf., also, http://www.historyofparliamentonline.org.

[10] Henry Pacey (1669-1729).

John Hopkins,[11] a successful stock jobber and merchant, was one of the lodge's Whig MPs, representing the pocket borough[12] of Eye from 1710-15,[13] and afterwards Ilchester, another pocket borough, from 1715-22.[14] Nicknamed 'vulture', Hopkins was immensely wealthy, partly from insider trading, especially in South Sea Company stock.[15] His estate was valued at over £300,000 at his death in 1732, the equivalent of perhaps some £300 million today.[16]

Other Whigs include Sir Thomas Samwell,[17] an MP for Coventry from 1715-22. A firm supporter of Sir Robert Walpole,[18] Samwell's fellow constituency MP was his cousin, Sir Adolphus Oughton,[19] a soldier, courtier and another freemason, a member of the Horn Tavern Lodge.

---

[11] John Hopkins (1663-1732).

[12] A 'pocket borough' was a parliamentary constituency controlled by one family; they were abolished in the nineteenth century with the passage of the Reform Acts of 1832 and 1867.

[13] Eye was in the control of the Cornwallis family whose estate was two miles away. The election was contested on only one occasion - in 1747, when John Cornwallis stood unsuccessfully against his brother's interest.

[14] Ilchester was controlled by the Lockyer family whose nominees generally voted with the government.

[15] Insider trading was made illegal in Britain only in the 1980s. It was made illegal in the USA in 1934.

[16] The comparison is based on a wage deflator not consumer prices.

[17] Sir Thomas Samwell (1687-1757), 2nd baronet. See appendix five.

[18] Robert Walpole, later 1st Earl of Orford (1676-1745). There are numerous biographies. Cf., for a summary, Stephen Taylor, 'Walpole, Robert, first earl of Orford (1676-1745)', *ODNB*, 2008 edn.

[19] Adolphus Oughton (1684-1736), 1st major and colonel Coldstream Guards, 1715; colonel 8th Dragoon Guards, 1733; brigadier general, 1735. MP for Coventry, 1715-death. He was knighted in 1722.

Sir Richard Everard mixed in the same social circles.[20] He was born at *Langleys*, a large estate at Much Waltham in Essex which his family had owned since the sixteenth century.[21] Sir Hugh, his father, had been receiver-general of taxes for the county of Essex but was so indebted at his death that his executors sold *Langleys* to pay his creditors. The house was purchased by Samuel Tufnell, a wealthy brewer and merchant, a member of the Bell Tavern Lodge in Westminster.[22]

Everard married shortly afterwards and acquired a smaller property at nearby Broomfield. His wife, Susannah, was one of two surviving daughters of Richard Kidder, the Bishop of Bath and Wells.[23] Everard had been a serving army officer at the time of his father's death and subsequently resigned his commission,[24] a decision that was probably linked to the time and expense incurred in defending litigation connected to his late father's estate.[25]

Everard petitioned successfully for the position of governor of North Carolina in 1725. It is no more than conjecture but since several members of the Rose Tavern traded actively with the Carolinas they would have had reason to recommend his candidacy.[26] Patronage and reciprocated favours were the currency of eighteenth-century business and politics, a means by

---

[20] Sir Richard Everard (c.1683-1732), 4th baronet. Cf., William S. Powell, 'Everard, Sir Richard, baronet (1683-1733)', *ODNB*, online edn, Jan 2008.

[21] Now 'Great Waltham'.

[22] Tufnell was later MP for Maldon (1715-22), Colchester (1727-34) and Great Marlow (1741-47).

[23] Richard Kidder (1633-1703), Bishop of Bath and Wells. He was killed in the Great Storm of 1703 when the chimney of the bishop's palace at Wells collapsed.

[24] Although the *ODNB* states that Everard resigned from the army in 1706, a newspaper report three years later refers to 'Sir Richard Everard's Company at Chelmsford', Essex, and to Everard being in command at that time: cf., *Post Boy*, 15-17 February 1709.

[25] NA, C 6/407/36; C 6/406/50; C 6/525/254; C 7/53/118; C 11/1978/15; C 11/2220/38 *et al*.

[26] Cf., John Pollexfen, *A Discourse of Trade and Coyn* (London, 1697).

which those with influence could benefit their family and associates and be benefited in return.

A family autobiography suggests that Everard also knew the Lords Proprietors socially: 'The Lords Proprietors were all particular friends of Sir Richard, and it has been understood in the family that his patrimony had been much reduced by adventuring in the South Sea bubble, and he accepted from the Proprietors the government of North Carolina to repair his estate.'[27] This is plausible and may explain why Everard was granted 5,000 acres in North Carolina in addition to his salary.[28]

A letter from the Proprietors dated 27 February 1725 announced Everard's appointment 'in the room of George Burrington Esq. against whom we have receiv'd many complaints.'[29] The nomination was received positively at the Board of Trade and just over a month later was advanced to the Privy Council[30] for royal consent.[31] The speed with which Everard's name was approved suggests that he was known to those crown officials concerned with Britain's American colonies: Martin Bladen at the Board of Trade and Charles Delafaye at the Southern Department. Not only was

---

[27] *Autobiography of David Meade II*: http://files.usgwarchives.net/va/nansemond/bios/meade01.txt, accessed 30 March 2016. Meade became Everard's son-in-law, cf., NA, C 11/1067/19.

[28] DNCB.

[29] Cecil Headlam and Arthur Percival Newton (eds), *Calendar of State Papers Colonial, America and West Indies: volume 34, 1724-1725* (London: HMSO, 1936), pp. 320-35, 27 February 1725. George Burrington (1682-1759). Governor of North Carolina from 1724-25 and again from 1731-34.

[30] The Privy Council was a body of advisers to the king (a 'private council') whose members comprised mainly senior politicians. It advised the sovereign on the exercise of royal prerogative and issued instructions in its own name through Orders in Council. It was also the final Court of Appeal. The Privy Council remains active today. Cf., http://researchbriefings.parliament.uk/ResearchBriefing/Summary/CBP-7460, accessed 11 October 2017.

[31] K.H. Ledward (ed), *Journals of the Board of Trade and Plantations: volume 5, January 1723 - December 1728* (London: HMSO, 1928), pp. 179-86, 2 June 1725.

upper middling London a relatively small community but all three were freemasons: Bladen a member of the lodge at the Rummer Tavern near Charing Cross, and Delafaye of the Horn Tavern in New Palace Yard, a short stroll away.

The rationale for Everard's appointment as North Carolina's new governor was as stated by the Proprietors: a requirement to replace the incumbent, George Burrington, following multiple allegations of misconduct in office.

Depositions and complaints from members of North Carolina's council had been made against Burrington and delivered to the Lords Proprietors in person by Christopher Gale,[32] the colony's chief justice.[33] A formal complaint was also raised with the Customs Commissioners, whose concerns were forwarded to the Board of Trade with a request that they 'enquire into the matter and be a means that the grievance complained of be redressed'.

So serious were the charges that Gale was ordered to attend the Board in person. His testimony to the Customs Office and his deposition to the Board are summarised in their respective minutes:[34]

Memorial of Christopher Gale to the Commissioners of HM Customs.

Memorialist has executed the office of Collector within the port of Beaufort, N. Carolina for two years. He had prepared the last quarterly accounts in order to be proved before George Burrington ... but before he had the opportunity to offer them, the said Governor insulted him in a public Court then in the execution of his office as Chief Justice (which office he hath executed for near twenty years with the general approbation of all persons).

---

[32] Christopher Gale (*c*.1679-1735).

[33] The petition was co-signed by seven members of the nine-man council.

[34] Cecil Headlam and Arthur Percival Newton (eds), *Calendar of State Papers Colonial, America and West Indies: volume 34, 1724-1725* (London: HMSO, 1936), pp. 302-20: Carkess to Popple, 28 January 1725.

A few days after he attempted to break into his house with intent to murder him, so that he was obliged to leave the Government and his office etc. He knows of no reason for such behaviour, unless it be for his supporting the Naval Officer and Collector of Customs in the port of Roanoke and advising them when applied to as Chief Justice, for the interest of HM Revenue and support of trade, when they were the one of them imprisoned and the other publicly threatened and insulted for only doing the duty of their office. Instances a seizure made in the Port of Roanake by the Governor himself of a Boston vessel on July 15 for illegal entry. After keeping her for two days he discharged her of his own authority without trial.[35]

Deposition of Christopher Gale. London, January 26, 1724.

The Governor at his first arrival, near two months before he saw deponent, gave out several menacing speeches against him, saying he would slit his nose, crop his ears, and lay him in irons etc. At the last General Court he grossly reviled Deponent, and his abusive interruptions caused the Court to be adjourned, ever since which he has continued to revile him, whereby his authority is weakened etc. Early on Sunday morning 23rd August, the Governor attempted to break into his house in Edenton with intent to murder him, to the very great terror of his family, but finding he could not break open the door, he broke the window all to pieces, cursing and threatening him, that he would have him by the throat speedily, and burn his house, or blow it up etc. etc. as preceding.[36]

True or otherwise, the allegations were taken at face value. Burrington's behaviour had been corroborated by other members of the council and Gale had standing in London. Among his patrons was Lord Carteret, one of the

---

[35] Ibid., 28 January 1725.
[36] Ibid.

more important Lords Proprietors, and Gale's family were members of Yorkshire's minor gentry. Gale himself had studied law as an articled clerk but left for America in 1700, one of many who sought to make their fortune in the colonies.[37] He succeeded, becoming a successful Indian trader and merchant. More importantly, Gale's marriage to Sarah Laker Harvey, the daughter of the former governor's widow, and Benjamin Laker, a member of the governor's council, provided Gale with entrée to the upper ranks of North Carolina society. It also placed him on the fast-track to political favour and provided access to financial capital.

Gale was appointed to the colony's Supreme Court and General Court in 1703, and the following year Governor Daniel[38] gave him the concurrent post of attorney general. Seeking to consolidate his position, Gale pressed his case personally with the Lords Proprietors and in 1715 obtained a patent as chief justice for North Carolina. Despite a four-year absence from 1717-21, which included a visit to England and a two-year commission as chief justice to the Bahamas, Gale was granted a second warrant as chief justice on his return.

GEORGE BURRINGTON

Burrington had been sworn to office as governor of North Carolina in January 1724. He succeeded William Reed,[39] who served as acting governor for two years following Charles Eden's death in office. Notwithstanding what would follow, Burrington's relationship with Gale had begun well. Within less than three months Gale was named to Burrington's council and members of his family given lucrative public offices in the colony. Gale's brother, Edmond, was appointed an assistant justice of the General Court,

---

[37] *DNCB*.
[38] Robert Daniel (*c.*1648-1718). Governor of North Carolina, 1703-5, and deputy (and acting) governor of South Carolina, 1716-17. Also written as 'Daniell'.
[39] William Reed (*c.*1670-1728), president of the council and thus acting governor, 1722-24.

and his sons-in-law, Henry Clayton and William Little, provost marshal and attorney general, respectively.[40]

But the initial harmony was short lived. Burrington's decision to consider an allegation of fraud in connection with Governor Eden's will triggered a passionate dispute, with Gale declining to implement Burrington's order that the governor's council convene as a Court of Ordinary to deliberate the matter. Gale's refusal was designed to protect his family and political allies, including John Lovick, the colony's secretary, and Clayton, his son-in-law. But whether Eden's will was drafted and executed deceitfully quickly became a secondary issue. Burrington was furious at Gale's decision to contradict his instructions and retaliated by insulting Gale in court and physically attacking his house in Edenton.

A combination of manufactured and justifiable alarm at Burrington's actions and threats drove Gale to decamp to London where he laid his and other depositions before the Lords Proprietors, each of which attested to Burrington's mercurial behaviour. Despite little hard evidence, the signatures of eight council members forced London's hand and within a few months Burrington's tenure was brought to a (temporary) close and Everard advanced as his replacement.

Everard Again...

Having posted financial security for his commission, Everard sailed to North Carolina in the spring of 1725. Burrington vacated his post formally in July, the same month that Everard was sworn to office in Edenton. Gale gained from his role in securing Burrington's dismissal and was invited to join the governor's nine-man council. And in the belief that he was now untouchable, Gale sought to exploit his authority and acquire greater political and judicial power.

---

[40] William Little (1691-1734).

Gale was opposed by a faction led by Edmund Porter,[41] an attorney who sat as sole judge of the Court of Vice-Admiralty, and John Baptista Ashe,[42] a prominent member of the assembly and its speaker in 1725 and 1726. Both had been associated with Burrington and with the ex-governor choosing to remain in the colony for another year, the relationship between the two sides became poisonous with the colony's principal and now rival courts firing legal broadsides at each other.

Gale and Porter's mutual antipathy set the jurisdiction of Gale's common law court against that of the crown and Porter's admiralty court; it was a fight that only the latter could win. Everard was drawn in to the dispute and issued writs of *nolle prosequi* - notices of abandonment - against a number of Gale's politically-motivated indictments.

Everard's support for Porter gave him the upper hand in the judicial face-off and Porter prosecuted and then imprisoned (albeit only temporarily) first the attorney general and then Gale, the chief justice.

At the same time and notwithstanding opposition from within the colony, Everard carried out his orders from London to restrict the issue of new land grants. This was highly unpopular, especially among the planters of the Lower Cape Fear where Burrington's expansionist settlement plans were put into reverse.

Everard's actions also worsened the political stand-off between the northern colonists from the Albemarle and Pamlico region, a clique supported by Gale and his allies, and the incomers from South Carolina who had acquired land around Brunswick and across the Lower Cape Fear. The dispute was economic and political, with the northern colonists seeking to

---

[41] Edmund Porter (1685-1737).

[42] John Baptista Ashe (d.1734). His marriage to Elizabeth Swann, daughter of Samuel Swann (1653-1707), procured allies with several leading families in the province, including the Moseleys and Moores, and brought Ashe firmly into the social and political elites.

retain their dominance in the assembly and council in the face of the influx of settlers to the south.⁴³

Burrington's land grant-friendly policies had increased the acreage under cultivation and led to higher economic growth in the Lower Cape Fear. But this was not the only issue that split north and south. The Cape Fear settlers feared that Everard's efforts to resolve the northern colonists' concerns over trade would be to the exclusion of their own.

With a high proportion of the Albemarle's exports shipped through Virginia, northern planters and farmers were hostage to the fees charged by Virginia's port officials, and Cape Fear's planters believed that valuable political capital was being expended in a fruitless attempt to convince the Board of Trade to intervene.

But the most significant issue overhanging Everard's tenure as governor was the impending change to the colony's ownership. It had been obvious since the early 1720s that the crown would acquire the Lords Proprietors' rights in North Carolina and in preparation for that event Everard established a joint commission with Virginia to finalise the boundary between the two colonies.

Commissioners were chosen to represent each side with Everard appointing four: Christopher Gale, John Lovick, William Little and Edward Moseley, who would subsequently become an opposition figurehead during Burrington's second term in office.⁴⁴ To state the obvious, the commissioners' remit facilitated land grabbing, which took place on a broad scale.⁴⁵

---

⁴³ Cf., William S. Price, Jr., 'A Strange Incident in George Burrington's Royal Governorship', *North Carolina Historical Review*, 51.2 (1974), 149-58.

⁴⁴ *DNCB*. Moseley sat as an assemblyman from 1705-34; he was speaker of the assembly from 1722-23 and again in 1731-34, and was afterwards appointed to the royal council.

⁴⁵ State Archives of North Carolina, North Carolina Land Grants Images and Data: www.nclandgrants.com.

What was less usual was the charge of abuse of office levied at Gale in 1729 by William Byrd, a member of Virginia's royal council.[46]

With the prospect of an imminent change from proprietary to crown ownership and in the knowledge that Burrington had rehabilitated his reputation in England and was benefiting from a groundswell of support within North Carolina, Everard was aware that his remaining time in office was limited. Perhaps it was this that drove him to change tack and allow land grants to resume in the Lower Cape Fear, with new warrants issued over some 400,000 acres, the majority via blank land patents. Everard also chose to disregard his instructions regarding money supply and approved the issue of new proclamation money. There is little doubt that he had been incentivised to do so:

> *Mr Porter to Governor Burrington.* Our session ended last Thursday, when Sir Richard confirmed several laws, one for raising £30,000 paper currency, who has a present for so doing of £500. How this latter conduct will be approved of in England, in respect it breaks one of the Articles of his Instructions, we are at a loss to judge. I prevailed with him for near a twelvemonth last past to stop warrants and patents for land, till H.M. pleasure was known; himself having wrote the Duke of Newcastle his resolutions etc. (v. 18th June), which now he is every day breaking through by signing patents.[47]

The Albemarle faction was furious at Everard's *volte face* and protested to the Lords Proprietors and to the Board of Trade. In August 1729 the Board agreed to examine the allegations and did so the following month. But although it was accepted that the charges against Everard were of a 'high and heinous' nature, the Board refused to censure him on the technical basis

---

[46] William Byrd (1674-1744), a planter and surveyor.
[47] Cecil Headlam and Arthur Percival Newton (eds), *Calendar of State Papers Colonial, America and West Indies: Volume 36, 1728-1729* (London: HMSO, 1937), pp. 527-40.

that 'no proofs had been transmitted'. The Board proposed instead that Burrington, now rehabilitated and nominated as the first royal governor of North Carolina, 'be directed to make strict enquiries into the truth of [the allegations], that exemplary justice may be done':[48]

> Order in Council of 22 January last, requiring copies of the papers of complaint from the members of the Council of North Carolina against Sir Richard Everard, Deputy Governor of that province, under the Lords Proprietors: as likewise of the complaint made by Sir Richard against the said Council, to put into the hands of Captain Burrington, now appointed Governor, for his examination into and report of the facts.[49]

Notwithstanding the supposedly indefensible nature of the accusations levied against Everard, there was little appetite or urgency to investigate.[50] Burrington delayed taking up his reappointment as governor for a further twelve months and in the interim Everard remained in office. And when Burrington finally arrived in the colony in February 1731, Everard was not arrested but allowed to depart for England by way of Virginia, where his elder daughter, Susannah, met and married David Meade,[51] a Nansemond County planter, merchant and ship owner.[52]

---

[48] Cecil Headlam and Arthur Percival Newton (eds), *Calendar of State Papers Colonial, America and West Indies: volume 36, 1728-1729*, pp. 475-85; and. K.H. Ledward (ed), *Journals of the Board of Trade and Plantations: volume 6, January 1729 - December 1734* (London: HMSO, 1928), pp. 119-28, 2 June 1730.

[49] K.H. Ledward (ed), *Journals of the Board of Trade and Plantations: volume 6, January 1729 - December 1734*, pp. 119-28, 2 June 1730.

[50] Ibid., pp. 114-9.

[51] David Meade (1710-1757). Cf., 'Meade Family History', *William and Mary Quarterly*, 13.1 (1904), 37-45, esp. 37.

[52] 'Virginia Gleanings in England (continued)', *Virginia Magazine of History and Biography*, 37.3 (1929), 253-5, esp. 255; and 'Walker and Wray Families', *William and Mary Quarterly*, 18.4 (1910), 289-91. Also Everard, *DNCB*; and Robert Polk

Everard died in February 1733 a short two years after his return to England; he was interred at Great Waltham in Essex.[53]

BURRINGTON AGAIN...

Burrington's two appointments as governor of North Carolina, the second as the colony's first royal governor, were supported by his patron, Thomas Holles, Duke of Newcastle, who was from 1724 secretary of state for the Southern Department.[54] Newcastle had sponsored Burrington before, most obviously in securing him a commission in the army at the age of seventeen and his promotion to captain.[55]

Burrington was also well-connected within London freemasonry and his lodges, the King's Arms in New Bond Street[56] and the Bear & Harrow in Butcher Row near Temple Bar,[57] were among London's more prestigious.

The sixty-plus members listed in the Bear & Harrow's 1730 membership return to grand lodge include many of freemasonry's most senior figures, not least the then grand master, Viscount Montagu,[58] and the deputy grand

---

Thomson, 'The Tobacco Export of the Upper James River Naval District, 1773-75', *William and Mary Quarterly*, 18.3 (1961), 393-407, esp. 407.

[53] *St James's Evening Post*, 17-20 February 1733 *et al.*

[54] Thomas Pelham-Holles, Duke of Newcastle (1693–1768), later prime minister (1754-56), eldest son of Thomas Pelham. Newcastle owned vast estates in eleven counties which allowed him to influence elections in numerous constituencies. He married Harriet Godolphin, the grand-daughter of the Duke of Marlborough.

[55] William S. Powell, 'Burrington, George (*c.*1685-1759)', *ODNB*.

[56] Constituted 25 November 1722. Previously meeting at the George and Dragon [or 'The George'], Charing Cross (1723), then The Lion, Brewers Street, Golden Square (1725), before moving to the King's Arms in New Bond Street in 1730. No. 10 in the 1729 list.

[57] Constituted either 26 February or 25 March 1730.

[58] Anthony Browne, 7th Viscount Montagu (1686-1767), GM 1732.

master, Thomas Batson.[59] Other current and past grand officers were J.T. Desaguliers, James Smythe, James Chambers, George Rooke and George Moody, alongside several grand stewards.

William Stewart, 3rd Viscount Mountjoy,[60] the future grand master of the Irish and Antients grand lodges, was also a member, as was Arthur Onslow, the influential speaker of the House of Commons and a close ally of Robert Walpole.[61]

Moreover, given his past zeal in issuing land patents, Burrington's return to North Carolina was likewise supported by Cape Fear's planters, their families in South Carolina and their parliamentary agents in London.

But although members of the Bear & Harrow may have influenced Burrington's return to North Carolina, it would have been those at the King's Arms Lodge who lent their support to his first appointment. They included Sir Thomas Samwell, MP for Coventry from 1715-22, another cousin of Sir Adolphus Oughton; and the Hon. William Herbert, the fifth son of the politically potent Earl of Pembroke, who sat in his family's interest as MP for Wilton.[62]

Several of Everard's allies in North Carolina suffered on Burrington's return but others were left relatively unscathed. Perhaps surprisingly their number included Christopher Gale who had returned to England in 1731,

---

[59] Thomas Batson, DGM 1731-4, a barrister and George Payne's brother-in-law, also a member of the Horn. He was a Trustee of the Georgia colony.

[60] William Stewart, 1st Earl of Blessington (1709-1769), an Anglo-Irish peer and member of the House of Lords; known as Sir William Stewart until 1728 and 3rd Viscount Mountjoy from 1728-45.

[61] Arthur Onslow (1691-1768), MP for Guildford (1720-27), then Surrey (1727-61). Onslow was secretary to the Chancellor of the Exchequer (his uncle), 1714-15; receiver-general of the Post Office 1715-20; and speaker of the House of Commons, 1728-61. Among other offices he was sworn to the Privy Council in 1728; appointed chancellor to Queen Caroline, 1729-37; and served as treasurer of the navy, 1734-42.

[62] The Herbert family exercised influence over the parliamentary constituencies of Newport and Wilton.

ostensibly to present a plan to the Board of Trade to assist the tobacco planters of Albemarle County:

> Mr Fitzwilliams, Surveyor General of the Customs in the southern part of America, and Mr Gale, Collector of the Customs in North Carolina, attending, presented to the Board a memorial from the inhabitants of the county of Albemarle in North Carolina, setting forth the great hardships they labour under for being denied the liberty of exporting their tobacco to Great Britain from the ports in Virginia, occasioned by virtue of two Acts passed there... and their Lordships taking the said memorial into consideration, as also both the Acts, gave directions for preparing the draught of a report for repealing the said Acts.[63]

A more important motive for Gale's journey to London was to assess whether he had a future in the colony and lobby for political protection. Gale was aware of the need to put his dispute with Burrington behind him; indeed, he attended a meeting of the Privy Council in November 1731 where he spoke in support of Burrington.

With the Proprietors having relinquished control of North Carolina, Gale needed new patrons and allies. It was that which underlay his meetings with the Bishop of London and the Society for the Propagation of the Gospel, an influential organisation which funded Christian missionaries across the American colonies. And although Gale was effectively neutered politically and never again sat as chief justice, when he returned to North Carolina in 1732 he was permitted to retain the lucrative post of customs collector at the port of Roanoke.[64]

Back as governor for the second time, Burrington acted to consolidate his position. One of his first moves was to compile a report to the Board of

---

[63] K.H. Ledward (ed), *Journals of the Board of Trade and Plantations: volume 6, January 1729 - December 1734*, pp. 216-23, 27 July 1731.

[64] Gale died three years later in 1735.

Trade that censured Everard's administration and described the now bleak conditions in the colony: 'the Government sunk so low that neither peace or order subsisted, the General Court suppressed, the Council set aside a year and a half, and some of the Precinct Courts fallen'.[65] Everard was critiqued as 'a very weak man … too easily put upon [whose] rash measures caused … heats and divisions'. And Edmund Porter, a previous ally, accused of having misused his position on the bench and 'run the country into disorders'.[66]

But not everything was negative. Burrington reported that he had taken steps to restore economic order and political stability, including proroguing the assembly. It had been in session for five weeks and Burrington explained his decision with the observation that 'the longer they sat the more their heats increased', as did their reluctance to adhere to the governor's instructions regarding quit-rents.

Burrington's orders from the Board of Trade specified that all official payments including quit-rents were now to be made in specie. This was not easy. Money supply was limited and credit scarce, which rendered the directive impossible to follow in some areas and caused hardship almost everywhere.

A lack of hard currency had been an issue in the colony for years. Burrington understood the problem and in the absence of proclamation money or reverting to barter and payment in kind, lobbied London to change his instructions, arguing that money 'is hardly to be raised … it being affirmed that there has not been cash enough at one time here to pay a year's rents'.[67] He contended that to do otherwise risked dissent: 'the people have another plea that the Grand Deed to the inhabitants of Albemarle (the name this Government was then called) in 1668, under which most part of

---

[65] Cecil Headlam and Arthur Percival Newton (eds), *Calendar of State Papers Colonial, America and West Indies: volume 38, 1731* (London: HMSO, 1938), pp. 151-61, 1 July 1731.

[66] Ibid. Porter had been nominated to Burrington's council in 1731.

[67] Ibid.

the lands are held, grants the lands to them on the same terms as in Virginia where the rents are paid in tobacco or money at the choice of the parties'.[68]

Burrington also updated the Board on his investigation into the allegations against Everard, announcing magnanimously that the former governor had not been dealt with fairly or candidly by the former council and that there was nothing material in their complaints against him. He ensured that Everard's reciprocal accusations were shelved and drew a line under the dispute by discharging the colony's secretary from Everard's litigation. Burrington nonetheless persisted with his own vendetta against Porter, accusing him of 'illegal and arbitrary proceedings' and complaining to the Board of Trade, who responded by indicating their unhappiness at him doing so. Rather than mediate, they instructed Burrington and Porter to deal directly with each other's allegations.

Mr Porter:
Ordered that a letter be wrote to Mr Porter with copies of such parts of Captain Burrington's letters as relate to him for his answer thereto.

Captain Burrington:
Ordered that in the next letter to Captain Burrington, copies of the above-mentioned representation and papers from Mr Porter be sent to him for his answer thereto.[69]

Leaving aside his feud with Porter, Burrington's letters to the Board focus principally on seeking consent to lift restrictions on land grants. Burrington emphasised the benefits of larger land holdings, writing that '50 acres to each person in a family [is] too little to produce much pitch and tar, because

---

[68] Ibid.
[69] K.H. Ledward (ed), *Journals of the Board of Trade and Plantations: volume 6, January 1729 - December 1734*, pp. 298-304, 21 June 1732; and 404-9, 1 August 1734.

1,000 acres of pine land of which 19 parts in 20 of the country consists, will hardly employ one slave,[70] so that, if not altered, this regulation will prove very detrimental to the revenue'.[71] He warned presciently that 'if people have so little land it will be a very long time before all the country is settled, and if men are obliged to live so near one another they must make their own apparel and household goods, because they cannot raise stock to purchase them brought from England'.[72]

Burrington argued that the colony's prospects hinged on expansion and developing larger farms. This was the case not only on the coastal plain but also inland, for 'it is by breeding horses, hogs and cattle, that people without slaves gain substance here at first, not by their labour'.[73] He was correct. With larger land holdings North Carolina was 'capable of being made a flourishing colony, and yearly will increase by the coming of people from the Northern settlements'. Nonetheless, Burrington was aware of the potential hurdles: 'the good lands lying commodiously are long since patented [and] the remainder, the greatest part of the country, are far from navigable waters'. The consequence was that trade was compromised and 'is now very miserable, except at Cape Fear River'.[74]

The constraints imposed by North Carolina's geography were considerable and Burrington spent months exploring the Lower Cape Fear to assess the prospects of establishing a plantation system similar to that in South Carolina,[75] and how to improve transport between the coast and the interior, and across the Atlantic. Inadequate ports, shallow and often blocked

---

[70] This was an exaggeration but the principal point is valid.
[71] Cecil Headlam and Arthur Percival Newton (eds), *Calendar of State Papers Colonial, America and West Indies: volume 38, 1731*, pp. 151-61, 1 July 1731.
[72] Ibid.
[73] Ibid.
[74] Ibid.
[75] *Calendar of State Papers Colonial, America and West Indies: volume 40, 1733*, pp. 107-18: Burrington to the Board of Trade, 19 May 1733.

rivers, and a coast ringed by sandbanks, were all obvious problems, but there were other issues that in theory could be overcome more readily.

With its output shipped largely through South Carolina and Virginia, North Carolina paid a premium to export and import: 'the merchants on James River in Virginia supply most of the inhabitants on the north side of Albemarle Sound and Roanoke River with British commodities at unreasonable rates, being brought in by land or in little canoes in small quantities'. To circumvent this, Burrington proposed a customs facility on Ocracoke Island 'where there is a good harbour for vessels of 300 tons' which would serve Roanoke, Currituck and Bath. Unsurprisingly, opposition from commercial interests in Virginia blocked the plan and Burrington's stratagem came to nothing.

Burrington may have been impulsive, emotional and thin-skinned, but he understood the economic challenges faced by North Carolina's colonists. His issuance of land patents against explicit orders was not designed to frustrate the Lords Proprietors' interests but rather the opposite - to enhance the value of their land by encouraging settlement. Indeed, he had expected his actions to be approved formally after the fact.[76] Land grants stimulated development and were beneficial for Britain, with an expansion in North Carolina's economy leading to higher incomes and thus greater demand for imported British manufactures. Regardless, Burrington faced almost continuous opposition from North Carolina's different domestic factions: 'a dangerous crew they are and unhappy must be every honest man that has anything to do with them'.[77]

Burrington's second term as governor would be almost as brief as his first. William Smith, the new chief justice and president of the royal

---

[76] ODNB.

[77] Cecil Headlam and Arthur Percival Newton (eds), *Calendar of State Papers Colonial, America and West Indies: volume 40, 1733* (London: HMSO, 1939), pp. 107-18: Burrington to the Board of Trade; reply to Mr. Popple's letter of 16 August 1732. Cf., also, pp. 1-15, 1 January 1733.

council,[78] resigned his post within a few months in protest at Burrington undermining his authority and returned to England to argue for the governor's dismissal. In his absence, Nathaniel Rice,[79] the secretary of the colony, the next most senior council member and another of Burrington's opponents, took over as president. Boxed-in, Burrington responded by appointing two allies to the council and simultaneously ousting Porter as the presiding judge at the Court of Vice-Admiralty.

On its own this would have been sufficient to elicit the Board of Trade's censure but Burrington compounded his problems by railing against his adversaries in a sequence of intemperate letters:

> Ashe is an ungrateful villain.[80] Cornelius Hamett[81] is a disgrace to the council. Bred in Dublin and settled at Cape Fear, he was set to be worth £1,000, but is now known to have traded with other men's goods and reduced to keep a public house. It is a misfortune to this Province and to the Governor in particular that there are not a sufficient number of gentlemen in it fit to be Councillors, Justices nor officers in the Militia. There is no difference to be perceived between the Justices, Constables and planters that come to a Court, nor between the officers and private men at a muster, which parity is in no other country but this. Sir Richard Everard had the meanest capacity and worst principles of any gentleman I ever knew. His administration was equally unjust and simple; he was under the direction sometimes of one set, then of others, who advised him for their

---

[78] Possibly a fellow member of the King's Arms Lodge in New Bond Street and/or the Blue Posts in Holborn, a lodge close to the Inns of Court. Grand Lodge *Minutes I*, pp. 20-1, 153. Other 'William Smith's' included members of the Queen's Head in Knave's Acre; the Goat at the Foot of the Haymarket; the White Bear in King's Street. Golden Square; and the Black Boy and Sugar Loaf in Stanhope Street etc.

[79] Nathaniel Rice (*c.*1684-1753).

[80] John Baptista Ashe (*d.*1734), rather than his son, John Ashe (1725-1781).

[81] Cornelius Harnett (*d.*1742), not his son, Cornelius Harnett Jr. (1723-1781), who is discussed below.

own interest, and being incapable of judging was led to do anything they put him upon, which brought infinite confusion on the country.[82]

The Board of Trade's response to Burrington suggests an almost tangible dismay:

> As to those paragraphs which relate to yourself and those who have disagreed with your measures, we cannot but take notice that they are couched in a very extraordinary style, particularly that where speaking of Mr Ashe's declining to come to England with the Chief Justice, you write in the following words 'by which failure of his Baby Smith will be quite lost, having nothing but a few lies to support his cause, unless he can obtain an instruction from a gentleman in Hanover Square'. Of these words we expect an immediate and distinct explanation.[83]

No acceptable explanation was forthcoming and a joint representation to the Duke of Newcastle from Rice, Ashe and Montgomery,[84] the attorney general,[85] in conjunction with a deputation to the Board from Porter, shaped opinion definitively against Burrington and lit the fuse on his dismissal:

> Mr Burrington, since his arrival here last, has been guilty of almost every crime, saving that of murder, and in that he hath bid very fair on ye person

---

[82] Cecil Headlam and Arthur Percival Newton (eds), *Calendar of State Papers Colonial, America and West Indies: volume 39, 1732* (London: HMSO, 1939), pp. 63-78: 20 February 1732, Burrington to the Council of Trade and Plantations.

[83] Ibid., pp. 156-8: Council of Trade and Plantations to Governor Burrington, 20 June 1732.

[84] John Montgomery (d.1744), chief justice, attorney general (1723) and assemblyman.

[85] *CSRNC*, volume 3, pp. 356-68: Memorial from Nathaniel Rice, John Baptista Ashe, and John Montgomery concerning their dispute with George Burrington, 16 September 1732.

of the King's Attorney General ... Mr Burrington has maliciously and undeservedly suspended [Porter] from the office of Judge of Vice-Admiralty because he would not come into his measures relating to the King's lands. If he had done so, it might have been a prejudice to the crown of above 500,000 acres, about 50,000 whereof Mr Burrington himself holds (as it is thought) by presents made him from Lovick, Little and Foster, besides 10,000 acres which he did unjustly acquire by a breach of the Lords Proprietors' Instructions in 1725.[86]

Burrington's subsequent letters in his defence were ignored and Newcastle was forced to accept that his lack of self-control and seeming paranoia had become too great a liability.[87] Burrington was dismissed in April 1733,[88] albeit that he remained in office until Gabriel Johnston, his replacement, arrived in November 1734.

Burrington's legacy can be regarded as mixed. His release of land in response to what he perceived accurately as a pressing need went against his orders and was criticised by London but nonetheless stimulated settlement and economic growth. At the same time, his attempt to promote infrastructure investment was far-sighted but had limited near-term success. And although he understood the colony's capabilities as an exporter of agricultural products and naval stores, and thus as a large-scale trading partner for Britain, Burrington was unable to neutralise South Carolina and Virginia's political influence and the additional costs imposed on North Carolina's foreign trade remained intact.

---

[86] Cecil Headlam and Arthur Percival Newton (eds), *Calendar of State Papers Colonial, America and West Indies: volume 40, 1733* (London: HMSO, 1939), pp. 154-63: Edmund Porter to William Popple, 15 August 1733.

[87] For example, Cecil Headlam and Arthur Percival Newton (eds), *Calendar of State Papers Colonial, America and West Indies: volume 39, 1732* (London: HMSO, 1939), pp. 240-58: Burrington to the Council of Trade and Plantations, 14 November 1732.

[88] *Country Journal or The Craftsman*, 7 April 1733, et al.

Burrington's reports to London demonstrate insight and intelligence, and his policies were designed to assist North Carolina to realise its economic potential. But his ability to effect change was undermined by personal and political insecurities, and an absence of self-control. His emotional and unrestrained rejoinders to almost all political opposition alienated many in London who might otherwise have been supporters and left Burrington marooned and without allies.

Burrington returned to England in May 1735.[89] He continued to take an interest in and comment on government policy towards North Carolina but remained embittered, at one point accusing Martin Bladen of an abuse of power and complicity in an attempt on his life.[90]

Burrington died London in February 1759, murdered in St James's Park during an attempted robbery.[91] His estates in the Carolinas were bequeathed to his son, also George, then aged twelve, later an army officer, who sold them just over a decade later to Samuel Strudwick[92] to settle family debts.[93]

---

[89] *General Evening Post*, 1-3 May 1735, et al.

[90] *Champion Or Evening Advertiser*, 16 January, 28 January and 11 February 1742.

[91] *Lloyd's Evening Post and British Chronicle*, 23-26 February 1759; *Universal Chronicle or Weekly Gazette*, 24 February - 3 March 1759, et al.

[92] Samuel Strudwick (d.1797), later a planter and member of the royal council. Cf., Strudwick Family Papers, 1728-1831, Collection Number 701, Southern Historical Collection, UNC.

[93] Wills Proved at Prerogative Court of Canterbury, 23 March 1759: LL ref: wills_1750_1759_2531398_585351. Also *ODNB*.

Chapter Two

London Calling

Martin Bladen and the Board of Trade

Established in 1734, Bladen County was named for Martin Bladen, the central figure at the Board of Trade and Plantations for almost three decades from his appointment in 1717 at the behest of the Duke of Newcastle until his death in 1746.[1]

Diligent and comfortable with detail, Bladen exercised influence across Britain's North American and Caribbean colonies but especially in North Carolina, where he was instrumental in appointing Nathaniel Rice, his brother-in-law, to the position of secretary. Bladen also sponsored Henry McCulloh, an Ulster-born merchant and land speculator, as inspector of quit-rents and land grants.[2] McCulloh had a considerable impact in the Carolinas and his reports to London resulted in the dismissal of John Hammerton, South Carolina's first provincial grand master, as receiver-general of the quit-rents.[3]

The son of a Yorkshire attorney and sometime Treasury official,[4] Bladen matriculated at St John's College Cambridge in 1697 and the following year,[5]

---

[1] Cf., Rory T. Cornish, 'Bladen, Martin (1680-1746)', *ODNB*, online edn, Jan 2008. Bladen's will was prove at Canterbury on 14 May 1747.

[2] Henry McCulloh (*c.*1700-1779), sometimes written as 'McCulloch'.

[3] For a discussion of John Hammerton, cf., *Loyalists & Malcontents*, pp. 22-42; and William A. Shaw, *Treasury Books and Papers, October 1735, Calendar of Treasury Books and Papers, 1735-8* (London: IHR, 1900), volume 3, pp. 53-4, 8 October 1735.

[4] Nathaniel Bladen (*bap.*1642), attorney and Treasury Receiver. Cf., E.K. Timings (ed), *Calendar of State Papers Domestic: James II, 1686-7* (London, 1964), pp. 402-18.

[5] Nathaniel Bladen was admitted to the Inner Temple on 19 October 1666; Martin Bladen was admitted on 23 March 1698: *The Inner Temple Admission Database* at www.innertemplearchives.org.uk, accessed 4 June 2017.

without graduating, was admitted to the Inner Temple, his father's alma mater, one of London's four Inns of Court.[6] But rather than pursue a legal career, Bladen bought a commission with his uncle, Colonel Fairfax's regiment, the 5th Foot, then stationed in Ireland. The War of the Spanish Succession led to the regiment's deployment to the Low Countries and then Spain and Portugal under a new colonel, Sir Charles Hotham, another Yorkshireman.[7] Bladen was promoted to captain, then major, and given the additional responsibility of provost martial and judge advocate. He was subsequently appointed aide-de-camp to Henri de Massue de Ruvigny, 1st Earl of Galway,[8] the commander-in-chief of British forces in the Iberian Peninsula whom Bladen had known while in Ireland.

Bladen received his colonelcy in 1709 and took command of an infantry regiment raised in Portugal, seeing action at La Gudina on the River Caia. The battle was a major defeat for the combined Portuguese and British army and despite heavily outnumbering the Spanish, around 4,000 allied troops were captured, wounded or killed. The Spanish lost barely a tenth of that number. Galway was castigated in the press[9] and the following year in a move that may have been related, the Treasury queried Bladen's regimental expenditures and called him to London to be questioned.

Profiteering was commonly accepted among army officers at all levels and it is plausible that part of the funds Bladen received for uniforms and provisions were diverted for other purposes, probably to acquire property in England and finance his wife's family's ongoing legal fees in connection

---

[6] The Inns of Court comprise Lincoln's Inn, Gray's Inn, the Inner Temple and the Middle Temple.

[7] The War of the Spanish Succession was fought from 1701-14; the 5th Foot served in Spain and Portugal from 1707-13. Charles Hotham (1663-1723), 4th baronet, was a staunch Whig from the Yorkshire gentry. He sat as MP for Scarborough (1695-1702), then Beverley (1702-23).

[8] Henri de Massue de Ruvigny, 1st Earl of Galway (1648-1720).

[9] Cf., for example, *Post Boy*, 19-21 May 1709; and *Daily Courant*, 23 May 1709.

with a contested inheritance. Bladen's censure was mild and he sailed from Falmouth to return to Portugal the following March.[10] Bladen nonetheless sold his colonelcy and resigned from the army three months later.[11] Galway returned to England shortly afterwards and Bladen accompanied him on the journey home.

Bladen failed to be elected MP for Saltash twice (in 1713 and 1715), but an alliance with two powerful friends, Robert Walpole, the Chancellor of the Exchequer, a member with Bladen of the loyalist Hanover Club,[12] and James Brydges, a past paymaster of the forces, bore fruit. Bladen gained the sinecure of comptroller of the Royal Mint in 1714,[13] and in 1715 was elected MP for Stockbridge in Hampshire, a notoriously venal seat with around 100 electors where success depended on securing the support of the local returning officer.[14]

Bladen's loyalty to Walpole led to other job offers, including that of envoy to Switzerland, which he declined. But when Galway was appointed a Lord Justice of Ireland in September 1715 alongside the young Duke of Grafton, Bladen agreed to become their first secretary. The role was equivalent to co-head of the Irish administration and was prestigious, politically significant

---

[10] *Post Man and the Historical Account*, 30 March - 1 April 1710.

[11] Bladen sold his commission on 26 June 1710 but nonetheless continued to be known by his military title; cf., of many examples, *Post Boy*, 6-8 August 1719.

[12] The Hanover Club met at Jenny Man's coffee house at Charing Cross. Cf., Nicholas Rogers, 'Popular Protest in Early Hanoverian London', *Past and Present*, 79 (1978), 70-100, esp. 78; also, Rae Blanchard, 'Some Unpublished Letters of Richard Steele to the Duke of Newcastle', *Modern Language Notes*, 48.4 (1933), 232-46; and Karen Proudler, *Martin Bladen: A Biography* (published privately, 2015), p. 45, quoting Addison to King, 4 October 1715, in *Report of the Royal Commission on Historical Manuscripts* (London: HMSO, 1870), volume 2, p. 249: 'Mr Walpole is the patron of [Martin Bladen]'.

[13] He held the sinecure from 1714 until 1728. Cf., *London Gazette*, 25-28 December 1714.

[14] Sedgwick, *History of Parliament: the House of Commons 1715-1754*.

and exceptionally well-paid.[15] As part of the package, Bladen was gifted a seat in the Irish House of Commons as a member for Bandonbridge, which he retained until 1727, and sworn to the Irish Privy Council.[16]

With Walpole's support Bladen later traded-up his English parliamentary seat for Maldon in Essex,[17] and in 1741 was invited to represent Portsmouth, despite not being a naval officer. The constituency was one of the safest in the country and in the gift of the government via the Admiralty.

Bladen's principal colleague in Ireland, the second secretary for Ireland, was Charles Delafaye (1677-1762), a brilliant and loyal Huguenot émigré plucked from the secretary of state's office in London whose father had been editor of the *French Gazette*, the foreign language version of the *London Gazette*, the government's propaganda mouthpiece.[18]

Bladen and Delafaye worked in tandem until January 1717 when Galway and Grafton stepped down as Lords Justices following Viscount Townshend, Walpole's brother-in-law's appointment as Ireland's Lord Lieutenant.[19]

Although Delafaye and Bladen remained in post, with Delafaye at Dublin Castle and Bladen in London at Whitehall, the new regime was short lived with Townshend's opposition to government policy leading to his dismissal after a bare three months. Bladen ensured that Delafaye was kept advised of the dynamics in Whitehall during the upheaval and was accurate in his remark that 'I have good reason to believe that My Lord Sunderland[20] will shortly take care of you in England fully to your satisfaction'.[21] Sunderland had been

---

[15] *St James's Evening* Post, 27-30 August 1715, *et al.*

[16] *British Weekly Mercury*, 28 September - 5 October 1715, *et al.*

[17] Bladen was elected in 1734.

[18] Cf., Berman, *Espionage, Diplomacy & the Lodge*.

[19] Charles Townshend, 2nd Viscount Townshend (1674-1738), *inter alia* Secretary of State for the Northern Department 1714-17 and 1721-30.

[20] Charles Spencer, 3rd Earl of Sunderland (1675-1722).

[21] NA, SP 63/375, quote from f. 428, 11 April 1717.

summoned back to office as secretary of state for the Northern Department[22] and within days of his appointment wrote to Delafaye requesting that he return to become his under-secretary, in essence his chief of staff.[23]

Delafaye continued as under-secretary under Sunderland's successors, Stanhope[24] and then Townshend, until March 1724, when Walpole, now in effect prime minister, transferred him to the Southern Department in the same position to support the Duke of Newcastle as the incoming secretary of state.[25] The role placed Delafaye even closer to the heart of the administration and gave him a direct link to Bladen at the Board of Trade.[26]

Delafaye was by then one of Britain's most highly regarded crown officials and in addition to serving as under-secretary was simultaneously secretary to the Lords Justices, the government's principal anti-Jacobite spy-master and, like Bladen, a senior justice of the peace on the Middlesex and Westminster benches.

Bladen and Delafaye were also committed freemasons, Delafaye a member of the Horn Tavern, a short distance from parliament and the offices of state, and Bladen a member of the predominantly military lodge at the Rummer, a

---

[22] As in Ireland, the role of under-secretary was unsalaried with compensation paid from the allowances and fees that passed through the office. In the eighteenth century the fees passing through the Southern and Northern Departments were pooled. They were divided equally between the under-secretaries in the two departments and supplemented by sinecures. The Northern Department was responsible principally for Protestant Europe and the Southern for remainder, together with the colonies. Domestic policy and intelligence matters were shared by both.

[23] Effectively chief-of-staff and the administrative head of the department.

[24] James Stanhope, 1st Earl Stanhope (1673–1721).

[25] Newcastle had previously served as Lord Chamberlain (1717-1724). He would spend twenty-four years as secretary of state for the Southern Department (1724-48) and a further six years at the Northern (1748-54).

[26] Of many examples, cf., Raymond Turner, 'The Excise Scheme of 1733', *English Historical Review*, 42.165 (1927), 34-57, esp. 36-7, 40-4.

few yards from the army's headquarters at Horse Guards. Their relationship was personal as well as political, and they co-operated to secure patronage for their family and associates, and to advance the political interests of the administration.[27]

Notwithstanding his position at the Board of Trade, Bladen had substantial assets in North America and the Caribbean. His estates in North Carolina were in part inherited through his wife, Mary, whose father, John Gibbs, had been a former governor of the colony.[28]

Mary's mother, Elizabeth Pride, was the niece of George Monck, 1st Duke of Albemarle,[29] one of the original Lords Proprietors, who had died without a direct heir. It encouraged the Pride family to pursue a lengthy and expensive court case to secure a portion of Monck's estate. The potential value was vast and christening their son 'George Monk Bladen' may have been a means of emphasising the legitimacy of Mary Bladen's case.[30] Nevertheless, after a decade of litigation and a 1709 ruling in the House of Lords in their favour,[31] the Pride family lost on final appeal and a perpetual injunction was issued that prevented further litigation.

Mary died relatively young in 1724 and in 1728 Bladen remarried. Frances, his second wife, was the widow of John Foche,[32] a West India merchant, and the niece and heir of Colonel Joseph Jory, a past agent for Nevis.[33]

---

[27] Cf., *Espionage, Diplomacy & the Lodge*, esp. chapters one and two.

[28] John Gibbs, Governor of North Carolina, 1689-90.

[29] George Monck, 1st Duke of Albemarle (1608-1670). Cf., Ronald Hutton, 'Monck, George, first duke of Albemarle (1608-1670)', *ODNB*, online edn, Sept 2012.

[30] He was christened in 1702 at St Martin-in-the-Fields, Westminster.

[31] *Journals of the House of Lords*, volume 19 (London, 1709), p. 39.

[32] John Foche (d.1725). Wills Proved at Prerogative Court of Canterbury, 12 October 1725; LL ref: wills 1720 1729 2531159 708544.

[33] Colonel Joseph Jory (d.1725). Jory also held properties at Bethnal Green, east of the City of London, and at Aldborough Hatch in Essex. Cf., Jenny Shaw,

She inherited his sugar plantations which passed to Bladen and converted him into a key supporter of the Caribbean bloc in parliament. He protected their interests and his own through the 1733 Molasses Act, among other means, which obliged the American colonies to buy sugar, rum and molasses from Britain's sugar islands and imposed heavy duties on competing products.[34]

Despite the obvious conflict of interest, Bladen's administrative acumen at the Board of Trade was acknowledged widely with a contemporary witticism referring to him as 'Trade' and to his colleagues as 'simply Board'. They had a point. In his first three years as a commissioner Bladen was present at 463 of 572 recorded meetings and in the 1730s attended numerous meetings where he sat alone.[35] Even in later years when the Board was dominated by placemen, Bladen's attendance is recorded on over 970 occasions.[36]

The Board was constituted as a committee of the Privy Council with a remit that covered the administration of Britain's colonies as well as overseas trade. Although it lacked formal executive authority, a power retained by the Privy Council and the secretaries of state, the commissioners had significant influence, albeit that their recommendations were not always accepted on matters of strategy and policy.

This was the case with a 135-page report produced by Bladen jointly with three fellow commissioners in September 1721 in which improvements to colonial governance were suggested.[37] Although the paper was in part a re-

---

Everyday Life in the Early English Caribbean (Athens, GA: University of Georgia Press, 2013), p. 187.

[34] Eveline Cruickshanks 'Bladen, Martin (1680-1746), of Aldborough Hatch, Essex' in Sedgwick, *The History of Parliament: the House of Commons 1715-1754*.

[35] Mary Patterson Clarke, 'The Board of Trade at Work', *American Historical Review*, 17.1 (1911), 17-43, esp. 22.

[36] Cornish, 'Bladen, Martin (1680-1746)', *ODNB*. The actual number is 978.

[37] K.H. Ledward (ed), *Journals of the Board of Trade and Plantations: volume 4, November 1718 - December 1722* (London: HMSO, 1925), pp. 318-22.

statement of official policy, it also tabled new ideas to improve administration, enhance security, and tighten control over the colonies.

One proposal was to replace the proprietary charters which, in Bladen's view, were being exploited by New England's colonists and in North Carolina to argue against changes to the quit-rent system and in favour of less restrictive land grants. Bladen also proposed that the number of regular troops in North America be increased and that new alliances with the first nations be negotiated to push back against opposing French interests. More contentiously, he raised the idea of an American confederation headed by a captain-general to be appointed by Britain and supported by a council with representatives from each of the thirteen colonies. The body would have the power to levy federal taxes and secure funding for military expenditure, avoiding the need to rely on the passage of annual money bills by the provincial legislatures.[38]

A second memorandum in 1727 dropped the idea of colonial union and proposed instead that the colonies be placed under the sole jurisdiction of the Board of Trade. Apart from giving the Board – and Bladen - considerably greater authority, the change in approach was based on an emerging view that colonial union could engender an organised opposition to London.

Regardless, Bladen reverted to promoting the idea of a federal government in a 1739 memorandum, suggesting that the colonies' defence against French and Spanish aggression would be more efficiently prosecuted under a bicameral American parliament. Bladen proposed that it might be based in New York with a crown-appointed upper house and an elected lower house configured to marginalise the influence of the New England charter colonies.[39] He argued that such a structure would remove

---

[38] Jack P. Greene, 'Martin Bladen's Blueprint for a Colonial Union', *William and Mary Quarterly*, 17.4 (1960), 516-30.

[39] Ibid., esp. 518-21.

the need for defence to be the subject of negotiation by individual governors with their assemblies and instead be dealt with at a federal level.

Although his strategic plans were shelved or adopted only in part, Bladen's impact was more pronounced in issues of day-to-day administration, not least with regard to those appointed to colonial office. A senior position in the colonies offered a path to potential wealth and the ability to nominate friends and family was prized commensurately. Patronage was of course not the exclusive preserve of Bladen and the Board of Trade. It was shared with others, including the two secretaries of state – Newcastle and Townshend, and the prime minister, with other parties weighing-in to support their own favourites. Delafaye also had significant influence, especially in the 1720s and early 1730s when Newcastle was limited by his lack of knowledge of the details of foreign policy and the responsibility of being Walpole's parliamentary manager.

But although the choice of placemen was the product of many voices, the most effective were generally those of Bladen and Delafaye.[40] Bladen's was probably paramount: 'what was common to the experience of numerous governors was a clash at some time or other in their careers with Martin Bladen … [whose] influence was widely spread'.[41] Indeed, despite their seniority, the secretaries of state could be frustrated in protecting their nominees where disapproval had been incurred or manufactured, or if prospective candidates were deemed to lack the required skills. Fitness for office and relevant experience may not have been the main considerations in choosing placemen but they were a component and a failure to perform provided an excuse to advance alternative names.

Historians frequently ignore the influence of senior crown servants notwithstanding that it was such men who developed and executed government

---

[40] But cf., Philip Haffenden, 'Colonial Appointments and Patronage under the Duke of Newcastle, 1724-1739' *English Historical Review*, 78.308 (1963), 417-35, esp. 420.

[41] Ibid., 421.

policy. This was especially true of Bladen, who was integral to the articulation of policy in North America and the Caribbean. Patronage was part of the methodology, with places awarded not simply to friends and family but to like-minded men willing to forge an administrative programme in their patron's interests as well as their own.[42] It was the nature of eighteenth-century politics to deem the well-being of the political elites identical to that of the nation as a whole. Little has changed.

The vacant governorship of the Bahamas in 1738 provides an example of Bladen's sway. There were two principal candidates. The first, the Earl of Essex's nominee, a Mr Colebrooke,[43] the brother of a London merchant, had the support of Edward Walpole, the prime minister's younger son,[44] and the Duke of Devonshire, among others.[45] John Tinker, his challenger, was a past agent for the Royal African Company at Cape Coast Castle, a fortified slave-trading post on the Gold Coast, who had been posted to Panama from where he had overseen the Asiento slave trade in the Americas. Tinker was willing to invest in the Bahamas and had the backing of several prominent City of London merchants whose interests he supported. He was also a well-connected freemason, a member of the Bear & Harrow in Butcher's Row.[46] But the most vital factor in his favour was

---

[42] But cf., James A. Henretta, *Salutary Neglect: Colonial Administration Under the Duke of Newcastle* (Princeton, NJ: Princeton University Press, 2015), esp. pp. 33, 79, 94, 103, 145, 248 and 321, for an argument that Newcastle's thirty-year tenure as secretary of state lacked coherence.

[43] Essex endorsed him as 'a very honest good sort of man and extremely unfortunate'. Cf., *Salutary Neglect: Colonial Administration Under the Duke of Newcastle*, p. 202.

[44] Edward Walpole (1706-1784).

[45] *Salutary Neglect: Colonial Administration Under the Duke of Newcastle*, pp. 202-4.

[46] Grand Lodge *Minutes I*, p. 178. That freemasonry was important to Tinker is underlined by his travelling from the Bahamas to attend the consecration of the first Masonic Lodge House in Lodge Alley, Philadelphia, in 1755. Alongside Benjamin Franklin, Tinker headed the procession of some 160 freemasons at the event.

that he was Bladen's son-in-law.[47] Tinker's appointment was approved by the Board of Trade on 2 April 1740 and subsequently endorsed by Newcastle.[48]

Bladen's influence can be seen elsewhere, including the appointment of Robert Hunter as governor of Jamaica,[49] and his nephew, Thomas Bladen, as governor of Maryland.[50] But with respect to North Carolina, the pre-eminent example is the appointment of Nathaniel Rice, his brother-in-law, as secretary, the third-ranked position in the colony behind the governor and chief justice. Rice had been an African slave trader and the Royal Africa Company's chief factor at Cape Coast Castle, where he worked alongside Tinker.[51] He returned to England in August 1726 and three weeks later married Anne Gibbs, Bladen's sister-in-law.[52]

Bladen's nomination of Rice as North Carolina's secretary was opportunistic rather than planned, but was significant nonetheless. Burrington had left two vacancies in the list of recommendations he presented to the Board

---

[47] BL, Add. MS. 32,691, fo. 374-5.

[48] K.H. Ledward (ed), *Journals of the Board of Trade and Plantations: volume 7, January 1735 - December 1741* (London: HMSO, 1930), pp. 326-30.

[49] Robert Hunter (1666-1734), governor of New York and New Jersey (1710-20), Comptroller of Customs (1720-27), and governor of Jamaica (1727-34). See *Espionage, Diplomacy & the Lodge*, chapters one and two, for details of Hunter's relationship with Delafaye.

[50] Thomas Bladen (1698-1780), governor of Maryland (1742-47). He was born in Maryland and educated in England where he married Williamza Henley (d.1731), the daughter of Sir Robert Henley and the sister-in-law of Charles Calvert, 5th Lord Baltimore, whose family owned the province. Baltimore, a prominent freemason and Whig politician, was part of the Duke of Richmond's social set. Thomas Bladen became MP for Steyning (1727-34), gifted the seat by the Duke of Chandos at Martin Bladen's request, and Ashburton (1735-41), before taking up the position of governor of Maryland. He relinquished office and returned to England in 1746.

[51] *Daily Journal*, 10 August 1726.

[52] *London Journal*, 3 September 1726. They married at St Clement Danes church in the Strand. Anne and Mary, Bladen's wife, were the daughters of John Gibbs, governor of North Carolina in 1689-90.

of Trade and Bladen took advantage to insert Rice as secretary and a member of the royal council,[53] and William Smith as chief justice and president of the council.[54] Burlington objected and made a personal plea to Newcastle, but Bladen's names were confirmed.

The nomination of William Smith was a political gesture to John Scrope (*c*.1662-1752), a Walpole loyalist and one of Bladen's parliamentary colleagues. Scrope, a barrister, the only son of Thomas Scrope, an affluent Bristol merchant, served as secretary to the Treasury from 1724-52 and chaired the parliamentary select committee on trade and finance whose support Bladen considered vital.[55] He sat as MP for Ripon (1722-7), then Bristol (1727-34), and finally Lyme Regis (1734-death), the last constituency having been procured by Walpole through Henry Holt Henley[56] when Scrope was rejected by Bristol's voters for having supported the Excise Bill.

Scrope was party to the inner machinations of government administration, including the disbursement of secret service funds and intelligence matters. In 1742 when summoned before the Parliamentary Committee of Secrecy he refused to testify so as not to implicate Walpole: 'the last thing he would do should be to betray the King and next to him the Earl of Orford'.[57]

---

[53] Rice was familiar with the Carolinas having acquired land in South Carolina in the late 1720s. The *DNCB* states that he had 'previously (*c*.1725) ... visited ... South Carolina'. Although this is possible it is unlikely. Rice was more probably in West Africa. Cf., *Daily Journal*, 10 August 1726 and *London Journal*, 13 August 1726.

[54] Cecil Headlam and Arthur Percival Newton (eds), *Calendar of State Papers Colonial, America and West Indies: volume 37, 1730* (London: HMSO, 1937), pp. 226-37, 6 August 1730. Cf., also, Henretta, *Salutary Neglect*, p. 118.

[55] R.S. Lea, 'Scrope, John (*c*.1662-1752), of Wormsley, in Stokenchurch, Bucks', in Sedgwick, *The History of Parliament: the House of Commons 1715-1754*.

[56] Henry Holt Henley (*d*.1748), a Walpole supporter whose family jointly controlled the borough of Lyme Regis.

[57] Horace Walpole to Sir Horace Mann, 17 June 1742 in *Horace Walpole's Correspondence, volume 17* (New Haven, CN: YUP, 1954), pp. 457-9. Walpole was created Earl of Orford in 1742 on his retirement from the House of Commons.

Despite this, Scrope retained his position at the Treasury for a further decade, described by Pulteney,[58] a fellow MP and briefly prime minister, as 'the only man I know that thoroughly understands the business of the Treasury and is versed in drawing money bills. On this foundation he stands secure and is immovable as a rock'.[59]

SMITH AND RICE IN NORTH CAROLINA

Smith and Rice were sworn to office in early 1731.[60] Burrington took their presence as a personal affront and was furious. Regardless, both men had the protection of key figures in London and became part of the anti-Burrington faction on the royal council, a bloc that included John Baptista Ashe and John Montgomery.

Smith found it impossible to work with Burrington and sailed from North Carolina in May to bring his complaints to London in person. In his absence, Rice assumed the presidency of the council and became the main focus of opposition to Burrington, heading the lists of signatures on petitions against the governor and hindering Burrington's administration of the colony.[61]

Burrington was dismissed from office in 1733 but remained in place as governor pending the arrival of his successor. However, when he temporarily left the province for South Carolina in April the following year, Rice took executive authority and assumed the role of acting governor.

---

[58] William Pulteney (1684-1764).
[59] *Correspondence of John, Fourth Duke of Bedford, volume I* (London: Longman, 1842), p. 7.
[60] *London Evening Post*, 19-21 January 1731.
[61] Cf., for example, Cecil Headlam and Arthur Percival Newton (eds), *Calendar of State Papers Colonial, America and West Indies: volume 39, 1732* (HMSO: London, 1939), p. 258, 17 November 1732.

Burrington was outraged and on his return suspended Rice from office, removed him from the council and accused him of planning an assassination attempt.

Gabriel Johnston arrived to replace Burrington two months later in November 1734. He restored Rice to the council, appointed him a magistrate for New Hanover County (1735) and to the bench of the General Court.

Rice died in January 1753. His will, dated 7 December 1752, was witnessed by James Potterfield, an assemblyman; David Lindsay, a merchant and one of Wilmington's town commissioners;[62] and Archibald MacLaine, also a town commissioner and an attorney and merchant.[63] It is not known whether Rice was a freemason, few contemporary records are extant, but it is possible. His third witness, MacLaine, was a member of Wilmington's St John's Lodge, one of only a handful of mid-eighteenth century Cape Fear freemasons whose names are known.

---

[62] David Lindsay (d.1757), a merchant, a partner in *Faris & Lindsay*, originally from Ulster; he owned a plantation, *Nell Town*, in north-west Cape Fear. Cf., *The Wilmington Town Book, 1743-1778*, p. 12.

[63] Cf., John R. Maass, 'The Cure for All Our Political Calamities: Archibald MacLaine and the Politics of Moderation in Revolutionary North Carolina', *North Carolina Historical Review*, 85 (2008). Also cf., *DNCB* and *Wilmington Town Book, 1743-1778*, p. 125.

Chapter Three

Johnston, Dobbs and the Land Grabbers

Gabriel Johnston

Gabriel Johnston was an improbable choice to become North Carolina's second royal governor.[1] A brilliant academic, he had been educated in Scotland at Edinburgh and St Andrews universities and in 1722, aged 24, been awarded the *Regius* chair of Hebrew at St Andrews.[2] Nonetheless, frustrated at academia's poor financial rewards,[3] Johnston resigned his position after five years[4] and left Scotland to take employment in the household of Lord Wilmington in London.[5]

Wilmington, a court favourite, had previously supported Walpole who had reciprocated, advancing Wilmington to speaker of the House of Commons and appointing him paymaster-general, a lucrative government position that allowed Wilmington to amass over £100,000 in the eight years he served.[6] Following George I's death in May 1727, George II determined

---

[1] Gabriel Johnston (1699-1752); governor of North Carolina, 1734-52.

[2] A *Regius* professor is appointed through royal patronage on government advice. The appointment is unique to Britain.

[3] NA, SP 55/12/83: Petition of Mr Gabriel Johnston Professor of Hebrew in the new college of St Andrews concerning the grant of annual allowances of £25 out of the bishop's revenues and £55 from His Majesty's establishment to the said office, 20 June 1724.

[4] NA, SP 54/19/15: James Hadow on the demission of Gabriel Johnston, professor of Hebrew at St Andrews University, asking that his replacement be carefully chosen, 11 March 1728.

[5] Spencer Compton, Earl of Wilmington (c.1674-1743). Speaker of the Commons 1715-27; Paymaster of the Forces, 1722-30; Lord Privy Seal, 1730; Lord President of the Council 1730-42; Prime Minister 1742-3.

[6] The value in current money can be obtained (roughly) by multiplying by 1,000 – an indication of earnings inflation (not price inflation) over the period.

to make Wilmington head of the incoming administration,[7] but his inability to realize the role soon became obvious - 'a plodding fellow ... with great application, but no talents',[8] and Wilmington was forced to rely on Walpole for political support. His embarrassment as having to do so triggered an enduring sense of grievance.

Despite Walpole advancing him to Lord Privy Seal, Wilmington allied himself with dissident opposition Whigs and Tories, and schemed to develop his claim as a potential successor to Walpole. This persisted until the Excise Bill crisis of 1732-33, when Wilmington and Walpole were nominally reconciled. Wilmington's backing was secured with the offer of the Order of the Garter, England's highest chivalric honour, and their temporary political rapprochement provides the context for Johnston's appointment as governor of North Carolina.

Johnston had been taken on by Wilmington to pen anti-Walpole articles for *The Craftsman*, an opposition mouthpiece established in 1726 which Wilmington co-financed and whose contributors included the Tory opposition peers Lords Bolingbroke, Harley and Pulteney.[9] Johnston's articles reflected the political views of his patron and both he and the paper were repeatedly investigated by Charles Delafaye, whose remit as under-secretary included 'press management' as part of his intelligence and counter-intelligence remit.[10]

---

[7] Wilmington had also been treasurer to the Price of Wales.

[8] John Hervey, *Memoirs of the reign of George the second, from the accession to the death of Queen Caroline*, (London: John Murray, 1848), volume I, p. 32.

[9] Henry St John, Viscount Bolingbroke (1678-1751); Edward Harley, 3rd Earl of Oxford and Mortimer (b.1699-1755); William Pulteney, Earl of Bath (1684-1764). Cf., Simon Varey, 'The Craftsman', Prose Studies, 6.1 (1993), 58-77.

[10] Cf., NA, SP 36/13/86, ff. 86-87. 'Examinations of persons upon criminal matters. Name of person examined: Richard Franklin, bookseller. By or before whom: Delafaye. Subject: Printing and publishing the paper called *The Country Journal* or *The Craftsman*, No. 158.' Also SP 36/15/82, ff.82-3; SP 36/28/221 and SP 36/29/13.

Johnston's appointment as governor can be viewed as an exercise in political appeasement. He had no relevant administrative or political experience and until 1732 was linked firmly to opposition interests. Reinforcing the argument, his nomination was introduced not through the usual channels via the Board of Trade but on Newcastle's direct instruction on Walpole's orders in early April 1733.[11] Johnston's commission was approved five weeks later at a meeting of the Privy Council on 10 May 1733 at which Wilmington presided.[12]

Although Johnston's appointment as governor was agreed in the spring of 1733, his briefing and the preparation of detailed orders lasted into 1734 and he left for Brunswick only in the second half of that year, arriving at the end of October. Burrington's reputation had by then reached a nadir and Johnston's arrival was welcomed across the colony, perhaps because it was thought that his lack of experience and sparse financial resources would make him malleable. It did, but not as the colonists might have hoped.

Johnston's political honeymoon was short. The tensions between the different factions in North Carolina, and the interests of the Board of Trade versus those of the colonists, created numerous problems. And with no wealth and limited income, Johnston found his induction into colonial politics harsh. His instructions from London included implementing a more rigid regime for land registration and improving quit-rent collection, both of which faced substantial local opposition. Johnston persisted nonetheless. His annual salary of £1,000 and the salaries of other placemen were paid from the proceeds of the quit-rents and their collection was a personal financial necessity,[13] but he was also driven by the respective political and commercial agendas of Martin Bladen and Henry McCulloh.

---

[11] K.H. Ledward (ed), *Journals of the Board of Trade and Plantations: volume 6, January 1729 - December 1734* (London: HMSO, 1928), pp. 338-40, 3 April 1733.

[12] Ibid., pp. 344-9, 14 June 1733.

[13] William S. Powell, 'Johnston, Gabriel (1698-1752)', *ODNB*. It took Johnston's estate forty-six years to receive his salary arrears which exceeded £13,000 at his death.

Henry McCulloh

There were two Henry McCullohs in North Carolina. The first, a relative unknown, was for two years the naval officer at Cape Breton in Canada. He returned to London in 1748 when the port reverted to France[14] and after six years of lobbying was appointed secretary of North Carolina and a member of the royal council, and made judge of the Court of Vice Admiralty. His time in the colony was brief and he died the following year.[15]

The second and more relevant Henry McCulloh,[16] a wealthy London-based Scots-Irish merchant, moved in the same social and political circles as Bladen.[17] Whether he was a freemason is not known - there are limited masonic records that cover this period - but he was associated with several influential figures who were freemasons, including Bladen, and freemasonry was a common fraternal association among London's elites and among the expatriate Irish merchant community in London in particular.[18]

Johnston was introduced to McCulloh during the period in which he was being briefed by Bladen prior to his departure for Cape Fear. McCulloh used the opportunity to place Johnston in his debt, figuratively and literally, advancing the fees for Johnston's patent as governor, funding the cost of his travel to North Carolina, and financing the furniture and household goods that were required of a colonial governor. McCulloh also provided Johnston with a line of credit since he had no income other than his

---

[14] Treaty of Aix-la-Chapelle (1748) which *inter alia* ended the War of the Austrian Succession

[15] *DNCB*. Also, John Cannon, 'Henry McCulloch and Henry McCulloh', *William and Mary Quarterly*, 5.1 (1958), 71-3.

[16] Henry McCulloh (*c*.1700-1779).

[17] Cf. Alan D. Watson, 'Henry McCulloh: Royal Commissioner in South Carolina', *South Carolina Historical Magazine*, 75.1 (1974), 33-48.

[18] Cf., *Schism*, appendix VI: 'The First Irish Lodge in London – the Ship behind the Royal Exchange'.

prospective salary - and the receipt of that was conditional. Within two months, Johnston's indebtedness to McCulloh stood at around £2,400, more than twice his annual salary.[19] The leverage it offered McCulloh is obvious.

Bladen had an administrative rather than commercial agenda: to counter the cabal of Cape Fear planters who had benefited from Burrington's land grants and threatened the political status quo in the colony.

The clique was known colloquially as 'the Family' and comprised a collection of wealthy inter-married South Carolina planters including two brothers, Maurice and Roger Moore, Edward Moseley, Eleazer Allen and John Porter, all of whom had settled in the Lower Cape Fear and taken advantage of Burrington's generous land grant policy to obtain large estates, especially around Brunswick.[20]

Between 1725 and 1740, Maurice Moore acquired at least 12 land grants covering some 12,600 acres; Roger Moore, 49 land grants over more than 30,000 acres; Eleazer Allen, 11 grants exceeding 7,200 acres; and Edward Moseley, 22 grants of around 42,000 acres.[21] Further grants were made in subsequent years and additional land acquired. The group became a political force with influence on the council and later in the assembly, creating a bloc that rivalled that of the Albemarle and Pamlico settlers.[22]

---

[19] Charles G. Sellers, Jr., 'Private Profits and British Colonial Policy: The Speculations of Henry McCulloh', *William and Mary Quarterly*, 8.4 (1951), 535-51, esp. 536.

[20] Maurice [also written as 'Morris'] and Roger Moore were brothers; John Porter was Maurice Moore's brother-in-law; Eleazer Allen was Roger Moore's brother-in-law. Edward Moseley was a friend not family.

[21] State Archives of North Carolina, North Carolina Land Grants database.

[22] Cf., for example, Cecil Headlam and Arthur Percival Newton (eds), *Calendar of State Papers Colonial, America and West Indies: volume 40, 1733* (London: HMSO, 1939), 19 May and 18 July 1733.

Burrington and Everard had each made use of blank land patents to promote settlement in the Lower Cape Fear and elsewhere. These gave the recipient the right to survey and occupy land prior to its formal grant but left the description of the land itself open. Some patents had been issued by land office officials for administrative convenience but many, perhaps most, were supplied corruptly.

Once a patent had been allotted in blank there was nothing to prevent the beneficiary from writing-in his own description of the property to be surveyed and extending its acreage. In doing so the holder obtained a pre-emptive claim and voided any requirement to pay tax or quit-rents until the land had been surveyed and recorded formally. The system was open to abuse and it was abused on a massive scale, allowing the Family and others to establish large estates at low cost and low risk.

Johnston set out the problem in several comprehensive letters to the Board of Trade.[23] He explained that the Lords Proprietors' instructions more than a decade earlier had prohibited land sales unless previously approved by London and set a price of £20 sterling per 1,000 acres. That had put a brake on settlement and the introduction of interim patents was a temporary work-around that gave colonists access to land and the ability to cultivate it on payment of an annual rent of 3*d* per hundred acres. It was intended that the patent holder would arrange a survey in due course and

---

[23] *CSRNC*, volume 4, pp. 296-9: Memorandum from Gabriel Johnston to the Board of Trade concerning blank land patents, 2 August 1735. Cf., also, K.H. Ledward (ed), *Journals of the Board of Trade and Plantations: volume 7, January 1735 - December 1741* (London: HMSO, 1930), pp. 173-7, 1 April 1737: 'Letter from Mr. Johnston, Governor of North Carolina, dated 29 November 1736, relating to Quit-rents, Blank Patents'; p. 264, 10 January 1739: 'two letters from Mr. Johnston… one dated 15 January 1738, and the other June 13 1738; in the first he complains of the great want of a decision of the disputes about the blank patents and validity of their laws'; pp. 396-401, 11 August 1741: 'two letters from Mr. Johnston… [the second] signifying his want of direction about passing a new Quit-rent Act, in the room of the last repealed'.

until that time would have pre-emptive rights so that his efforts to clear and farm the land would not be unrewarded.

But although prudent in theory, the practice had caused 'a long train of artifices and threats', and the 'weakness and necessities' of earlier governors had allowed patents to be 'drawn up in form and signed and sealed with the persons' names, the number of acres, the description of the boundaries and the sums paid for them in blank'.[24]

Given the problems he now faced, Johnston expressed his concern at London's failure to respond: 'It is impossible to go on with public business until the fate of the blank patents is determined. I dare not give up so much of the only revenue the king has here and the fund from whence the officers' salaries are paid, without orders or at least a permission from home. If the Attorney [General]'s opinion should not come these seven years (this is now the third year that it has been lying before him…) all our affairs must remain in suspense till then'.[25]

Johnston implemented London's instructions nonetheless and legislation was drafted to remove blank land patents and require quit-rents to be paid at higher rates and in specie. But he faced opposition. Swayed by the Cape Fear faction, the council and the assembly declined to pass the necessary legislation.

Johnston reacted by relocating to Cape Fear and cooperating politically with rival planters and merchants, including James Innes,[26] James Murray,[27]

---

[24] Ibid.

[25] K.G. Davies (ed), *Calendar of State Papers Colonial, America and West Indies: volume 43, 1737* (London: HMSO, 1963), pp. 250-70: Johnston to Alured Popple, 6 October 1737.

[26] James Innes (c.1700-1759), appointed a justice of the peace for New Hanover County (1733) and recommended by Johnston for the council.

[27] James Murray (1713-1781), a merchant, planter and colonial official. Appointed a justice of the peace for New Hanover County (1737), deputy naval officer for Brunswick (1739), and a member of the council (1739).

Matthew Rowan,[28] Robert Halton[29] and Samuel Woodward,[30] in an attempt to diminish the Family's influence. His crackdown on the issuance of land patents and related land fraud was also supported by William Smith, who had returned to the colony and resumed his place as chief justice.

A political stand-off persisted nonetheless until 1739, when Smith issued a judicial ruling that quit-rents could be demanded in specie. The judgment gave rise to opposition in the legislature and elsewhere, and the Family and their allies took advantage to move that the assembly impeach Smith.

The vote took place on 13 February and was relatively close, with the motion defeated by six votes. Johnston retaliated within a week, calling on his supporters in the assembly to incorporate the town of Wilmington and thereby create a rival to the Family's power base at Brunswick.[31]

The lower house passed the resolution but the vote in council was tied with four on each side. Smith, as president of the council and chief justice, determined that he could and would have the deciding vote, and voted the bill through. Wilmington's incorporation and the transfer of the principal port facilities and seat of government away from Brunswick cut the ground from under the Family, who were obliged to acquiesce and accommodate Johnston.

During the preceding five years McCulloh had used his hold over Johnston and influence with Bladen and the Board of Trade to obtain numerous

---

[28] Matthew Rowan (d.1760), an assemblyman (1727); subsequently a member of the council (1731) and later its president and acting governor. A merchant and ship owner, he was born in County Antrim, Ulster, and migrated to North Carolina in the 1720s. Rowan County is named in his honour.

[29] Robert Halton (d.1749), appointed a justice of the peace for New Hanover (1734), collector of quit-rents, usher of the Exchequer Court (1735), town commissioner (1740) and assistant justice of the General Court (1743).

[30] Samuel Woodward, a justice of the peace. Cf., *CSRNC*, volume 2, pp. 377-80: Minutes of the North Carolina Governor's Council, 4 April 1720; also *CSRNC*, volume 4, pp. 8-10: Gabriel Johnston to the Board of Trade, 25 May 1735.

[31] Wilmington was incorporated with effect from 1740.

land grants for himself and his associates.[32] The first instance had been in November 1735, when Johnston informed the council that he had 'received a letter from Mr Dobbs[33] and some other gentlemen of distinction in Ireland and Mr Henry McCulloh, merchant in London, representing their intention of sending over to this province several poor Protestant families with design of raising flax and hemp ... [they] had appointed Captain Woodward[34] as their attorney ... and now applied for a grant of 60,000 acres for that purpose on Black River in North Hanover'.[35] Johnston announced that he intended to accede to the request and grant the land once surveyed. The council concurred and approved the grant subject to Board of Trade consent.[36]

The land warrant that followed granted 54,000 acres and named as beneficiary 'divers persons, then and now unknown' – in effect, nominees, albeit that the actual beneficiary was McCulloh. He sold the part of the rights to other speculators, including 6,000 acres to Arthur Dobbs, who would succeed Johnston as governor in 1753. The terms of grant obliged the beneficiaries to pay quit-rents immediately but only Dobbs did so.[37] Indeed, not only did McCulloh not pay but four years later when holding a commission to investigate and reform the collection of the quit-rent system he ensured that those who had acquired land from him were allowed to continue to avoid payment.[38]

---

[32] Cf., for example, *Calendar of State Papers Colonial, America and West Indies: volume 42, 1735-1736* (London: HMSO, 1953), p. 160-1: Council of Trade and Plantations to the Committee of Privy Council - Report upon petition of Mr McCulloh, 2 March 1736.

[33] Arthur Dobbs, (1689-1765), governor of North Carolina (1754-death).

[34] Samuel Woodward, as above noted.

[35] *CSRNC*, volume 4, pp. 72-3: Minutes of the North Carolina Governor's Council, 29 November 1735.

[36] Ibid. Cf., also, *CSRNC*, volume 4, pp. 209-15: Minutes of the Board of Trade, 6 February and 12 February 1736.

[37] *CSRNC*, volume 4, pp. 696-8: Minutes of the North Carolina Governor's Council, 9 March 1744.

[38] Ibid.

Having gained part of what he wanted, McCulloh followed-up with two applications to the Privy Council for land grants 'on the branches of Cape Fear River wherein few or no settlements have been made within these twelve years'.[39] The first application was with respect to 72,000 acres and the second for 60,000. In return, McCulloh committed to install 'three hundred Protestants in the space of ten years and to increase that number', and to produce naval stores and agricultural goods, but with one caveat. Given the self-described 'very great hazards' he expected to face, McCulloh argued that both grants should be exempt from quit-rents for ten years.[40]

Further statements in favour of McCulloh's applications were tabled the following month: 'North Carolina hitherto has been very inconsiderable as to trade and though there is near 40,000 whites in that Colony, which is one-third more than in the South, yet their produce is not equal to one-tenth part and we have not had so much as one ship from that Colony this last year, which plainly shows what necessity there is to encourage those that are willing and capable to introduce trade and commerce amongst them.[41] It is to be presumed from this state of the Colony it will appear that a settlement carried on in the manner above hinted at, by trading people, will answer all the ends proposed in giving such grants to the undertaker; - For trade naturally occasions an increase of people, and in such case the settlement becomes lasting. And at the same time puts those that are already settled there on new methods of industry, which will enrich the Colony and make it useful to its Mother Country.'[42]

---

[39] *Calendar of State Papers Colonial, America and West Indies: volume 42, 1735-1736* (London: HMSO, 1953), pp. 151-6, 24 January 1736.

[40] Ibid.

[41] For reasons discussed in the Introduction, this was the received view in London, albeit that McCulloh exaggerated the position to bolster his argument.

[42] *Calendar of State Papers Colonial, America and West Indies: volume 42, 1735-1736*, pp. 156-60, 12 February 1736.

Convinced by his arguments, the patents were approved by the Board of Trade in March 1736 and by the Privy Council a month later.[43] McCulloh retained the larger of the two grants and brought in around 40 Swiss and 150 Irish migrants. The 60,000 acre grant on the north-west Cape Fear he made out in favour of Johnston. As a *quid pro quo*, it was agreed that McCulloh's settlers' accommodation and subsistence would be financed by Johnston and James Murray, one of McCulloh's agents who would later become one of the most successful traders in Cape Fear and a leading figure in Wilmington, appointed to the royal council in 1739.[44]

The following month, the Privy Council received a petition from 'Messrs Murray Crymble & James Huey, London merchants',[45] 'on behalf of themselves and several others' requesting a grant of 1.2 million acres in North Carolina.[46] Six months later following questioning, Crymble and Huey confirmed that 'our names were made use of in the said Petition only in trust for Henry McCulloh ... and that the said tracts of land when granted is to be for the proper use and benefit of the said Henry McCulloh'.[47] Despite the seeming deception and notwithstanding the scale of the proposed grant, discussions at the Board were concluded in McCulloh's favour within the following six months and the grant approved by the Privy Council in May 1737.

McCulloh had put forward a seemingly viable proposal and persuaded the Board that 'where there are vast tracts of land, neither cultivated nor claimed by any person' the issuance of land grants would 'be the

---

[43] Ibid., pp. 160-72, 2 March 1736.

[44] *DNCB*.

[45] It was not a coincidence that Crymble and Huey were involved substantially in trade with Ireland. Cf., *Reports from Committees of the House of Commons, volume 2, Miscellaneous Subjects, 1738-1765* (London: House of Commons, 1803), reprint, p. 68.

[46] *CSRNC*, volume 4, pp. 255-6, 9 June 1736.

[47] *CSRNC*, volume 4, p. 1093, 13 December 1736.

means of increasing HM quit-rents, improving the trade of the Province, and extending their settlements by protecting their frontiers'.[48] The Privy Council agreed and issued an order instructing Johnston to approve McCulloh's grant and to survey the land; it also granted a ten-year exemption from quit-rents during which 6,000 Protestants were to be settled.

McCulloh dispatched a copy of the grant to Johnston so that rival claims could be prevented and informed him that instructions as to how to divide the land would follow. But Johnston chose not to wait. Unfortunately for McCulloh, his financial hold over Johnston had been compromised by the governor's marriage. Johnston's wife, Penelope, the step-daughter of the late Governor Eden, was one of the wealthiest women in the province having inherited the estates of three husbands.

Colonel William Maule (1690-1726), her first, the colony's surveyor-general, had died having amassed more than 16,000 acres, including three plantations in which she had a half share. John Lovick (d.1733), her second, a sometime secretary of the province, had been chief justice and surveyor general of the colony under Burrington and had owned Roanoke Island. And George Phenney (d.1737), her third, an ex-governor of the Bahamas, had been customs collector and surveyor-general for Southern America, an area comprising Pennsylvania, Maryland, Virginia, both Carolinas, Jamaica and the Bahamas. Penelope inherited Phenney's estate after probate in June 1737 and this and her other property passed to Johnston on their marriage later that year, including Eden House, the former governor's plantation opposite Edenton.[49]

Having received McCulloh's letter and a copy of the land grant, Johnston saw an opening to profit at McCulloh's expense.[50] North Carolina's

---

[48] *Calendar of State Papers Colonial, America and West Indies: volume 42, 1735-1736* (London: HMSO, 1953), pp. v-xxvii, Introduction.

[49] DNCB.

[50] Charles G. Sellers, Jr., 'Private Profits and British Colonial Policy: The Speculations of Henry McCulloh', *William and Mary Quarterly*, 8.4 (1951), 535-51.

surveyor-general had died and with the position vacant, Johnston installed Matthew Rowan, now a political ally, as an interim replacement and agreed with him that his surveying fees would be shared with Samuel Woodward, McCulloh's former attorney, who in turn would pass back a proportion to Johnston.

Johnston instructed Rowan to begin the survey immediately and directed him to locate the land grant in the west of the province and to survey it as a single rectangle. Without waiting for McCulloh's detailed instructions, Rowan began the survey, dividing the grant into twelve 100,000 acre lots in line with the terms of the grant, rather than the 12,500 acre parcels that McCulloh required. This was intentional. If the land had to be re-surveyed to reduce the unit size, the surveyor (and Woodward and Johnston) would be entitled to additional fees.

When he discovered what had happened, McCulloh was incensed and looked to recover his losses. His opening came through the still unresolved issue of blank land patents.

North Carolina's royal council and assembly had continued to withhold their consent for reform until existing land holdings and land rights had been recognised. McCulloh used the impasse to appear before the Board of Trade to offer technical advice.[51] His knowledge of the issues and apparent willingness to assist at no charge convinced the Board that his intentions were honourable.[52] And with the Board in his pocket, McCulloh exploited his friendship with Bladen to persuade him to encourage Walpole to grant a commission that would allow McCulloh to propose a solution.

---

[51] *Calendar of State Papers Colonial, America and West Indies: volume 43, 1737* (London: HMSO, 1963), pp. 1-21, 17 January 1737; pp. 250-70, 6 October 1737.

[52] *Calendar of State Papers Colonial, America and West Indies: volume 44, 1738*, (London: HMSO, 1969), pp. 43-59, 14 March 1738; and pp. 109-26, 27 May 1738. Also *Journals of the Board of Trade and Plantations: volume 7, January 1735 - December 1741* (London, 1930), pp. 282-9, 1 June 1739.

The suggestion was approved in-principle and when McCulloh presented a formal proposal to the Privy Council listing the defects in the quit-rent system and advancing prospective remedies, he obtained authorisation to put his ideas into effect.[53] A warrant naming McCulloh 'Commissioner for Supervising, Inspecting and Controlling His Majesty's Revenues and Grants of Land in North and South Carolina' was granted in May 1739. He would be paid a salary of £600 per year and receive a £200 allowance for clerical support, both to be funded 'out of such quit-rents in North and South Carolina as shall be recovered and improved by his means'. McCulloh was also granted investigatory powers and given authority to enforce the quit-rent regulations and recommend reforms. A request that he be appointed an extraordinary member of the royal council in both North and South Carolina was however rejected following opposition from Governor James Glen.[54]

But as McCulloh prepared to leave for Charleston a despatch arrived from Johnston informing the Board that a compromise to the blank land patent problem had been negotiated and settled. All sides had agreed that 150,000 acres of land grants issued under blank land patents would be recognised formally under a new law that would at the same time introduce a new quit-rent structure.

The proposal had the approval of the Family, the Albemarle settlers and Johnston's own supporters in Cape Fear, and it provided a viable solution to the political stalemate that had prevailed for years. But one person would lose out - McCulloh. As a letter from James Murray made clear, McCulloh had been blind-sided and risked seeing his land grants dismembered by rival claims: 'Roger Moore alleges that he has an old patent (which is now confirmed by the quit-rent law) that he says is within your 72,000 acres ... You'll

---

[53] *Calendar of State Papers Colonial, America and West Indies, 1739* (London: IHR, 1969), vol. 45, pp. 90-111, 16 May 1739.

[54] Ibid. Cf., also, Sellers, Jr., 'Private Profits and British Colonial Policy', 542. James Glen (1701-1777), had been appointed South Carolina's governor in 1738 but did not leave London for Charleston until 1743.

observe a clause in the Quit Rent Law that all disputes between Proprietors' Patents and those lately issued are determinable by the Governor in Council, who I hope will take care that no injury be done to you.'[55]

McCulloh responded swiftly to the threat to his interests and approached the Privy Council to argue that the new law was against Britain's interests and should be disallowed; he also persuaded other Carolina merchants in London to lobby Bladen and the Board of Trade to make the same argument. They succeeded, and the Quit Rent Law was nullified.

In light of his failing hold over Johnston, McCulloh's aims were now three-fold: to safeguard his North Carolina land grants from any claims that might arise from outstanding blank land patents; to dismantle any co-operation between the hitherto competing interests in North Carolina that would render his commission irrelevant; and to validate his actions by confronting outstanding quit-rent and land grant issues in South Carolina.

His first move was to attack John Hammerton, the incumbent receiver-general of the quit-rents based in South Carolina.

Shortly after arriving in Charleston, McCulloh demanded that Hammerton provide a statement of quit-rent arrears, a copy of his receipts, and a list of all land grants made in both Carolinas since 1730. Hammerton declined to comply, arguing that his clerks had insufficient time. His refusal opened a window of opportunity for McCulloh and in his first report to London he complained that his work was being obstructed by members of the royal council intent on protecting their own interests and certain crown officers, notably Hammerton.[56]

McCulloh set out a copy of his orders to Hammerton and noted that he did not expect Hammerton to co-operate: 'he is in arrears with the Crown at least £1,500 and, from his books, indebted to the Crown up to

---

[55] Nina Moore Tiffany (ed), *Letters of James Murray, Loyalist* (Boston, printed privately, 1901), p. 54-5.
[56] *Calendar of Treasury Books and Papers* (London: IHR, 1901), 8 November 1741

the 1738 March quarter date as to over £1,280". McCulloh alleged fraud, accusing Hammerton of crediting his own account for 'several sums paid as he alleges but for which vouchers are not forthcoming'.

In the report that followed McCulloh stated that he had examined the treasurer's accounts and had estimated what tax was payable. His conclusion was devastating: the outstanding quit-rents could be collected but *only* if Hammerton were to be removed from office. The missive was delivered to London in August 1742 and, despite his protests, Hammerton was replaced as receiver-general for both Carolinas within months.[57]

McCulloh faced more effective opposition in North Carolina where his motives were better understood. Counter-reports from the colony persuaded London to disregard McCulloh's complaints of obstruction and, equally ominously, Horatio Walpole, the auditor-general, stopped his salary, arguing that the collection of quit-rents was not yet improved. But if McCulloh lost this battle he nonetheless won the war. He managed to obtain a copy of the fee-sharing agreement between Rowan and Woodward and used this to blackmail them into issuing his land grants; McCulloh deployed the same means to persuade Johnston to pay most of the outstanding surveying fees for which McCulloh was liable.[58]

Ninety-six land patents of 12,500 acres each were issued in 1746 which encompassed the entirety of McCulloh's 1.2 million acre grant. Thirty-four went to McCulloh directly; sixteen to Arthur Dobbs to discharge a mortgage in relation to another grant held by McCulloh; and with one exception the balance was placed in trust for McCulloh's children or McCulloh himself. The exception comprised sixteen patents totalling 200,000 acres made out to John Selwyn.[59]

---

[57] Cf., *Loyalists & Malcontents*. An excellent commentary is given in Watson, 'Henry McCulloh: Royal Commissioner in South Carolina'.

[58] This was expressed as Johnston settling his outstanding debts to McCulloh.

[59] John Selwyn (1688-1751).

McCulloh's link to Selwyn, then MP for Gloucester,[60] circles the story back to freemasonry. Selwyn was an exceptionally well-connected member of London society, a loyal government supporter in parliament and a prominent member of the Bear & Harrow Lodge.[61] His links to the political and masonic establishment went back decades, including serving as aide-de-camp to the Duke of Marlborough and colonel of the 3rd Foot from 1711-13, when Charles Churchill, one of Walpole's closest confidantes, was one of Selwyn's senior officers.

Selwyn had been elected MP for Truro in 1715, a pocket borough controlled by Hugh Boscawen, later 1st Lord Falmouth,[62] a loyal Whig, and the following year was appointed clerk to the household of the Prince of Wales, a position obtained through the patronage of Viscount Townshend, a member of the Horn Tavern Lodge. It was around this time that Selwyn acquired his house in St James's, close to the palace.

When Walpole and Townshend returned to office in 1720 Selwyn was rewarded for his loyalty with the profitable position of receiver-general and comptroller of the customs. He held the office from 1721-27,[63] albeit that convention required that he resign his seat in parliament on appointment.

Selwyn subsequently acquired a large estate in Whitchurch, Hampshire, which gave him control of one of that constituency's two seats and secured his return to parliament in 1726. In addition to other more minor offices,[64]

---

[60] Selwyn was MP for Truro (1715-21), Whitchurch (1727-34) and Gloucester (1734-death).
[61] Grand Lodge *Minutes I*, pp. 177-8.
[62] Hugh Boscawen, 1st Viscount Falmouth (*c*.1680-1734).
[63] University of Reading: Special Collections, MS 3: Receiver General and Cashier of the Customs, Account of John Selwyn, 1725-26.
[64] Including Chief Clerk, Register and sole Examiner in the Court of Chancery in Barbados, and Clerk of the Crown for Barbados: Cecil Headlam and Arthur Percival Newton (eds), *Calendar of State Papers Colonial, America and West Indies: Volume 34, 1724-1725* (London: HMSO, 1936), pp. 166-7.

he was appointed groom of the bedchamber to George Augustus, as Prince of Wales as well as king – George II, and in 1730 secured the post of treasurer to Queen Caroline, most probably through the influence of his wife, Mary Farrington, one of the queen's favourite ladies of the bedchamber.[65]

Selwyn extended his influence in 1733 with the purchase of Ludgershall Manor in Wiltshire. The city's reservoirs were on his estate which gave him power over Gloucester's MPs.[66] Selwyn was subsequently elected for Gloucester and his seat at Whitchurch was passed to his son, also John, which allowed Selwyn to influence or control three parliamentary seats.[67]

Horace Walpole's view of Selwyn as a 'shrewd silent man … reckoned very honest … he had made his court and his fortune with as much dexterity as those who reckon virtue the greatest impediment to worldly success' may have been misguided.[68] Given McCulloh's venality and the way in which his other patents were allocated, the sixteen grants obtained by Selwyn can be explained plausibly as recognition of the services he almost certainly rendered.[69]

Selwyn's North Carolina property was passed from his son to his grandson, George Augustus Selwyn (1719-1791). The town of Charlotte, later the county seat, was chartered on a small part of the Selwyn grant around the time his grandson inherited. Henry Eustace McCulloh[70] and three others - Abraham

---

[65] Sedgwick, *History of Parliament: the House of Commons 1715-1754*. Charles Selwyn (1689-1749), John's brother, was a fellow Whig MP; their father, William Selwyn (1658-1702), a major general, had been governor of Jamaica. Selwyn later served as paymaster of the marines (1747-8) and was briefly treasurer to the Prince of Wales.

[66] Gloucestershire Archives, D149/E33: Agreement between Gloucester Corporation and John Selwyn of Matson for supply of water, 1741.

[67] John Selwyn Jr. predeceased his father in 1751 by a matter of months.

[68] Horace Walpole, *Memoirs of George III* (London: Lawrence and Bullen, 1894),

[69] For obvious reasons there is no evidence as such.

[70] Henry Eustace McCulloh (1737-1810), Henry McCulloh's son.

Alexander, Thomas Polk and John Frohock - were appointed trustees and directors of the new town.

ELEAZER ALLEN

McCulloh may have been ultimately responsible for Hammerton's removal as receiver-general of the quit-rents in the Carolinas but he was building on foundations laid by others.[71] Hammerton's relationship with each of South and North Carolina's respective governors had been dysfunctional. In South Carolina Hammerton had been initially excluded from office by Robert Johnson, who appointed his son instead. And in North Carolina, Gabriel Johnston became disenchanted with Hammerton's inefficiency, arguing in a letter to the Board of Trade that it was more advantageous to have a local man: 'as the Receiver General is Secretary and Receiver General of the province of South Carolina, he is by virtue of his said offices obliged to reside within the said province, by which means the receipt of his Majesty's rent is here neglected'.[72]

Johnston accompanied his words with action and in 1735 appointed Eleazer Allen (d.1750), a member of the Family and Brunswick landowner, to replace Hammerton. Allen had been nominated to the royal council by Burrington in 1730 but had declined, preferring to remain in Charleston where he had trading interests and was clerk of the assembly.[73] Allen's wife, Sarah Rhett, came from a wealthy family in South Carolina. Her sister had married Roger Moore and it was Moore who encouraged Allen to apply

---

[71] Hammerton returned to London where he lobbied unsuccessfully for reinstatement. Pursued by his creditors, he was subsequently incarcerated for debt at the Fleet Prison.

[72] *Treasury Books and Papers*, October 1735, *Calendar of Treasury Books and Papers, 1735-8* (London: IHR, 1900), vol. 3, pp. 53-4, *8 October 1735*. Reinforcing the point, Johnston also argued that Hammerton should be censured and dismissed.

[73] Allen was elected/re-elected Clerk 1727-32. He represented St Philip's Parish 1725-31.

for land grants in North Carolina. Allen did so, accumulating grants from c.1725 onwards.[74] He relocated to Brunswick in 1734 and settled on an estate adjacent to Moore's.

Johnston also invited Allen to join the royal council. Allen accepted and was subsequently made a magistrate and appointed an assistant judge of the Court of Oyer and Terminer.[75] His appointment as receiver-general was confirmed later the same year. Nonetheless, when Allen joined with other members of the Family and Brunswick's planters writ large to frustrate Johnston's land registration and quit-rent reforms, his relationship with the governor soured.

Johnston's promotion of Wilmington over Brunswick forced Allen to make peace and the governor responded positively, appointing Allen to the influential post of surveying officer to map the Granville District.[76] Allen subsequently served as public treasurer for North Carolina (1749) and as president of the royal council. He was also reconciled with Nathaniel Rice, described in Allen's will as 'my good friend'.[77]

One of Johnston's principal aims as governor was to encourage immigration, especially from Scotland in the wake of the defeat of the Jacobite Rising. But notwithstanding that migration was vital to the colony's population growth, which more than doubled from around 35,000 to approximately 73,000 during Johnston's tenure, another key component was the rising number of slaves which tripled from an estimated 6,000 in 1730 to almost 20,000 in 1750.

---

[74] Allen and Moore each received initial land grants of 640 acres. Cf., Edgar & Bailey, *Biographical Dictionary of the South Carolina House of Representatives*, volume II, pp. 32-3.

[75] Effectively a circuit judge or judge of assize.

[76] Brunswick suffered economically to the extent that it became necessary to legislate to promote settlement in the town.

[77] J. Bryan Grimes, *Abstracts of North Carolina Wills*, p. 9.

Slaves were worked predominantly on the plantations and farms on the coastal plain, but slavery was also present further inland. The majority were purchased through Charleston's slave markets[78] or from the ranking slave merchants in the Carolinas: Henry Laurens, Miles Brewton, Joseph Wragg and Benjamin Smith. Laurens was treasurer of Solomon's Lodge in Charleston[79] and a provincial grand steward under Peter Leigh, and Smith the provincial grand master of South Carolina from 1744-54 and then both Carolinas from 1761-67.[80]

Gabriel Johnston died in 1752 and Nathaniel Rice as president of the council took over as acting governor. Rice died the following year and was replaced in turn by Matthew Rowan, who had become the council's president on Rice's death.[81] Arthur Dobbs arrived a year later.

Arthur Dobbs

Arthur Dobbs (1689-1765), has been described as an Enlightenment visionary, a reformer, and one of the earliest theoretical economists. He was a Whig and loyal to the concept of Empire, if not always the detail. And in keeping with the mores of his social and business circles he was an avid land speculator.

In addition to the land patents he obtained through McCulloh in the 1730s, and a further 200,000 acres in 1746, Dobbs acquired land in his own right and eventually owned more than 400,000 acres across North

---

[78] Walter E. Minchinton, 'The Seaborne Slave Trade of North Carolina', *North Carolina Historical Review*, 71 (1994), 1-61.

[79] Elected 1754.

[80] W. Robert Higgins, 'Charles Town Merchants and Factors Dealing in the External Negro Trade 1735-1775', *South Carolina Historical Magazine*, 65.4 (1964), 205-17.

[81] Matthew Rowan served as acting governor from 1753-54.

Carolina.[82] Indeed, at least one source suggests that Dobbs' land holdings exceeded one million acres. Even before becoming governor, Dobbs was intent on promoting settlement on his lands, encouraging migrants from his estates in Ulster and reportedly describing one group who sailed from Ballycarry and Carrickfergus in 1751 as his 'tenants, neighbours and friends'.[83]

Dobbs had been born in Scotland to Ulster-Protestant parents. His father, Richard, fought as an officer in William III's army during the Williamite-Jacobite War in Ireland and had sent his wife to Scotland for safety.[84] He owned a 5,000 acre estate at Carrickfergus in north-east Ulster and been High Sheriff of County Antrim. Dobbs inherited in 1711 and subsequently relocated to Ireland. He became High Sheriff in 1720 and in 1727 was elected to represent Carrickfergus in the Irish parliament.

Hugh Boulter, the archbishop of Armagh and a keen promoter of the British interest in Ireland, introduced Dobbs to Walpole, who became his patron and in 1733 secured him the positions of engineer-in-chief and surveyor-general of Ireland. The latter office gave Dobbs a 5% commission on public works, which included the construction of Ireland's new parliament building in Dublin.[85] The income was substantial and it was around this time that the construction of a new house - Castle Dobbs - at Carrickfergus was completed.

Walpole's exit from government in 1742 proved to be no more than a temporary set-back for Dobbs and substitute patrons were found in the Earl

---

[82] Robert M. Calhoon, 'Dobbs, Arthur (1689–1765)', *ODNB*; online edn, Jan 2008.

[83] http://www.carolana.com/NC/Royal_Colony/adobbs.html, accessed 2 February 2018.

[84] Richard Dobbs (1660-1711); he enlisted in William III's army and fought in Ireland.

[85] Edward McParland, 'The Office of the Surveyor General in Ireland in the Eighteenth Century', *Architectural History*, 38 (1995), 91-101.

of Hertford[86] and the Earl of Holdernesse,[87] and especially George Montagu Dunk, Earl of Halifax.[88]

Dobbs' understanding of Ireland's economic distress led him to argue against mercantilism. He believed, correctly, that Britain was exhausting Ireland's working capital.[89] The Irish Treasury had been instructed to co-fund the military establishment in Ireland, as well as the Royal Navy, Britain's regiments in North America, and the salaries of absentee army officers. The Irish pension list had been extended to include foreign nationals whose pensions were awarded as patronage.[90] And payments to English-resident owners of Irish estates drained another £1-1.5 million from Ireland annually, around a fifth of domestic output.

The result was a monetary squeeze and economic depression: 'we are daily running in debt; our public funds prove deficient; our trade is diminished; our farmers are breaking condition; the value of land is lessened; money is scarce to a degree, and consequently our credit sinking'.[91]

London was not willing to consider let alone resolve Dublin's difficulties. Received wisdom viewed Ireland as a subservient not a co-equal state,

---

[86] Algernon Seymour, 7th Duke of Somerset (1684-1750), Earl of Hertford until 1748.

[87] Robert Darcy, 4th Earl of Holderness (1718-1778), Secretary of State for the Southern Department, 1751-54.

[88] George Montagu Dunk, 2nd Earl of Halifax (1716-1771).

[89] Cf., William Connolly to the duke of Grafton, 18 October 1720, quoted in Patrick Walsh, '"The Sin of With-Holding Tribute", contemporary pamphlets and the professionalization of the Irish Revenue Service in the early eighteenth century', *Eighteenth-Century Ireland/Iris an dá chultúr*, 21 (2006), 48-65.

[90] Cf. A.P.W. Malcolmson, *Nathaniel Clements: Government & the Governing Elite in Ireland* (Dublin: FCP, 2005); also, Alice E. Murray, *A History of the Commercial & Financial Relations between England & Ireland from the Period of the Restoration* (New York: Burt Franklin, 1970), reprint, first published 1903.

[91] Anonymous, *An Inquiry into Some of the Causes of the Ill Situation of the Affairs of the Irish* (Dublin, 1731), p. 3.

and the function of a colony was simply to serve the purposes of its colonial masters - 'to advance the interest of England'.[92]

Britain's one-sided policy was exemplified by a Declaratory Act,[93] which re-asserted the right of the British parliament to legislate for Ireland[94] and transferred to the British House of Lords the powers of a supreme court for Ireland. Economic imperialism was allied to social disdain, captured in Barnard's comment that Irish peers were 'shouldered aside' in the procession marking the wedding of the Prince of Orange to George II's eldest daughter.[95] And although William Molyneux, an Anglo-Irish critic, may have been a lone voice in the 1690s, forty years later the political context had changed and Jonathan Swift could rouse Ireland to nationalism. The threat was met by a tactical retreat by Britain but its strategy remained unchanged.[96]

Dobbs' assessment of America's economic potential was founded on his experience in Ireland. He argued for increased trade and in favour of strengthening the thirteen colonies militarily in anticipation of another war with France. His views were not dissimilar to those of Halifax, who had been appointed president of the Board of Trade in 1748.

The most influential commissioner since Bladen,[97] Halifax had secured an Order in Council in 1752 that placed the nomination of colonial governors in the Board's hands. And while Halifax may not have agreed with

---

[92] John Cary, *An Essay on the State of England in relation to its trade, its poor and its taxes* (Bristol, 1695).

[93] 'An Act for the better securing the dependency of the Kingdom of Ireland on the Crown of Great Britain', 6. Geo. I, c. 5 (1719).

[94] Poynings' Act of 1495, known as Poynings' Law, had made Ireland subservient to England in matters of parliamentary legislation more than two centuries earlier. The act was passed by Ireland's parliament and voluntarily restricted its powers to the approval or rejection of bills drawn up in London.

[95] Toby Barnard, *Improving Ireland?* (Dublin: FCP, 2008), p. 123.

[96] Ibid., esp. 166, 169, 173, 181-3.

[97] Halifax was president until 1761 apart from a short interval between June 1756 and October 1757.

everything Dobbs suggested, he was impressed by the concept of an integrated empire and proposed Dobbs as Johnston's successor.[98] The order confirming Dobbs as governor was issued on 25 January 1753,[99] and Dobbs arrived in the colony the following year to take up his post.

Dobbs' political objectives for North Carolina included pushing back against the assembly's accumulation of legislative power and preserving the governor and the Board's influence over taxation and appointments. Given his experience in Ireland, Dobbs understood that passage of the money bills were central to London's administrative control but although he had some tactical successes Dobbs could not reverse the accretion of power by John Starkey,[100] North Carolina's public treasurer, nor the more frequent exercise of local prerogatives. Although Dobbs faced down attempts by the assembly to control the office of colonial printer, which in practice often determined the supply of paper money in the province, he failed to overcome the assembly elsewhere and was frequently bested by Samuel Swann, its speaker.[101]

Like his predecessors, Dobbs was obliged to expend political energy mediating between the Cape Fear and Albemarle factions in the legislature. It was this that underlay his attempt to establish a new capital near Kingston, mid-way between the two. The assembly had met at Edenton from 1726-36 but was afterwards peripatetic. A law passed in 1746 had made New Bern the permanent capital but this was vetoed by London, partly because of objections from opposing political factions. But although the assembly voted

---

[98] J. Russell Snapp, 'An Enlightened Empire: Scottish and Irish Imperial Reformers in the Age of the American Revolution', *Albion*, 33.3 (2001), 388-403. Cf., also, C.R. Fay, 'Arthur Dobbs, Adam Smith and Walpole's Excise Scheme', *Historical Journal*, 4.2 (1961), 203-7.

[99] *CSRNC*, volume 5, pp. 16-7.

[100] John Starkey (c.1697-1765), elected to the assembly in 1734, he was elected treasurer of the Southern District in 1750.

[101] Samuel Swann (1704-1774), elected to the assembly in 1725. Cf. Jack P. Greene, 'The Role of the Lower Houses of Assembly in Eighteenth-Century Politics', *Journal of Southern History*, 27.4 (1961), 451-74.

the money to purchase the land at Kingston (from Dobbs himself, albeit at cost), London refused its assent. And when Kingston was removed from consideration, Dobbs took the seat of government to Brunswick where he had acquired *Russellborough*, a plantation, which he renamed *Castle Dobbs*.[102]

Dobbs' decision to relocate the capital to Cape Fear may have reflected his sympathy with the southern faction's anxieties over inadequate credit and limited money supply, but these concerns were shared across the colony.[103] The legal obligation to pay quit-rents and taxes in specie rather than commodities had been in the face of established practice and caused severe problems everywhere. Dobbs understood the issues well. There was a direct parallel with Ireland where a shortage of money supply had constrained economic growth,[104] and Dobbs believed the result would be the same in North Carolina if the colony's concerns were ignored.

But Britain was adamant that its trade policies would continue unchanged. The Navigation Acts were designed to capture the benefits of trade within the Empire. They prevented the colonies from trading directly with competing countries, obliged exports to be shipped on British-owned vessels, and required 'enumerated' goods to pass through British or colonial ports. Regardless, Dobbs wrote to London recommending repeal.[105] He

---

[102] Dobbs' estate in Brunswick was next to Roger Moore's *Orton* plantation, where he met and married Moore's niece in 1762. It was his second marriage. She was 15. He was 73. The capital moved again, to New Bern, in 1766 when the assembly agreed to fund William Tryon's office and mansion.

[103] A more valid reason may be that Brunswick offered Dobbs the opportunity to purchase *Russellborough* at one shilling per acre: http://www.nchistoricsites.org/brunswic/russellborough.htm, accessed 1 November 2017.

[104] Cf. Anthony Malcolmson, *Nathaniel Clements: Government & the Governing Elite in Ireland*; Alice Murray, *A History of the Commercial & Financial Relations between England & Ireland*; and William Connolly to the duke of Grafton, 18 October 1720, quoted in Patrick Walsh, "The Sin of With-Holding Tribute".

[105] For a general if one-sided overview, cf., Desmond Clarke, *Arthur Dobbs, Esquire, 1689-1765: Surveyor-General of Ireland, Prospector and Governor of North Carolina* (Chapel Hill, NC: UNCP, 1958).

had made a similar argument when in Ireland, writing that 'a flourishing trade gives encouragement to the industrious ... increases the power of the nation; [and] puts it in the power of every prudent and industrious man in it to enjoy more of the innocent pleasures of life ... to promote the happiness of [their] nation [and] increase its power and wealth'.[106]

Dobbs may have been correct that the principles of mercantilism were flawed and legislation that treated Ireland and America as competitors was as pointless as penalising 'the rest of England against London'.[107] But his reasoning was ignored and the British parliamentary mind-set that held mercantilism to be optimal remained unchanged.

Dobbs also failed to persuade London to address the shortage of currency. He had suggested that North Carolina be permitted to mint small denomination coins using local copper,[108] and presented calculations to London to demonstrate the advantages, but his proposals were ignored. North Carolina was forced to explore other options and to use Spanish dollars and French écus, as well as barter.

Proclamation money - promissory notes and bills of credit created locally to fund the cost of public works – offered another solution. The money was intended to be withdrawn when returned in tax payments but in practice remained in circulation to finance general expenditure.

Dobbs was aware that uncontrolled issuance of proclamation money would damage the colony's credit and diminish its currency's value. And when an attempt was made in 1760 to create paper bills of credit, Dobbs was forced to dissolve the assembly to prevent the legislation being passed.[109] In this in-

---

[106] Arthur Dobbs, *An Essay of the Trade and Improvement of Ireland* (Dublin: J. Smith, W. Brude, 1729 and 1731).

[107] Ibid, pp 27-8.

[108] K.H. Ledward (ed), *Journals of the Board of Trade and Plantations: volume 10, January 1754 - December 1758* (London: HMSO, 1933), pp. 160-72.

[109] For example, *CSRNC*, volume 6, pp. 216-20: Dobbs to the Board of Trade, 19 January 1760.

stance his concerns were shared by London and in 1764 parliament approved the Currency Act to control proclamation money across the America colonies as a whole, and in 1773 banned almost all money issuance.[110] But it was too late; by the early 1770s the nominal value of proclamation money had risen to stand at around £350,000 in North Carolina alone.[111]

Was Dobbs a freemason? Perhaps not while he was in North Carolina. But he had been part of Anglo-Irish circles in Dublin and London where freemasonry was current. And there is little doubt that the Dobbs family writ large had multiple connections to freemasonry. William Dobbs, a cousin, the middle son of the Rev. Richard Dobbs, Dobbs's uncle, was present at the elite lodge at the Yellow Lion in Dublin in June 1725[112] and makes a second documented appearance in 1731.[113] Richard Dobbs, probably Dobbs's younger brother, is recorded as a member of Lodge No. 430 at Ballyclare in County Antrim on 14 June 1769.[114] And after his father's death, Dobbs's step-mother, Margaret, married William Ruxton (d.1783), surgeon-general of Ireland, who in 1769 was installed as deputy grand master of Ireland.[115]

---

[110] The 1764 Currency Act was passed by parliament to regulate the issue and legal tender status of paper money in the colonies. It was an extension of the 1751 Currency Act that applied to the New England colonies and imposed the same principles on Britain's other American colonies.

[111] *Encyclopedia of North Carolina* (Chapel Hill, NC: UNCP, 2006) http://www.ncpedia.org/currency.

[112] *The Dublin Weekly Journal*, 26 June 1725. No extant minutes, personal correspondence or other documents have been identified.

[113] *Faulkner's Dublin Journal*, 18-21 December 1731. Cited in Lepper & Crossle, *History of the Grand Lodge of Free and Accepted Masons in Ireland* (Dublin, Lodge CC, 1925), volume I, p. 90.

[114] *Grand Lodge of Freemasons of Ireland Membership Registers, 1733-1923.*

[115] Ibid., p. 201. Cf., also, *Biographies of Members of the Irish Parliament 1692-1800*, Ulster Historical Foundation. The Ruxton family were landowners who controlled the borough of Ardee in the Irish parliament.

Dobbs's links to freemasonry would have been significant in two senses: first, in that it was an elite fraternal association shared by men of a similar class and outlook; and second, in that it offered opportunities to associate with influential figures in government, commerce and elsewhere, and played a significant role in social advancement.

Chapter Four

Benjamin Smith

The First Provincial Grand Master of North and South Carolina

The Grand Lodge of England appointed twenty-one provincial grand masters in Britain's thirteen American colonies between 1730 and 1776.[1] Of these, five patents were for the Carolinas. Three were in respect of South Carolina: John Hammerton in 1736; Peter Leigh in 1754; and his son, Sir Egerton Leigh, in 1770.[2] And one in respect of North Carolina: Joseph Montfort in 1771.[3] The fifth, granted on 14 October 1761, deputed Benjamin Smith (1717-1770) to be provincial grand master for both South and North Carolina.[4]

London's decision to appoint a provincial grand master for both Carolinas is significant. The provinces had been administratively separate for half a century and the expansion of Smith's remit to include North Carolina confirms that freemasonry had become established and suggests that Smith was in a position to interact with the relevant people and lodges. Although he was based in Charleston, Smith had business and family networks across North Carolina, and especially with those South Carolina planters and merchants who had relocated to Cape Fear.[5]

---

[1] See appendix one. Other provincial grand masters were elected locally without apparent input from London. Cf., *Loyalists and Malcontents*.

[2] *Masonic Year Book, Historical Supplement* (London: UGLE, 1969), 2nd edn, p. 47.

[3] The minutes of the Grand Lodge of England for 6 February 1771 record the appointment of Montfort as 'Provincial G. M. for North Carolina'.

[4] Ibid.

[5] The Moores were among the earliest settlers at Cape Fear. Maurice Moore (d.1743), and Roger Moore (d.1751), were South Carolinians from Goose Creek and related to Smith through his mother.

Smith had been born in South Carolina to Thomas Smith,[6] a middling planter, and Sabina, whose family owned more than 24,000 acres.[7] He inherited a 2,000 acre plantation at St James Goose Creek and later purchased the *Accabee* plantation on the Ashley River. But despite his planter background, Smith was determined to build a career as a merchant-trader and in his teens sought a clerkship - an apprenticeship - with James Crokatt, arguably South Carolina's foremost merchant. He became Crokatt's protégé and when Crokatt left Charleston for England to establish what would become London's pre-eminent Carolina trading house, the preparations for his departure included an invitation to Smith to become one of three founding principals in a new partnership.

Simmons, Smith & Crokatt was owned equally by its three founders and began trading in September 1738.[8] Operating from Crokatt's landmark building in Broad Street in central Charleston, the business took over *Crokatt & Co.'s* client base. The benefits were obvious. Crokatt maintained access to the Carolina market through a partnership in which he held a one-third equity stake, and Simmons and Smith gained a relationship with the most astute and best-connected Carolina merchant in London. Their clients also benefitted, retaining commercial continuity on the same trading terms as before: two years credit and the ability to exchange agricultural commodities directly for imported goods.

In 1745 at the expiry of *Simmons, Smith & Crokatt*'s seven-year term, Smith opened his own trading house but continued to cooperate with Crokatt, co-investing in several vessels including the 200-ton *Flamborough's Prize* and the 100-ton brigantine *Charming Nancy*.[9]

---

[6] Thomas Smith (1691-1724).

[7] Edgar & Bailey, *Biographical Dictionary of the South Carolina House of Representatives, 1692-1775*, volume II.

[8] Ebenezer Simmons had been the senior clerk at *Crockatt & Co*.

[9] R. Nicholas Olsberg, 'Ship Registers in the South Carolina Archives 1734-1780', *South Carolina Historical Magazine*, 74.4 (1973), 189-299.

Smith formed *Smith & Palmer* with John Palmer, two years later. It lasted until 1752 when he established *Benjamin Smith & Co.* with two junior partners, Miles Brewton and John Jones. A partnership with Brewton alone followed and in 1761 a final partnership, *Smith, Brewton & Smith*, that included Thomas Loughton Smith, his son.[10]

One of South Carolina's most significant merchants for more than two decades, Smith's client base extended across both Carolinas. His trading and factoring businesses included the export of naval stores, deerskins and agricultural products to Britain and Europe, and the reciprocal import of dry and manufactured goods, and wine and spirits. In the deerskin trade, *Simmons, Smith & Crokatt* was responsible for twenty-three cargoes; *Simmons & Smith* for eighteen; *Smith & Brewton*, *Smith & Palmer* and *Benjamin Smith & Co.* for a further thirty-four.[11] All were similarly active in rice exports. In the import trade, *Smith & Brewton* and *Smith, Brewton & Smith* were among South Carolina's top ten firms in general merchandise and luxury goods, aggregating more than a hundred consignments.[12] And in the transatlantic slave trade, Smith handled twenty-three cargoes directly from 1739-66, with up to 600 slaves trafficked on each vessel.[13]

Smith's commercial network was predominantly across the coastal plain where he had, in Henry Laurens's words, an 'extensive acquaintance and ability in dispatch of business [and] influence with the planters at least equal to those of any other man in the province'.[14] Although it is not pos-

---

[10] Thomas Loughton Smith (c.1740-1773).

[11] Moore, 'The Largest Exporters of Deerskins from Charles Town, 1735 - 1775', 144-50.

[12] Stumpf, 'South Carolina Importers of General Merchandise, 1735-1765', 1-10.

[13] Higgins, 'Charles Town Merchants and Factors Dealing in the External Negro Trade 1735-1775', 205-17.

[14] Henry Laurens quoted in Kenneth Morgan, 'Slave Sales in Colonial Charleston', *English Historical Review*, 113.453 (1998), 905-27; quote from 910.

sible to know precisely how his trading connections were reinforced by freemasonry, it is not unreasonable to assume an association, especially with his counterparts in Wilmington.

By the 1750s Smith had become one of America's wealthiest traders and his co-owned fleet one of the largest in the South. His shipping partners testify to the breadth of his relationships and include many of Charleston's principal merchants.[15] The *Charles Town*, a 180-ton ex-French privateer, had eight investors including Edmund Cossens, John Palmer, Robert Pringle, George Inglis and Jacob Motte, the public treasurer of South Carolina from 1743-70. The equity partners in *Charming Nancy*, a 130-ton vessel built at James Island, include Ebenezer Simmons, James Crokatt and Charles Crokatt, his son. And the *Couper River*, a 200-ton ship taken from the French, was jointly owned with Henry Laurens and Joseph Pickering, among others. Equally if not more profitably, Smith also had an equity share in the *Charles Town*, a privateer co-owned with Robert Pringle.[16]

Smith retired in 1762 at the age of 45 having earned at his peak an estimated £10,000 per annum. He was lauded by his peers, including Laurens, like Smith a leading Carolina merchant, politician and freemason, who described him as 'in the first rank of company in Carolina and for a great many years at the head of a house of very extensive trade'.[17]

Smith's commercial achievements were mirrored in his political status. Elected to the assembly in 1746, Smith served as speaker of the South

---

[15] Cf., *Loyalists & Malcontents*.

[16] Theodore Corbett, *St Augustine Pirates and Privateers* (Charleston, SC: History Press, 2012), p. 110. Also, Walter B. Edgar (ed.), *Letter Book of Robert Pringle 1737-1745* (Columbia, SC: USC Press, 1972). The commonly held view that few activities were 'near so profitable as a proper vessel or two well-fitted out for privateering' was broadly correct: Carl E. Swanson, 'American Privateering and Imperial Warfare, 1739-1748', *William and Mary Quarterly*, 3rd series, 42.3 (1985), 357-82; quote from 366.

[17] Henry Laurens, *The Papers of Henry Laurens* (Columbia, SC: USC Press, 1968), pp. 500-1, Henry Laurens to William Fisher, 16 July 1763.

Carolina assembly from 1755-63,[18] and was offered but declined membership of the royal council in 1760.

Smith's introduction to freemasonry had been via his mentor, James Crokatt.[19] His elevation to the chair of Solomon's Lodge in 1738 in succession to Crokatt was recorded in the *South Carolina Gazette*, as was the St John's Day parade a year later in December 1740:

> Saturday last being the festival of St John the Evangelist, the day was ushered in with the firing of guns at sunrise from several ships in the harbour with all their colours flying. At 9 o'clock all the members of Solomon's Lodge belonging to the Ancient and Honorable Society of Free and Accepted Masons, met at the house of Benjamin Smith, Master of the said lodge, and at 10 proceeded from thence, properly clothed, with the ensigns of their Order, to the house of the Provincial Grand Master, James Graeme, where a Grand Lodge was held...[20]

Smith had been elected master of Solomon's Lodge at the age of 22 and afterwards rose rapidly through South Carolina's provincial grand lodge, becoming provincial grand master only three years later and remaining in the chair until Peter Leigh, the colony's new chief justice, arrived from London in 1754 with a provincial grand warrant. Following Leigh's death in 1761, Smith was confirmed as his successor by the Grand Lodge of England and his remit extended to both Carolinas.[21]

---

[18] In addition to St Philip's Parish, Smith represented St George Dorchester, 1749-51; St James Goose Creek, 1766-68; and Sir John Colleton Parish, 1770. He did not serve in the eighteenth and twenty-eighth assemblies.

[19] *South Carolina Gazette*, 28 December 1738.

[20] *South Carolina Gazette*, 1 January 1740.

[21] Smith was acting PGM following the death of his predecessor, Peter Leigh. His deputation was issued by London the following year.

Under Smith's stewardship freemasonry became immensely popular to the extent that attendance at the 1764 St John's Day feast in Charleston exceeded a hundred 'gentlemen of distinction' and a guest list that boasted the lieutenant-governor, William Bull.[22]

The lodge had by then become integral to Southern colonial society, providing a link between South Carolina's planters and merchants and their compatriots in Cape Fear and elsewhere in North Carolina. Trade tied the sister colonies together, with the bulk of North Carolina's exports shipped to Britain, Europe and the Caribbean from South Carolina's ports, especially Charleston, and imports following the reverse route. Charleston's merchants worked with wholesale and retail counterparts in North Carolina to distribute manufactured, luxury and other goods. And other connections were forged through slave factoring, with Charleston's markets the principal source of North Carolina's slaves, and shipbuilding, with vessels operated and owned by South Carolina's merchants built in Beaufort, Brunswick and elsewhere in North Carolina.[23]

Citing declining health, Smith gave notice of his intention to resign as provincial grand master in December 1767.[24] Egerton Leigh took over on an acting basis the following year. Smith died in 1770 while visiting Rhode Island. His body was brought back to South Carolina and reinterred in Charleston.

Smith's death did not end the family's connection to freemasonry. His nephew, also Benjamin (1756-1826),[25] was later grand master of North Carolina, serving from 1808-10. A planter, lawyer and bencher at London's Middle Temple, he was also related to the Moore family at Cape

---

[22] *South Carolina Gazette*, 31 December 1764.
[23] Olsberg, 'Ship Registers in the South Carolina Archives 1734-1780', 189-299.
[24] *South Carolina Gazette*, 1 January 1768.
[25] The son of Thomas Smith (1720-1790), of Broad Street in Charleston, SC.

Fear. Smith was an aide-de-camp to Washington; a three-term member of North Carolina's lower house; a state senator, serving eighteen-terms, five as speaker; and the state governor in 1811. He was also one of many North Carolina freemasons who supported the University of North Carolina, donating warrants over 20,000 acres in Tennessee[26] and acting as a trustee of the university from 1789-1824.

---

[26] He received more than 100,000 acres in land warrants for war service. The 20,000 acre donation was later sold by UNC for USD 14,000.

CHAPTER FIVE

FREEMASONRY AT CAPE FEAR

CORNELIUS HARNETT JR. AND WILMINGTON TOWN

Cornelius Harnett Jr.,[1] Wilmington's leading politician and merchant-trader, owned a portfolio of commercial interests that stretched across the Lower Cape Fear and included forestry, farming and shipping, as well as a sawmill, distillery and tavern. Part had been inherited from his father,[2] a first generation Irish migrant who served on Burrington's council, albeit that the two fell out, and as a magistrate for Bladen County and New Hanover County, where he was also sheriff. His son was equally active in public life. Appointed a town commissioner for Wilmington in 1750 and justice of the peace for New Hanover County the same year, Harnett represented Wilmington in the general assembly from 1754 through to Independence.

Harnett was master of St John's Lodge Wilmington in 1764 when he issued a warrant to constitute the Royal White Hart Lodge in Halifax. The authority by which he did so, if any, is unclear. There was no provincial grand lodge in North Carolina and Harnett was not the provincial grand master. But there are at least two possible explanations. First, that he was deputed by Benjamin Smith;[3] and second, that he issued the warrant in

---

[1] Cornelius Harnett Jr. (1723-1781).

[2] Cornelius Harnett (d.1742). Born in Dublin, he migrated in 1720. Although Crowe refers to Harnett having founded a lodge at Norfolk, VA, in 1741 (Frederick J.W. Crowe, *A Concise History of Freemasonry*, Revised Edition (London: Gale & Polden, 1951), p. 336), this is improbable. Cf., *DNCB*.

[3] There were strong links between Charleston and Wilmington. Although there is no extant correspondence between Smith and Harnett, cf. Guerard to Harnett, 23 October 1753, *Guerard Letterbook, 7 March 1752 - 17 June 1754*, South Carolina Historical Society, Charleston, SC; also, Bradford J. Wood, *This Remote Part of the World: Regional Formation in Lower Cape Fear, 1725-1775* (Columbia, SC: USC Press, 2004), fn. 53. p. 307.

his own right, making Royal White Hart a daughter lodge to St John's. Although there are no minutes for St John's Lodge from the 1760s, those of the Royal White Hart have survived and it may be significant that in 1765 Frederick Schultzer is described as 'grand master' rather than 'master', perhaps implying that masters of certain lodges assumed a wider authority than over a single lodge.[4]

Harnett epitomised the patriotic wing of North Carolina's eastern political establishment, heading opposition to the Stamp Act and chairing the Sons of Liberty in Cape Fear. He jointly led the protest march in Brunswick in 1766 and in 1770 chaired the committee charged with enforcing non-importation in protest against Townshend's duties.[5] Perhaps less conventionally, Harnett also advocated government reform in an attempt to curb the abuses that had sparked the Regulator Movement, notwithstanding that he opposed the violence that threatened to damage his and his peers' economic interests.

As resistance to Britain grew from the early 1770s, Harnett emerged as one of North Carolina's principal revolutionary leaders. He was instrumental in establishing a committee of correspondence in 1773 and the following year was elected chair of the Wilmington-New Hanover committee of safety, a body comprised mainly of his fellow plantocrats and freemasons.

When Governor Josiah Martin fled the colony in 1775 and a provincial council of safety was formed, Harnett became its president and the *de facto* head of the executive branch. He subsequently served in the second, third, fourth and fifth provincial congresses, becoming president of the fifth, and was one of the state's delegates to the continental congress in 1777. His spearheading of anti-British resistance was such that when Sir Henry Clinton[6] tabled an amnesty in 1776 that offered to pardon those Carolinians who agreed to cease hostilities and submit to British law, Harnett was one of

---

[4] Minute Book of the Royal White Hart Lodge (1765-1818), p. 5, 18 April 1765.
[5] Named after Charles Townshend (1725-1767), Chancellor of the Exchequer (1766-7).
[6] Sir Henry Clinton (1730-1795), a British general.

only two men excluded.[7] He was captured in Wilmington in January 1781 and died a prisoner of the British three months later.

St John's Lodge

The warrant constituting St John's Lodge was issued by the Grand Lodge of England in 1754, payment for which was acknowledged on 27 June. The following year the lodge was assigned No. 213 on the grand register and it continued to be recognised nominally as an English lodge until 1813.[8]

There are only a few details of the lodge's early years. *The Wilmington Town Book* refers to a 'Masons' Lodge' valued in 1756 at £140 for rateable purposes and taxed at '£1 8s', placing the building in the upper third of properties in Wilmington ranked by taxable value.[9] This is significant. It demonstrates not only that a permanent lodge building existed in the town in the 1750s but that the members had financial substance and were relatively numerous. The reason that lodge meetings were afterwards held at other locations, including St James's Church and the county courthouse, or met in member's houses, including those of Harnett and William Hooper,[10] a wealthy lawyer, is not known. But a probable explanation is that the lodge building had been wrecked by fire, a constant danger in Wilmington as in other towns.

Several ordinances were passed to reduce fire risk, including the provision of a mobile pump – a 'fire engine', tighter regulations covering the

---

[7] The other was Robert Howe (1732-1786), in 1775 colonel of the 2nd North Carolina Regiment and in 1776 a brigadier general in the Continental Army.

[8] St John's Lodge was subsequently assigned No. 158 (1770); 126 (1780); 127 (1781); and 114 (1792). Cf., Lane's *Masonic Records*. Although the Grand Lodge of North Carolina was formed on 9 December 1787, St John's remained on the English register until 1813. The lodge is No. 1 on the register of the GLNC.

[9] *The Wilmington Town Book, 1743-1778*, pp. 95-6. By way of comparison, Harnett's house was assessed at £200 and taxed at £2 0s.

[10] William Hooper (1742-1790).

storage of flammable goods, and the proscription of wooden and clay chimneys. But despite this Wilmington continued to suffer destructive fires, including two in 1756 and 1766, respectively, that devastated the town. The latter led the town commissioners to introduce a 2% tax on properties to pay for two boreholes and yet more fire-fighting equipment.[11]

Although the names of only a handful of lodge members have survived from the colonial period, those that have were from the town's elites.[12] In addition to Harnett and Hooper, they include Archibald MacLaine,[13] Caleb Grainger, Richard Hellier,[14] Robert Howe[15] and Joshua Toomer.[16]

Of Scots-Irish ancestry, MacLaine had been born in Banbridge County Down and migrated to Philadelphia in 1750, from where he travelled to Cape Fear. He married in November 1752. His wife, Elizabeth, was the step-daughter of Matthew Rowan, president of the royal council and later acting governor.

MacLaine initially traded in partnership as a merchant but gave it up to study law when his business partner died. With the assistance of his wife's family, he later built a successful law practice and gained appointment as clerk of the provincial Supreme Court.

Despite his late father-in-law's position in the colony, MacLaine opposed the Stamp Act and took a leading role in the Sons of Liberty. He was elected to Wilmington's committee of safety in 1774 and served in the provincial congresses in 1775 and 1776, sitting on the committee that drafted the bill of rights and the state constitution. The following year he co-drafted the law establishing North Carolina's court system and chaired the committee on

---

[11] Cf., Alan D. Watson, 'Fire and Fire Control in Colonial Wilmington', *Lower Cape Fear Historical Society Bulletin*, 18.3 (1975), 1-4.

[12] *The Wilmington Town Book, 1743-1778.*

[13] Archibald MacLaine (1728-1790).

[14] Richard Hellier (*d.*1756).

[15] Robert Howe (1732-1786).

[16] Joshua Toomer (1712-1763).

internal security. He was elected to the general assembly in 1780-81, and again in 1783-87, but twice refused election to the continental congress. He also declined to sit as a judge of the superior court.

Despite his support for independence, MacLaine was criticised for his willingness to defend loyalists under the law, a moral stance that on at least one occasion sparked a minor riot with MacLaine assaulted and seriously injured.[17] He was also a Federalist and a delegate to the Hillsborough convention in 1788, where he voted in the minority that the Constitution be adopted. The *DNCB* considers that MacLaine 'provided a model for those who would advance the theory of conservative and radical continuity in early American politics'. It was probably to further such aims that he became one of the first trustees of the University of North Carolina.

Caleb Grainger, the son of one of Cape Fear's earliest settlers,[18] became an alderman, mayor and a town commissioner;[19] a member of the assembly from 1746; county sheriff from 1749-52; and a captain, major and then colonel in the North Carolina militia.[20] Grainger's will, written and amended with codicils between 1761-65, the year of his death, reveals the extent of his estate which included plantations, a wharf, a 'general stock of negroes', and properties at Wilmington, Smith's Creek and Masonboro. Grainger specified that his executors should ensure his burial 'in a decent manner and as a Mason', 'and that my dear and ever-worthy Friend Mr Corn. Harnett have purchased out of my estate a neat mourning ring which I beg he may wear in remembrance of his sincere friend & [masonic] brother'.[21]

---

[17] Maass, 'The Cure for All Our Political Calamities: Archibald Maclaine and the Politics of Moderation in Revolutionary North Carolina'; cf., also, *DNCB*.

[18] Joshua Grainger (1702-1745).

[19] For a period Wilmington held a borough charter. Cf., Lee, *The Lower Cape Fear in Colonial Days*, pp. 117-44.

[20] *The Wilmington Town Book, 1743-1778*.

[21] Bryan, *North Carolina Wills and Inventories*, pp. 202-7. Two of Grainger's sons were named for Harnett.

His fellow town commissioner, Richard Hellier[22] had migrated to Cape Fear from Somerset in south-west England where he owned an estate at Prestleigh.[23] He was subsequently appointed town clerk and surveyor. *The Wilmington Town Book* notes that 'until his death in 1756, he belonged to the Masonic Order'. His financial standing was seemingly no more than upper middling, underlined by the rateable value of his house at £50, 10s paid, and a modest seven land grants of around 5,000 acres across Bladen and New Hanover counties.[24]

Born in Boston to a Scottish minister and the daughter of an affluent Massachusetts merchant, William Hooper graduated from Harvard in 1760, studied law in Boston, and moved to Wilmington in 1764 to open what would become a successful legal practice.[25] He was appointed deputy attorney general of North Carolina five years later.[26] His marriage to Ann Clarke connected Hooper directly to the planter elites in Cape Fear and eased his election to the assembly where he represented Campbellton in 1773 and thereafter New Hanover County.

Hooper was involved closely in Governor Tryon's move against the Regulators and present at the Battle of Alamance, but his loyalist politics reversed in the 1770s. Self-interestedly or otherwise, Hooper acknowledged

---

[22] Also written as 'Hillier'. He was appointed a town commissioner in 1743: *The Wilmington Town Book, 1743-1778*, p. 2.

[23] *New Hanover County Deed Book D*, p. 519, Death Record.

[24] *The Wilmington Town Book, 1743-1778*, p. 78; State Archives of North Carolina, North Carolina Land Grants database.

[25] William Hooper (1742-1790). Cf., Benson J. Lossing, *Lives of the Signers of the Declaration of Independence* (Aledo, TX: WallBuilder Press, 1995), p. 201-4, originally published 1848.

[26] William Hooper's younger brothers, Thomas and George, achieved success as Cape Fear merchants to the extent that they opened an office in Charleston. Thomas later entered into partnership with Newman Swallow and established *Hooper & Swallow*.

that the colony was 'striding fast to independence'[27] and joined the committees of safety and correspondence accordingly. He was selected as a delegate to all five provincial congresses and attended the second continental congress in Philadelphia where he co-signed the Declaration of Independence.

Hooper returned to North Carolina in May 1777 and was elected to represent Wilmington. The British occupation of the town and the destruction of his estates at Wilmington and Masonboro led Hooper to relocate to Hillsborough. He remained there until his death in 1790.

Robert Howe, the son of wealthy South Carolina planters who had settled at Cape Fear, had been born in New Hanover County. Educated in England, he married into another planter dynasty - his wife, Sarah, was a direct descendant of Sir John Yeamans. Their later divorce was due to his womanising.

Howe owned rice plantations across the Lower Cape Fear and other estates, including a plantation in Bladen County, which he represented in the assembly from 1760-62, and land in Brunswick, which he represented from 1764, re-elected six times. He also sat as a justice of the peace for both counties and on the Wilmington Town committee of safety.

Howe saw active service with the militia in the 1760s and had command of Fort Johnston for almost seven years. He fought with Virginia's troops in the French and Indian War, and served as a colonel of artillery in Tryon's expedition against the Regulators. In 1775 he was given command of the militia, leading them against Fort Johnston that July. He was promoted colonel of the 2nd North Carolina Regiment two months later and commanded the troops that captured Norfolk.

The continental congress promoted Howe to brigadier general in 1776 and the following year to major general, when he succeeded James Moore as

---

[27] Jo. Seawell Jones, *Defence of the Revolutionary History of the State of North Carolina* (Raleigh, NC: Turner & Hughes, 1834), p. 314.

commander of the Southern Department. As with Harnett, his reputation as an unbending patriot led to his exclusion from Clifton's proposed amnesty.

Personal and political animosities led to Howe being stripped of command and transferred to New York, where he served under Washington. He was accused of attempting to defect but whether this is accurate or an aspersion is unclear. The latter is more probable given Howe's history and that he helped to quell mutinies in the Pennsylvania and New Jersey lines. He returned to *Kendall*, near Orton, his principal plantation, in 1783. Howe died three years later in December 1786 on route to a sitting of the North Carolina Commons.

The last known member of the lodge, Joshua Toomer, a tanner born in St Andrews Parish in Charleston,[28] had moved to New Hanover in around 1747.[29] He supposedly left Charleston in disgrace owing money to Henry Laurens.[30] Toomer's aunt, Elizabeth, had married Joshua Grainger in 1722, making Caleb Grainger his first cousin. With family support, Toomer acquired a tavern in Wilmington and over 1,600 acres of land grants around Duncan's Creek. He prospered, becoming a notary public, postmaster and county coroner,[31] and a town commissioner and alderman. Anthony Toomer, his grandson, was also a member of St John's Lodge.[32]

---

[28] Henry Toomer (*d.*1739), his father, was resident in South Carolina as early as 1709. Edgar & Bailey, *Biographical Directory of the South Carolina House of Representatives*, volume II, p. 677.

[29] DNCB.

[30] Henry Laurens, *The Papers of Henry Laurens: Sept. 11, 1746-Oct. 31, 1755* (Columbia, SC: USC Press, 1968), p. 38.

[31] CSRNC, volume 6, pp. 58-60: Memorial from the Vestry and parishioners of St James Parish, New Hanover County concerning the work of Michael Smith. 1 October 1759.

[32] Joshua's son, Henry Toomer (1738-*c.*1799), a merchant and financier, was a member of the Wilmington committee of safety (1775-76) and commissary for various units of the North Carolina Militia. His name does not appear in the extant lodge membership registers.

CHAPTER SIX

JOSEPH MONTFORT

JOSEPH MONTFORT - 'GRAND MASTER OF AND FOR AMERICA'

Joseph Montfort was not born to aristocratic parents in England in 1724,[1] nor was he initiated into freemasonry before migrating to America.[2] He was born in Hampton in Warwick County Virginia on an estate close to Old Point Comfort where the Montfort family had settled in the early seventeenth century. It was from here - not England - that Montfort left for North Carolina, most probably via the Roanoke River.[3] He was not a member of the English nobility but middling and named for his father, also Joseph, a grandson of Colonel Thomas Montfort.[4]

Montfort arrived in Edgecombe County in the early 1750s and in 1752 acquired 419 acres on Quankey Creek,[5] around five miles west of where

---

[1] Inaccurate information appears on Montfort's gravestone, which is a modern replacement. The date and place of birth were probably derived from Gowen. See fn. below.

[2] Harry W. Gowen, *The Story of the Right Worshipful Joseph Montfort* (Halifax, NC: Gowen, 1907). With respect to his supposed 'noble parentage', the title of 'Lord Montfort' has been created twice in the English peerage. First in 1295, when John de Montfort was created Baron Montfort. The title became extinct in 1367). And second in 1741, when Henry Bromley (i.e. not Montfort), previously MP for Cambridgeshire, was created Lord Montfort, Baron of Horseheath. That title became extinct in 1851 on the death of the third baron.

[3] John N. Martin, 'Stokes Notes', *William and Mary Quarterly*, 8.2 (1928), 124-35, esp. 124-5.

[4] W.G. Stannard, 'Abstracts of Virginia Land Patents', *Virginia Magazine of History & Biography,* 6.1 (1898), 91-100, esp. 95-9. Also 'Virginia Quit Rent Rolls, 1704', *Virginia Magazine of History and Biography,* 30.4 (1922), 341-7.

[5] '419 acres lying on both sides of Quankie Pocoson': NC Land Patent Book No. 11, Land Grant File No. 1400.

Joseph Montfort (d.1776)
Copied from an eighteenth-century miniature
Jacques (James) Littlejohn Busbee (1870-1947)
From the Collection of the Grand Lodge of North Carolina

Halifax Town would be founded.[6] The land was surveyed in early 1753 and entered into the records of the Granville Land Office in November the same year.[7] Other members of his family migrated with him, including Sarah, his sister,[8] married to David Stokes of Virginia, a planter and justice of the peace. Their names are documented in the early membership registers of the Royal White Hart Lodge. Montfort is recorded in 1765 and Henry, his son, in 1783, although both were initiated earlier.[9] David Stokes appears in the minutes in 1765, and John[10] and Montfort Stokes[11] in 1783.[12]

Like many incomers, Montfort's business success had two important foundations: first, family money to begin the process; and second, an efficacious marriage that brought additional resources and the right connections.

Montfort's wife, Priscilla, was the daughter of Benjamin Hill,[13] a trader and merchant in Bertie County who had made his fortune exporting pelts

---

[6] The town was established in 1757 and named for George Montagu-Dunk, Earl of Halifax, president of the Board of Trade.

[7] W.D. Bennett, *Granville Proprietary Land Office: Deeds and Surveys, 1752-1760*, (Raleigh, NC: Bennett, 1989). John Carteret, 2nd Earl Granville, was the only descendant of the original Lord Proprietors of Carolina not to sell his lands to the crown. His holdings covered a strip of land roughly 60 miles wide abutting the border with Virginia and his agents were instructed to register vacant lands granted to settlers and collect quit-rents from them.

[8] Sarah Stokes (1717-1800).

[9] Henry Montfort is described in the minutes of the Royal White Hart Lodge as a 'visiting brother': Minute Book of the Royal White Hart Lodge, 24 January 1783, p. 54.

[10] John Stokes (1756-1790).

[11] Montfort Stokes (1762-1842).

[12] Montfort Stokes was David and Sarah's eleventh child. He is discussed below.

[13] Colonel Benjamin Hill (1697-1752).

and deerskins to England via Virginia.[14] He also acted as an agent for Henry McCulloh,[15] the land speculator.[16] With affluence came influence. Hill served on Burrington's royal council from 1731-34, was appointed a justice of the peace in 1732,[17] and thereafter commissioned a colonel in the militia. He represented Bertie County in the assembly from 1736-46,[18] and had been one of many legislators who objected volubly to changing the practice for the payment of quit-rents and taxes that had ruled since the seventeenth century.[19]

Aside from Priscilla, Hill had two other daughters.[20] Sarah,[21] his second, was married to Henry McCulloh's nephew, Alexander McCulloch.[22]

---

[14] Priscilla inherited a share of her father's estate following his death in 1752. It included £400 cash, a horse and five slaves - 'Negroes Cesar, Hanna, and Jenny, being the three children born of my Negro Flora, and Negro Penne, born of Teresa, and Negro Flora'. Cf., J. Bryan Grimes, *Abstracts of North Carolina Wills*, p. 164. The will was proved in 1753.

[15] *CSRNC*, volume 4, pp. 1097-100: Benjamin Hill to Henry McCulloh, 23 July 1750.

[16] K.H. Ledward (ed), *Journals of the Board of Trade and Plantations: volume 9, January 1750 - December 1753* (London: HMSO, 1932), 27 June 1751, p. 215.

[17] *Calendar of State Papers Colonial, America and West Indies: volume 41, 1734-1735* (London: HMSO, 1953), 'America and West Indies: 7 October 1734', pp. 249-54.

[18] *Calendar of State Papers Colonial, America and West Indies: volume 43, 1737* (London: HMSO, 1963), 'America and West Indies, 29 March 1737', pp. 93-9; *CSRNC*, volume 4, pp. 1097-100: Benjamin Hill to Henry McCulloh, 23 July 1750, *et al.*

[19] *CSRNC*, volume 4, pp. 115-55: Minutes of the Lower House of the North Carolina General Assembly, 15 January 1735 - 1 March 1735, *et al.*

[20] Hill also had two sons, Henry (1723-1772) and Benjamin (1732-1750).

[21] Sarah Hill (1716-1771), married Alexander McCulloch in 1734.

[22] Alexander McCulloch (1715-1798), deputy auditor of Edenton (1745), clerk of the Bute County Court (1772). Also written as 'McCullock'. An officer in the Orange County militia until 1754, he was appointed colonel of the Edgecombe County militia in 1760. At his death McCulloch owned 70 slaves and plantations across Halifax and Warren counties. Cf., *DNCB*; also, Thomas W. Cutrer,

An Ulsterman like his uncle, McCulloch migrated to North Carolina in the early 1740s and acquired an estate at nearby Elk Marsh.[23] He was involved in trading and land deals on his own account,[24] and for his uncle, for whom he held a joint power of attorney.[25] Active in public office, McCulloch secured an appointment as deputy auditor for North Carolina, was elected to the assembly in 1760 representing Halifax County, and obtained a colonelcy in the militia the same year. He was appointed to the royal council in 1762, remaining a member until 1775 when the council was disestablished.[26]

Hill's eldest daughter, Mary,[27] had married equally well. John Campbell,[28] originally from Coleraine in Ulster, had purchased land in Hertford County in the late 1730s and established a plantation. He also traded successfully as a merchant from Edenton and accrued considerable wealth, eventually amassing over 8,000 acres, a ferry, and the *Lazy Hill* estate in Bertie County.[29] Dobbs refers

---

Ben McCulloch and the Frontier Military Tradition (Chapel Hill, NC: UNCP, 1993), p. 9; and State Archives of North Carolina, North Carolina Land Grants database.

[23] The plantation was in the north of Halifax County. It appears as Elk Marsh on Collet's map published in 1770 but is renamed 'Marsh Swamp' on Price's 1808 map. Cf., *CSRNC*, volume 15, pp. 418-9: Benjamin McCulloh to Jethro Sumner, 16 January 1781.

[24] Alexander McCulloch acquired land across North Carolina from the late 1730s onwards. His grants exceeded 4,600 acres.

[25] *CSRNC*, volume 5, pp. 779-82: Power of attorney for Alexander McCulloch and John Campbell (his brother-in-law) to act for Henry McCulloh, 19 July 1757.

[26] Although a royalist until the revolution, McCulloh was not censured thereafter and retained his assets. He was on good personal terms with many patriots, including Wylie Jones and John Baptiste Ashe, both of whom he appointed as executors to his will.

[27] Mary Elizabeth Hill (1725-1753), married John Campbell c.1740.

[28] Captain John Campbell (c.1701-1781).

[29] When his estate was sold it was listed as 'One tract of land known as "Lazy Hill" lying in Bertie County on the west side of Chowan River, containing 800 acres. It is a beautiful situation well-watered; on its premises are a good dwelling

to him in a memorandum to the Board of Trade as 'the most eminent trader in this province',[30] and named Campbellton on the Upper Cape Fear River in his honour. He was also praised in the *Journal of a French Traveller in the Colonies*:

> *Friday, March the 29th, 1765* ... Mr Campbell ... is a man generally esteemed and of the greatest property of any man in this part of the province. He received me with the greatest civility possible, and notwithstanding all I could do, would not let me go from his house for a fortnight, during which time he accompanied me to different places. His house is pleasantly situated on the south side of Chowan River on a fine hill or eminence which [is] a rarity in this country; the river is about two miles broad here although 100 ms. from the Bar, and large sloops and schooners go up 50 miles above this place. The river separates into two branches, called Nattoway and Meharin,[31] this last is navigable far up in the country, the vessels that go up it bring great quantities of corn, some wheat and staves, which they carry to the norward to different parts, the difficulty of the Bar makes all these commodities sell cheaper than elsewhere.[32]

Alongside his plantations and trading house, Campbell co-owned a small merchant fleet in partnership with his brother, James, who acted as his agent in England. Naval stores, agricultural produce and tobacco were exported

---

house, kitchen store, warehouse, workhouse, barns milk and meat house, stables. Together with a good shad and herry fishery, a good apple and peach orchard and two vegetable gardens.' Cf., Bertie County Historical Association.

[30] *CSRNC*, volume 6, p. 286: Memorandum from Arthur Dobbs to the Board of Trade.

[31] Nottoway and Meherrin.

[32] 'Journal of a French Traveller in the Colonies', *American Historical Review*, 26 (1921), 737-8.

to London, Liverpool, Whitehaven[33] and Glasgow, and wine, spirits and manufactured goods imported back to North Carolina.[34] They also shipped tobacco to the Caribbean.

Campbell had been elected to the legislature in 1744 and with his father-in-law led the faction opposing Governor Johnston's attempts to increase the representation of the southern – Cape Fear - counties. He became speaker in 1754 but resigned citing ill health only a year later. He returned to the assembly the following decade as a representative for Bertie County (1767-9), was elected again in 1773, and was thereafter nominated to four provincial congresses.[35] He was in addition a magistrate and a commissioner for Roanoke Port, a lucrative post.[36]

Montfort's familial alliance with Alexander McCulloch and John Campbell helped to boost his standing in the province and aided his accretion of public offices and properties. He purchased and was awarded land grants across Edgecombe County and adjacent Granville County, acquiring 1,780 acres in 1762-63 alone, and in Mecklenburg County, where he obtained 8,400 acres in 1765 and a further 800 acres a few years later. Montfort also developed land in partnership with others, including Solomon Alston and Willie Jones. Jones, a member of the Royal White Hart Lodge, would later marry Montfort's daughter, Mary.

---

[33] Whitehaven was a prominent centre for tobacco imports in the seventeenth and eighteenth century, and accounted for around 10% of total British imports, much of which was re-exported to Ireland. J.E. Williams, 'Whitehaven in the Eighteenth Century', *Economic History Review*, 8.3 (1956), 396-7; and Percy Ford, 'Tobacco and Coal: A Note on the Economic History of Whitehaven', *Economica*, 26 (1929), 192-6.

[34] Thomas C. Parramore, 'The Saga of "The Bear" and the "Evil Genius"', *Bulletin of the History of Medicine*, 42 (1968), 321-32.

[35] Member of the assembly 1744-60, 1767-75; speaker 1754-55; member of the first four provincial congresses, 1774-76.

[36] *CSRNC*, volume 5, pp. 779-82.

North Carolina's planters could commonly generate investment returns of 15-20% per annum, a rate that allowed an efficient planter to double the value of his assets in around five to six years. The pace at which Montfort accumulated wealth suggests that he did so. The State Archives of North Carolina's land grant database hold thirty-four entries for Montfort across five counties from 1753-71, and indicate that he acquired more than 30,000 acres.

Montfort's land purchases and property developments were funded by his profits from trading and income from public offices, including that of clerk to the Edgecombe County Court, a position he secured in 1754 which gave him a share of the fees levied on judicial business. When the county was divided in 1759 with the creation of Halifax County from part of Edgecombe, Montfort's income increased with his appointment as clerk of Halifax County Court and the Halifax District Superior Court. Similarly significant were his positions as a Halifax Town commissioner and provincial treasurer for the Northern District of North Carolina, roles that offered considerable influence. As treasurer, he was obliged to post a bond of £10,000 sterling, a vast sum;[37] his co-guarantors were Alexander McCulloch and John Campbell.[38]

It was not unusual to underwrite such bonds jointly and three years later Montfort was a co-signatory with Cornelius Harnett Jr. and Richard Caswell for Caswell's bond for his commission to sign and stamp debenture bills.[39]

---

[37] The equivalent today would be somewhere between £2 million (labour value) and £15 million (purchasing power parity).

[38] *CSRNC*, volume 7, p. 671: Bond from Joseph Montfort for performance as Treasurer for the Northern District of North Carolina, 15 January 1768. Montfort's subsequent bond for £50,000 Sterling issued on 6 March 1773 was counter-signed by Alexander McCulloch, John Harvey, John Sampson, John Campbell, Benjamin McCulloch, Thomas Person and William Dry: *CSRNC*, volume 9, pp. 591-2.

[39] *CSRNC*, volume 9, pp. 74-5: Bond from Richard Caswell for performance as commissioner to sign and stamp debenture bills, 23 December 1771.

Montfort represented Halifax County in the general assembly in 1762 and again in 1764.[40] He subsequently represented Halifax Town in five assemblies from 1766-74, and in 1775 was nominated to the second provincial congress, albeit that his poor health prevented him from attending.

Alongside his plantations and land speculation, Montfort was one of a number of prominent Halifax merchants and traders who jointly led the construction and development of Halifax Town. Their efforts focused on building the physical infrastructure and on raising the town's commercial and social profile. And it is in the latter context that the petition for a warrant to establish a lodge at Halifax can best be understood.

Freemasonry was a mark of sophistication and the lodge a dedicated space for elite fraternal association. English freemasonry set the example. London was the pre-eminent global hub, the capital of Britain's expanding Empire, and the largest metropolis in Europe with a population that in the 1760s was three times that of North and South Carolina combined. It was the commercial, political and social heart of Empire, and since most colonists considered themselves British, not American, London was their constitutional and spiritual capital.

London offered a confluence of connections and an obvious destination for those seeking to exploit the multiple opportunities made possible by Empire. The city contained the best and worst that the eighteenth century could offer. Conspicuous wealth and grand architecture; fine art, music and theatre; and discussion of the latest literature and scientific discoveries, all jostled against poverty and depravity. And for the elites amidst the mêlée of coffee houses, inns and taverns, and London's many clubs and societies, one organisation reigned supreme - the Ancient and Honourable Society of Freemasons.

---

[40] *CSRNC*, volume 6, pp. 800-12, 13-19 April 1762, *et al.*

In the mid-1730s up to a quarter of London's gentry and upper middling, some 4,000 men, were freemasons.[41] And although many lodges failed or relocated, more than a hundred remained affiliated to the Grand Lodge of England with most meeting every two weeks.[42]

English freemasonry was synonymous with exclusivity. Led by a parade of celebrity and well-connected grand masters, freemasonry enjoyed often sycophantic press coverage at home and overseas, with a membership that included influential and wealthy politicians, merchants, senior public officials and military officers. Newspaper reports of 'distinguished gentlemen' becoming members appeared on a regular basis and joining a lodge became an *arriviste* statement. The Craft was seemingly endowed with a history deemed to date from time immemorial, provided commercial connectivity and, perhaps most importantly, validated social position.

It would have been surprising had freemasonry *not* developed across Britain's Empire. And it was fully understandable that America's east coast lodges were championed by those emulating London's fashions and tastes in precisely the same vein that South and North Carolina's Palladian homes were modelled on the latest architectural designs of William Kent[43] and James Gibb.[44]

THE LODGE AT HALIFAX

A masonic lodge – probably an Irish lodge – was meeting at the Marsh Store on or close to Alexander McCulloch's estate at Elk Marsh in the early

---

[41] Grand Lodge *Minutes I*. Comprehensive masonic membership records are limited to the 1720s and 1730s.

[42] *AQC*, 68 (1955), 129-31.

[43] William Kent (1685-1748), a protégé of Lord Burlington and one of Hanoverian England's most fashionable architects and furniture designers.

[44] James Gibbs (1682-1754), another popular and influential British architect.

1760s.[45] But Montfort and his colleagues wished to establish a new and more prestigious English lodge in Halifax Town and it was to this end that they sought and obtained a warrant from St John's Wilmington.

Members of the Royal White Hart Lodge at the first recorded meeting of the lodge 18 April 1765 [46]

Frederick Schultzer	Grand Master
Daniel Lovel	Deputy Master
William Martin	Secretary
Robert Goodloe	Senior Warden
John Matt Ince	Junior Warden
William Wilson	Senior Steward
John Geddy	Junior Steward
David Stokes	}
Joseph Long	}
Henry Dowse	}
Andrew Troughton	}
Joseph Montfort	}
Peter Thompson	} Brothers

Harnett's warrant cemented the legitimacy of the new lodge and at its first meeting the members agreed to send a delegation of John Deloach, James Ince and Joseph Long to speak with their Elk Marsh counterparts to 'settle and make division' of the lodge's monies and assets between those who wished to remain at Elk Marsh and those who preferred to meet in Halifax Town.

---

[45] J. Hugo Tatsch, *Freemasonry in the Thirteen Colonies* (New York, NY: Macoy, 1933), p. 99. Cf., also, Haywood, *The Beginnings of Freemasonry in North Carolina and Tennessee*, p. 5.

[46] Minute Book, Royal White Hart Lodge (1765-1818), 18 April 1765.

The Marsh Store lodge is not known to have been warranted by any of the home grand lodges. But since McCulloch was an Ulsterman, as were many others who had settled in the area, not least John Campbell, it would not have been unusual for the lodge to have worked Irish ritual.[47] Regardless, Harnett's warrant ensured that the new lodge at Halifax would be allied with the Grand Lodge of England.

There are no minutes to indicate the names of those who remained at Elk Marsh but the lodge ceased to exist after the war and in 1794 the former lodge treasurer was instructed to give up the remaining assets to the Royal White Hart.[48]

The early minutes suggest that the members of the Royal White Hart were adamant that the lodge would be socially prestigious. This was expressed in the furniture and assets they acquired, and in their rules and regulations.[49] The meetings were to have 'dignity and harmony', and the membership fee was set at 40 shillings Virginia currency with new members admitted only after 'sufficient recommendation'.[50]

Montfort's masonic advancement began almost immediately in June 1765 with his election as treasurer and at the following meeting as master. Montfort occupied both offices concurrently for a period thereafter, giving him effective control of the lodge.

---

[47] It may or may not be relevant but a David McCulloch is recorded as a founder member of lodge No. 313, Antrim, on 5 April 1759. Cf., *Grand Lodge of Freemasons of Ireland Membership Registers, 1733-1923*.

[48] *DNCB*, volume 4, pp. 289-90.

[49] *Minute Book of the Royal White Hart Lodge, No. 403 (No. 2), 1765-1818*, p. 3: for example, 'that the Dignity and Harmony of the lodge shall not be violated by any Indecent Behaviour [or] Profane words', and no member shall '[exit] the lodge while sitting without leave from the Master or speaking without Rising and addressing the Master... [and] no Person [shall] be admitted... without being sufficiently recommended'.

[50] Minute Book, Royal White Hart Lodge, 18 April 1765, p. 3.

The impetus to elevate and promote the Royal White Hart accelerated in 1767 following the initiation of James Milner (c.1735-1772), and the lodge thereafter purchased a new bible, prayer book, a copy of Anderson's *Constitutions*, and a large quantity of drinking vessels.

The minutes record that in December 1767 Andrew Miller, the senior warden, was instructed to 'get for the use of the lodge' a collection of bespoke glassware and porcelain.[51] This would comprise seventy-two wine glasses, twelve half-pint glasses, twenty-four pint glasses and three dozen punch glasses, all with expensive 'worm'd stalks', in addition to forty-two quart decanters and four one-gallon punch bowls, the latter produced by the Bow factory and glazed with the lodge name.[52]

Bow was one of England's most exclusive porcelain manufacturers and probably recommended by John Campbell. He had visited the London factory in the 1740s and supplied white china clay.[53]

The same minutes mention a public procession and a ball at the Halifax Town court house to celebrate St John's Day, a strong indication that the lodge had arrived on the town's social map.

A NEW ENGLISH CHARTER

Montfort had not been present at the December lodge meeting in Halifax. He was away from the province in England with Alexander McCulloch, almost certainly in connection with their tobacco and other transatlantic

---

[51] Ibid., 28 December 1767.

[52] Ibid., p. 19.

[53] Pat Daniels & Ross H. Ramsay, 'Bow porcelain: New primary source documents and evidence pertaining to the early years of the manufactory between 1730-1747, and John Campbell's letter to Arthur Dobbs', *Southern Institute of Technology Journal of Applied Research (SITJAR), NZ* (2009), esp. pp. 8, 10-3.

trading activities.[54] His time in London provided an opportunity to seek a more prestigious lodge warrant directly from the Grand Lodge of England under the hand of its grand master, the Duke of Beaufort.[55]

Montfort produced the charter to the Royal White Hart on 20 May 1768.[56] Lane's *Masonic Records* note that the warrant was dated 21 August 1767, with the lodge assigned No. 403 on the grand register.[57] The same date and number appear in the Royal White Hart minutes. The members' satisfaction with their new warrant – 'unanimously and gratefully received' - is almost tangible, and the secretary was instructed to send a letter of appreciation to London.

Montfort then formally closed the lodge before reopening it in 'ample form' by virtue of the new charter. He took the master's chair with Joseph Long as senior warden and Matthew Brown as junior warden. Montfort appointed John Thompson as treasurer; James Milner, secretary; William Martin and Peter Thompson, stewards; and Joseph Gray, tyler. He ended by instructing that a committee be constituted, comprising Thompson, Miller, Milner and himself, to produce a new set of by-laws.

Montfort visited London at least twice, in 1767 and 1771, and acquired furnishings to take back to North Carolina, including the masonic floor cloth purchased in 1771 and presented to the Royal White Hart in March the following year. He also sat for a formal masonic portrait.[58]

---

[54] Two of Whitehaven's leading tobacco merchant families, Lowther and Senhouse, were freemasons. Nevil Lowther was a member of the lodge at the Coash & Horses in Maddox Street, and Allen Senhouse the master of the Cheshire Cheese in Arundel Street.

[55] Henry Somerset, 5th Duke of Beaufort (1744-1803), grand master of the Grand Lodge of England, 1767-72.

[56] Minute Book, Royal White Hart Lodge, 20 May 1768, p. 20.

[57] Lane's *Masonic Records*.

[58] Minute Book, Royal White Hart Lodge, [14?] March 1772, p. 49.

A Floor Cloth purchased by Joseph Montfort in London, England, in 1771
Image from the Collection of the Grand Lodge of North Carolina

The painting was almost certainly executed by Nathaniel Dance,[59] a renowned society portraitist who had probably been selected on the recommendation of the Duke of Beaufort - Dance had recently painted his second son, Charles Somerset. Although commissioned, the portrait was not shipped to America. Dance would have taken time to complete the work and Montfort, suffering from declining health, did not return to London after 1771. The outbreak of war and Montfort's death in March 1776 prevented further contact. The portrait remained in Dance's London studio and two of the original attributes – a vibrant pink coat and distinctive masonic regalia - were subsequently over-painted, after which it was sold into the British market. Dance retired as an artist shortly afterwards to become a member of parliament.

The painting may hold a clue as to why North Carolina did not experience the bruising friction between Moderns and Antients freemasonry that was prevalent in South Carolina. Montfort's masonic collar jewel incorporates a 'Royal Arch' symbol and sunburst, perhaps suggesting that Montfort straddled both branches.[60] There is additional anecdotal evidence of an Irish connection in his issue of a warrant to the Royal Arch lodge at Cabin Point in Virginia and, of course, in his past membership of McCulloch's Elk Marsh lodge.

Deputed as Provincial Grand Master

Whether in person or by letter or both, Montfort persuaded the Grand Lodge of England, or at least the grand master, that he should be appointed provincial grand master for North Carolina. The timing was opportune.

---

[59] Sir Nathaniel Dance-Holland, 1st baronet (1735-1811), a founder member of the Royal Academy and notable English portrait painter who later became a politician. He was the third son of George Dance the Elder, the architect.

[60] There was no 'standard' or uniform design for a master's or grand master's masonic jewel in the eighteenth century.

Benjamin Smith had resigned in December 1767 and been replaced on an acting basis by his deputy, Egerton Leigh.[61] And when Leigh's appointment was made permanent in March 1770 he was given jurisdiction over South Carolina alone. Eleven months later, having paid a fee of ten guineas, Montfort obtained masonic authority over North Carolina.[62]

Montfort was away from Halifax and unable to attend any lodge meetings during 1771 and his new provincial grand warrant was presented to the Royal White Hart the following year on 13 March 1772. He wrote to the grand secretary in London later the same year to acknowledge receipt and inform him that several new lodges had been granted charters of incorporation for which Montfort would be forwarding contributions to the grand charity. He also advised that Douglas Hamilton, a member of Royal White Hart, would convey the remittances to London. Montfort concluded with a promise to send a report on the general state of freemasonry in North Carolina, with full details of the lodges formed.[63]

London's rationale for appointing Montfort appears straightforward. Unlike his predecessor, Benjamin Smith, Egerton Leigh lacked a network of business contacts and family relationships in North Carolina. And a dedicated provincial grand master for North Carolina could accelerate the development of regular freemasonry in the province and put a brake on the expanding influence of the Antients. Montfort, smitten with London Society and all that it offered, and a wealthy man, would have been regarded as 'one of us' and a safe pair of hands. He was also willing to pay the required fee.

Although the minutes of the Grand Lodge of England for 6 February 1771 record Montfort's appointment as provincial grand master for North Carolina, the deputation is worded differently, appointing him provincial grand master 'of and for America'. There is a long-standing debate

---

[61] *Loyalists & Malcontents*, p. 86.

[62] Minutes of the Grand Lodge of England, 6 February 1771.

[63] Joseph Montfort to James Heseltine, 20 December 1772: UGLE Library & Museum, GBR 1991 HC 28/G/7.

in North Carolina as to whether the wording signifies that Montfort was *de jure* the first and only 'Grand Master of America', the text carried by the North Carolina Historical Marker on U.S. 301 in Halifax.[64] This is not the case.

Although the wording is incontestable, Montfort did not have delegated masonic authority across all of Britain's thirteen colonies, not least because the minutes of the Grand Lodge of England refer to North Carolina alone and there were other provincial grand masters of longer standing.[65] Nonetheless, precedents exist where deputations to office reached into other provinces. One example is the 1768 warrant appointing John Rowe 'Provincial Grand Master of North America' and extending his jurisdiction to 'the territories … where no other provincial grand master is appointed'.

Montfort's appointment should be viewed similarly but in practice he exercised authority almost entirely in North Carolina and predominantly within its north-eastern quadrant. The only warrant granted outside the province was to the Royal Arch lodge at Cabin Point Virginia, where the lodges were otherwise Irish or Scottish. And Royal Arch was probably a one-off case.

Cabin Point's port focused on tobacco exports and would have been used by Montfort, Campbell, McCulloch and others in Halifax for that purpose.[66] The members of the Virginia lodge, local merchants and officials, would have been known to Montfort,[67] and a warrant from the provincial grand master 'of and for America' viewed as an honour, cementing

---

[64] North Carolina Highway Historical Marker E-8 at U.S. 301 Bypass at U.S. 301 Business north of Halifax, NC.

[65] Montfort's warrant is dated 14 January 1771, indicating that Grand Lodge was approving an event that had already occurred.

[66] Cf., Cabin Point, VA: Historical Marker K 222.

[67] Robert Polk Thomson, 'The Tobacco Export of the Upper James River Naval District, 1773-75', *William and Mary Quarterly*, 18.3 (1961), 393-407, Table on 407.

a commercially-valuable trading relationship.[68] Nonetheless, the name - 'Royal Arch' - suggests that the lodge was Irish, Scottish or Antients, and that Montfort had no objection to that ritual.

One of Montfort's first acts as provincial grand master was to issue a new charter for St John's Lodge New Bern, ranking the lodge second behind Halifax and raising a question over the seniority and standing of St John's Lodge Wilmington. The New Bern charter is dated 10 January 1772 but was not received until the following August. Parramore suggests that the delay was a result of 'the necessary materials' being unavailable and hints that it may have been back-dated to ensure New Bern's primacy over Richard Caswell's lodge at Kingston.[69] But Parramore passes by another aspect. There was no pressing reason for Montfort to issue a warrant to New Bern other than to establish his authority as provincial grand master. The lodge had been in operation since at least the mid-1750s and outranked Halifax in terms of longevity and thus seniority. Indeed, it could be argued that the purpose of the warrant was not so much to legitimise New Bern as to give Halifax primacy.

Kingston's warrant raises another issue: the lodge may have been Irish or Antients rather than Moderns. It was possibly for this reason that Richard Caswell agreed to a second initiation when he attended the Royal White Hart on 28 December 1772. The minutes of the meeting are quoted by Stearns in his paper on Caswell.[70] Other than as a joke, which is improbable, or the specious argument that Kingston had not been chartered by Montfort when Caswell was first initiated and was thus not 'properly constituted', there are

---

[68] Montfort carried his warrant with him. Cf., Minute Book, Royal White Hart Lodge, 13 March 1768, p. 48.

[69] Parramore, *Launching the Craft: The First Half-Century of Freemasonry in North Carolina*, p. 27.

[70] *NOCALORE*, 4.3 (1934), 204. The minutes of this meeting appear not to have been scanned and are not available online at http://library.digitalnc.org/cdm/compoundobject/collection/ncmemory/id/235888/rec/1.

few other explanations for Richard Cogdell's[71] request that Caswell, a visitor to the lodge, 'take the obligation again, having passed the different degrees of Masonry formerly, tho' not in a regular Constituted Lodge'.[72]

The gravitation of masonic prestige away from Wilmington and the Lower Cape Fear to Halifax and the north-east of the province was consolidated by Montfort's choice of provincial grand officers. His ally, James Milner, a relatively recent arrival in Halifax, was made deputy provincial grand master and subsequently took over as master of the Royal White Hart, and another Halifax man, William Brimage, later deputy attorney at New Bern, was endowed with the pivotal position of provincial grand secretary.[73]

Milner has been mentioned above. Like Montfort, he had migrated from Virginia where his family property in Sussex County was a day's ride from Montfort's father's estate. He arrived in Halifax in 1766, opening a law practice and joining the lodge almost immediately, perhaps to meet prospective clients. Regardless, his success at the Bar was such that within three years he had acquired *Green Hill*, a plantation, investment properties across the town, and held land elsewhere.

In 1770, Milner won a legal action against Herman Husband,[74] a central figure in the Regulator Movement, and was awarded title to Husband's 200-acre estate in Guildford County, around 150 miles away.[75] The debt for which Milner had sued Husband involved unpaid legal fees, probably his own, and the case encapsulates why the Regulators resented if not hated eastern-appointed lawyers

---

[71] Cogdell was a member and sometime master of St John's Lodge, New Bern.

[72] *NOCALORE*, 4.3 (1934), 204.

[73] *CSRNC*, volume 8, pp. 507-11, and volume 11, p. 539.

[74] Herman Husband (1724-1795), a planter, author and preacher, and a leader of the Regulator Movement.

[75] The *DNCB* suggests that from 1755-62, Husband acquired more than 10,000 acres in Orange and Rowan counties and land along Sandy Creek, in addition to property lots in Hillsborough.

and court officials.[76] A letter to a fellow advocate, John Williams, suggests that Milner was afterwards understandably fearful of practicing in the Piedmont.[77]

Milner encouraged and supported Montfort's drive to elevate freemasonry's status in Halifax. They were successful and the lodge attracted many of the town's more prominent political and commercial figures. These included Montfort's brother-in-law, John Campbell; James Auld, who would succeed Montfort as clerk of the Halifax Court; Charles Bruce, a planter and merchant; John Geddy, a fellow planter; Joseph Dickinson, a lawyer and a member of several other lodges; Andrew Miller and Alexander Telfair, both leading merchants; and John Thompson, a prosperous tavern owner whose sister was married to Telfair.[78]

Milner died in late 1772 following a fall from his horse. He may have been drunk since his fall followed a ball held to celebrate his election to the assembly. Montfort and Miller were executors to the estate, which was one of the more remarkable of the period. In addition to his plantation and investment properties, Milner had owned an extensive library of more than 620 books, and scientific equipment, including a microscope, telescope and other instruments.[79]

Following Milner's death a rumour circulated that he had been engaged in counterfeiting, although this was denied and nothing was proven.[80] It may be no more than a coincidence but Montfort had been the focus of a similar

---

[76] Cf., chapter nine. Also *CSRNC*, volume 8, pp. 184-5: Minutes of the Hillsborough District Superior Court, North Carolina, Superior Court (Hillsborough District), 25 March 1770.

[77] *CSRNC*, volume 9, pp. 346-7: James Milner to John Williams, 22 October 1772.

[78] Parramore gives a list of known early lodge members in *Launching the Craft*, pp. 215-7.

[79] Grimes, *Abstracts of North Carolina Wills* (1912), pp. 514-22.

[80] Cf., Kenneth Scott, 'Counterfeiting in Colonial Virginia', *Virginia Magazine of History and Biography*, 61.1 (1953), 3-33.

report. There was a serious problem with paper currency counterfeiting in North Carolina in the late 1760s,[81] and Montfort had come under suspicion. Access to the printing press and plates was restricted to just a handful of men: the two provincial treasurers, John Ashe for the south and Montfort for the north; and the public printer, James Davis[82] and his assistants. An investigation found no one to be culpable and no charges were brought. Instead new printing plates and a more robust strong box were ordered.[83]

Montfort invited Cornelius Harnett Jr. to succeed Milner as deputy grand master, a move designed perhaps to extend the basis of Montfort's masonic authority by including a respected and senior figure from Cape Fear within the provincial grand lodge hierarchy. But it also served another purpose: to demonstrate Montfort's masonic seniority to Harnett, despite him having granted the Royal White Hart's first charter.

There are many indicators that point to the civic standing of the Royal White Hart Lodge and the affluence of its members but the most powerful is their willingness to fund a purpose-built masonic temple in Halifax.[84] The largest donation was given by Montfort personally.

> Whereas we, the subscribers esteem it publicly beneficial to promote society and laudably to increase the means of obtaining benefit and happiness to those whom we are most nearly connected, and whereas it is proposed and agreed to improve a lot in the town of Halifax, to wit: No. 111, so that the accommodation thereon may serve for various purposes,

---

[81] Cf., for example, William S. Powell (ed), *The Correspondence of William Tryon* (Raleigh, NC: Department of cultural resources, 1981), pp. 17-8, 24-5, 488-97 *et al*. The Committee of the Assembly to Governor Tryon, 16 January 1768.

[82] James Davis (1721-1785).

[83] Cf., William Tryon to Messrs. Drummond & Co., 2 February 1768, ordering 'plates for stamping of Bills in Proclamation Value ... to the following Rates and Denominations ... and a proper strong Treasurers Chest with three good Locks'.

[84] Royal White Hart Lodge Minutes, April 1769.

particularly that of a Masonic Hall and Assembly room, we therefore obligate ourselves, our Heirs, Executors and Administrators respectively, to pay or cause to be paid on demand… the sums annexed to our respective names, for the purpose of improving the said lot…

Joseph Montfort	a lot and house, deed executed.
Andrew Miller [85]	£10
J.O. Long	£10
Frederic Schulzer	£10
John Thompson	£10
Alexander Telfair	£10
James Milner	£10
Charles Presten [86]	£10
William Martin	£10
F. Stewart	£10
David Stokes	£5
Peter Thompson	£5
Joseph Campbell	£5
James Auld	£3 [87]

Those named include several firm loyalists, most notably Andrew Miller, Alexander Telfair, and his brother-in-law, John Thompson, all of whom later fled the province.[88] Other loyalists appear in the minutes as officers of the lodge, members and visitors.

---

[85] Andrew Miller, a Halifax merchant. Miller was reported by the Committee of Observation of Halifax County in 1775 when he refused to sign an agreement not to engage in trade with Britain. Cf., *DNCB*: 'Committees of Observation'.

[86] Possibly 'Preston'.

[87] Cf., Gowen, *The Story of the Right Worshipful Joseph Montfort*, pp. 5-6.

[88] Cf., for example, Robert O. Desmond, *The Loyalists in North Carolina during the Revolution* (Durham, NC, Duke University Press, 1940).

There is unfortunately no primary source material concerning Montfort's provincial grand lodge other than as detailed above, and no records of it having met as such. Regardless, sources such as the *Freemason's Monitor* state that the provincial grand lodge 'convened occasionally at New Bern and Edenton, at which latter place the records were deposited previous to the revolutionary war'.[89] There is no basis for this statement and it is probably erroneous. As Parramore notes, Webb also comments that 'the [provincial grand lodge] records were destroyed by the British army', an account that ignores the fact that the British neither occupied nor attacked Edenton.[90]

REFLECTIONS

As the first provincial grand master for North Carolina, Montfort's place in masonic history is assured whether or not he was 'Provincial Grand Master of and for America' other than in name.

Montfort was a founder member of the Royal White Hart in Halifax and thereafter its master, and as provincial grand master issued warrants to and regularised at least seven lodges. But notwithstanding his masonic success, it would be wrong to ignore one of his most dominant characteristics – self-interest.

Among several examples, the *DNCB* notes that Montfort was exceptionally unhelpful when Governor Tryon[91] requested funds for his military campaign against the Regulators. As northern treasurer, Montfort was obliged to assist but claimed that no money was available.[92] The reality was that

---

[89] Thomas S. Webb, *Freemason's Monitor; or, Illustrations of Masonry* (New York: Southwick and Crooker, 1802), p. 286.

[90] *Launching the Craft*, pp. 30-1. It is feasible that Brimage removed the records when he fled North Carolina.

[91] Governor William Tryon (1729-1788), royal governor of North Carolina (1765-71) and of New York (1771-80).

[92] *DNCB*.

financial support from the northern treasury would have required promissory notes to be issued with repayment from higher taxes and reduced spending, both anathema to Montfort and his allies. Moreover Montfort was under a personal obligation as northern treasurer. He had lodged a £10,000 Sterling bond in 1768.[93] It was subsequently increased to £50,000.[94]

Montfort was equally unhelpful when he gained entree to the Granville Land Office as vice-auditor to the proprietary, refusing to give the administration access to the records until he was granted the deeds to a dozen vacant land grants and what Montfort claimed was a promised annual salary of £200.[95] To remove the impasse, Governor Martin[96] negotiated a compromise in June 1774, allowing Montfort ten grants over some 7,000 acres and re-confirming him in office.[97] Martin was nonetheless privately appalled at Montfort's actions, labelling him untrustworthy and having 'a certain slyness [and] a character [that] nobody pretends to understand'.[98]

Montfort's declining heath from 1773 and his death in 1776 drew a line between colonial and post-colonial freemasonry in North Carolina. Without a provincial grand master and on the cusp of war with Britain, North Carolina's provincial grand lodge ceased to operate and freemasonry fell into abeyance. Activity resumed only slowly after the war and a state-wide governance structure under a grand lodge was not organized until 1787, the same year that the U.S. Constitution was adopted.

Montfort's Royal White Hart Lodge appears to have ceased to meet shortly before the war and did not resume until 1783. Dissent between

---

[93] *CSRNC*, volume 7, p. 671.

[94] 6 March 1773.

[95] Joseph Montfort to Josiah Martin, 31 March 1774: Granville Proprietary Records.

[96] Governor Josiah Martin (1737-1786), the last royal governor of North Carolina (1771-75).

[97] Thornton W. Mitchell, *The Granville District and Its Land Records* (Raleigh, NC: NC Office of Archives & History, 1993), volume 70, pp. 103-29.

[98] *DNCB*.

loyalists and patriots within the lodge may have been a principal reason, something especially poignant given that Montfort's relationship with the Grand Lodge of England had been integral to his masonic stature in the province. The lack of lodge activity explains why his son, Henry, was initiated at Unanimity Lodge in Edenton in January 1776, rather than at Halifax.

Montfort is regarded as a patriot. Ill health prevented his attending the general meeting at New Bern in 1774[99] but not that at Halifax Town where he was one of many who voted for a resolution condemning British behaviour: 'Americans can be taxed only by those persons who legally represent them; that the distance between Great Britain and America is so considerable that it would be impracticable for our representatives to sit in parliament, therefore the power assumed by the British parliament over the Colonies, is an invasion of those rights which as free people we have enjoyed [since] time immemorial.'[100]

In December 1775 the provincial council appointed Montfort one of several commissioners for Port Roanoke tasked with purchasing arms, procuring a vessel, and recommending officers 'to protect the Trade and Commerce of this Province'.[101] It is unlikely that he was sufficiently well to have taken an active role. Montfort died on 25 March 1776. His will has not survived but his weapons and stockpile of black powder were passed to his son to support the war effort.[102]

---

[99] *CSRNC*, volume 9, p. 1041: Resolutions by inhabitants of Halifax (town) concerning resistance to parliamentary taxation and the Provincial Congress of North Carolina, 22 August 1774.

[100] Ibid.

[101] *CSRNC*, volume 10, p. 353: Minutes of the North Carolina Provincial Council, 21 December 1775.

[102] *CSRNC*, volume 10, pp. 633 and 691: Minutes of the North Carolina Council of Safety, 19 June and 1 August 1776.

CHAPTER SEVEN

THE MONTFORT LODGES

Excluding Royal Arch Lodge in Virginia, the charters issued by Montfort in the years between his appointment as provincial grand master and his death in 1776 were to lodges in North Carolina's north-east. Several had been in existence for some years and Montfort's purpose was not to create new lodges *per se* but to establish a formal masonic structure in North Carolina as in South Carolina, and to cement his position at its head.

The Montfort Lodges [1]

Name	Number(s)	Location	Year Chartered
St John's Lodge	No. 2 (now 3)	New Bern	1772
St John's Lodge	No. 3 (now 4)	Kingston	1772
Royal Edwin Lodge	No. 4 (now 5)	Windsor	1773
Dornoch Lodge	No. 5 (extinct)	Bute County	1773/4
Royal William Lodge	No. 6 (extinct)	Winton	1774
Royal Arch Lodge	No. 7 [2]	Cabin Point VA	1775
Unanimity Lodge	No. 9 (now 7)	Edenton	1775

---

[1] The biographical data in this section is drawn principally from *DNCB*, *CSRNC* and other sources as specified. The dates given are those on which an individual is recorded in the relevant source material (newspaper, pamphlet, lodge and GLNC records). Unless the context suggests otherwise, they are not dates of initiation.

[2] The history of freemasonry set out in Virginia's *Ahiman Rezon* contends that the lodge was constituted by the Grand Lodge of Scotland on 5 April 1775 under the name 'Cabin Point Royal Arch'. Cf., John Dove, *The Virginia text-book: containing a history of Masonic grand lodges, and the constitution of masonry, or Ahiman Rezon: together with a digest of the laws, rules and regulations of the Grand Lodge of Virginia* (Richmond, VA: 1866), 3rd edn, p. 315. It is feasible however that the lodge held two warrants or held successive warrants.

The failure to issue warrants to lodges in the Piedmont and elsewhere in North Carolina is not easily explained. One possibility is that Montfort simply did not have time, especially since he would have travelled less in 1775-76 given his poor health. A second is that most lodges beyond the Fall Line were Irish, Scottish or Antients, independent of the Grand Lodge of England and with pro-Regulator members, both of which militated against submission to an eastern masonic hierarchy.[3] Such lodges are discussed in chapter ten.

ST JOHN'S LODGE, NEW BERN

A masonic lodge had existed at New Bern since the mid-1750s, almost two decades prior to the receipt of a charter from Montfort. The names of the master, Andrew Scott, and wardens, John Clitherall and Joseph Carruthers, are set out in a contemporary pamphlet printed by James Davis, North Carolina's first public printer: *Sermon, Preached in Christ-Church, in Newbern, in North-Carolina, December the 27th, 1755, Era of Masonry, 5755, Before The Ancient and Honourable Society of Free and Accepted Masons.*[4]

All three were leading figures in the town. Andrew Scott, the master, was a recent migrant from Prince George's County in Maryland to which his brother, George, had migrated in the early 1730s to become a merchant and planter.[5] Scott joined him in Maryland in 1736[6] and opened a medical

---

[3] There were exceptions. See 'The Regulator Movement' below regarding Herman Husband's comment with respect to freemasonry and Colonel Edmund Fanning.

[4] James Davis (1721-1785), was appointed North Carolina's first public printer in 1749; he printed *The North Carolina Gazette* from 1751-c.1760.

[5] Different sources suggest that the family came from either Scotland or Ulster, the latter being more probable.

[6] George F. Frick, James L. Reveal, C. Rose Broom, and Melvin L. Brown, 'The Practice of Dr Andrew Scott of Maryland and North Carolina', *Maryland Historical Magazine*, 82 (1987), 123-41.

practice the following year.[7] It was sufficiently successful to allow Scott to acquire a 200-acre tobacco plantation, *The Hermitage*, in December 1737, and 144 acres at *Bacon Hall* in April 1739. However his hopes of social preferment and a position as county sheriff came to nothing.[8]

Scott married the following year and from this point his life in Maryland descended into chaos. His wife, Mary Abington, was a wealthy widow with four children, three of whom were minors. Scott became their guardian and took control of both his wife and his wards' properties. Two years later he was charged with maladministration and misappropriation: 'Destroying Orphans Land and Timber in his Possession'.[9] Although he escaped conviction, Scott was embroiled in lawsuits over the next several years and sued repeatedly by his wife, his wards, and their elder sister and her husband; he was also charged with mistreating two servants for which he was found guilty and fined.

In mid-1744, the court ruled that Scott should provide detailed accounts for the Abington estate. He failed to do so. Two years later, his wards petitioned successfully to choose a new guardian and Scott was ordered to deliver their estate accordingly. He did not and in June 1747 was ruled in contempt. Scott finally settled his obligations in 1751 and left for North Carolina shortly afterwards.[10]

New Bern in the 1750s was a small town with a population of no more than 500, probably less. Scott would have been one of a modest number of trained medical doctors in what he described some years later as the 'remote wilderness' of Rowan County.[11] Nonetheless, it was a profession that could

---

[7] Ibid., 126.

[8] Ibid. Scott sent several botanical specimens to Hans Sloane and afterwards asked for his assistance in obtaining the post of sheriff and that he intercede with Lord Baltimore, whose family owned Maryland.

[9] 'The Practice of Dr Andrew Scott of Maryland and North Carolina', 128.

[10] Ibid., 128-31. Cf., also, Leland Ormond Scott, Jr., *The First Scotts* (Winston Salem, NC: Wayne County Historical Association and the Old Dobbs Genealogical Society, 1982).

[11] Rowan County, North Carolina Tax Lists, 1757-1800.

command high fees from those able to pay, albeit that this was probably not his main source of income.[12]

As in Maryland, Scott was also active as a land speculator, buying and selling property lots in New Bern and acquiring land grants further inland. They included more than 320 acres on Deep River in Cumberland County and over 240 acres in Rowan County along the Reedy Branch of Crane Creek.[13] It is around this time that Scott's name appears on a petition to Earl Granville seeking an exemption from quit-rents and church taxes, and requesting arms and ammunition in order to defend the settlement.[14]

By the mid-1750s, Scott had become one of New Bern's leading figures having gained the social status that had eluded him in Maryland, and in May 1758 Governor Dobbs appointed him justice of the peace for Craven County, an office he held until 1763.

Scott's position as master of the lodge linked him to other prominent local men, including Joseph Carruthers,[15] his junior warden. Carruthers had benefited from Dobbs's patronage, who appointed him sheriff, and from his friendship with Scott, who was one of two justices instrumental in Carruthers' appointment as inspector of commodities for New Bern's port. In return, Carruthers named Scott and Joseph Leech, the second justice, as his deputies, with Scott also named as one of three examiners of Carruthers' financial accounts as sheriff.

Scott was similarly friendly with Richard Spaight (1730-1763), Dobbs's nephew, to whom Dobbs had given several sinecures and provincial offices, including that of secretary.[16] And with his senior warden, John Clitherall, a successful merchant. Clitherall's wealth can be gauged by his ability to pay for

---

[12] Cf., Lawrence Lee, *The Lower Cape Fear in Colonial Days*, pp. 199-200.
[13] State Archives of North Carolina, North Carolina Land Grants database.
[14] Rowan County, North Carolina Tax Lists, 1757-1800.
[15] Joseph Carruthers (*b*.1724).
[16] His son, Richard Dobbs Spaight (1758-1802, also a member of the lodge, would become the eighth governor and *inter alia* a UNC trustee.

his son, James,[17] to study medicine in Scotland at the University of Edinburgh, and to fund his subsequent medical apprenticeship in England. Following his return, James left New Bern to establish a medical practice in Charleston.

Scott died in 1766. As his two largest creditors, Richard Cogdell, a fellow lodge member, and Philip Ambrose were appointed administrators to his estate, which was realised within the year.

The lodge is mentioned next in December 1764 when the *North Carolina Magazine or Universal Intelligencer*,[18] another Davis venture, published a report of the St John's Day feast at which the attendance of the newly appointed lieutenant governor, William Tryon, was given prominence.[19]

Eight years later, the lodge petitioned Joseph Montfort for a warrant.[20] The charter was issued in 1772 and counter-signed by James Milner and William Brimage. It gave the lodge the legitimacy of a formal constitution and reconfirmed the then incumbents in office: Martin Howard, the chief justice of North Carolina, as master; Joseph Leech and Richard Cogdell, as wardens; and Thomas Haslen and William Brimage, as treasurer and secretary, respectively. Brimage, a member of the Royal White Hart Lodge and provincial grand secretary provides an obvious connection to Montfort, as

---

[17] James Clitherall (c.1744-c.1801).

[18] *The North-Carolina Magazine or Universal Intelligencer* was the first magazine periodical to be printed in North Carolina. Published by James Davis, the first issue was dated 1-8 June 1764; it continued in print until 1768 at an initial cover price of 4*d* and was funded principally by advertisements.

[19] 'On Thursday, being the feast of St John the Baptist, the members of the Ancient and Honorable Society of Free and Accepted Masons, belonging to the lodge in this town, met in their lodge room; and after going through the necessary business of the day, retired to the Long Room in the courthouse to dine where was served up an elegant dinner; the Lieutenant Governor honored them with his company; where also dined many other gentlemen. The usual and proper healths were drank; and at drinking 'the King and the Craft' the artillery fired 3.3.3.'

[20] Among the signatories were Martin Howard, Joseph Leech, Richard Cogdell, Richard Ellis, William Brimage, Thomas Haslen and Bartholomew Rooke.

does Martin Howard, who would have known Montfort and Milner through their shared legal connections.

Members of St John's Lodge, New Bern (1770-1774) [21]

Simon Alderson	Moses Almond
J. Anderson	A.M. Ausborn
David Barron	John Benners
William Brimage	William Brown
William Bryan	John Burnside
William Cannon	Richard Caswell
Richard Cogdell	Joseph Dowse
Richard Ellis	Duncan Fergus Finley
Richard Graham	Peleg Green
Thomas Haslen	Josiah Holt
Martin Howard	Joseph Leech
Alexander McAuslan	James McConnell
- McDowell	James McInce
John McKay	Andrew Mack
Jacob Milligan	John Parker
James Parrott	John Patton[22]
John Richardson	Bartholomew Rooke
Henry Vipon	Edward Winslow
Thomas Woods	

The resolutions passed by the lodge on 9 January 1772 underline that membership was restricted to the more affluent in the town:

---

[21] As from Minute Book No. 1, St John's Lodge No. 3 at http://library.digitalnc.org/cdm/compoundobject/collection/ncmemory/id/248112/rec/2, accessed 14 April 2017.

[22] Also written as 'Patten'.

Agreed at this Meeting

First, That a Lodge be held Monthly (viz.) the first Thursday in every month.

Second, That a Quarterly Meeting be held the first Thursday in March, June, September and December at each of which the Members are to pay five Shillings into the Treasury.

Third, That every Candidate admitted to the Degree of an entered Apprentice, shall pay into the Treasury, Five Pounds, To the Tyler of the Lodge Eight Shillings, and shall also pay the Expences of the Night.

Fourth, That every entered Apprentice raised to the Degree of FellowCraft, shall pay Twenty Shillings; to the Tyler five Shillings; together with the Expences of the Night.

Fifth, That every Fellow Craft raised to the Degree of Masters shall pay into the Treasury Twenty Shillings, together with the expense of the Evening.

Sixth, That the Elections of Members be by Ballot…

Resolved, that any person who shall have been Entered, Passed, or raised in any other Lodge, on application to become a Member of this, shall be Balloted for, and if approved of, shall be admitted on payment of Thirty Shillings into the Treasury.[23]

The members of the lodge were a mix of planters, merchants and officials linked by family and business connections. Many were active in the assembly or held local public office, with Martin Howard one of the most prominent.[24]

Originally from Rhode Island, Howard had studied law at Newport under James Honyman, Jr., later the attorney general. In 1754 he had been chosen as a delegate to the Albany Congress[25] and two years later was

---

[23] Minute Book No. 1, St John's Lodge No. 3, New Bern, pp. 7-8.

[24] Martin Howard (c.1725-1781).

[25] The conference was held to debate Benjamin Franklin's plan of union, how to improve relations with the Mohawk and Iroquois, and military cooperation against the French.

elected to Rhode Island's assembly. Staunchly conservative, Howard supported Britain's right to tax the colonies, not least to fund the cost of British military and naval protection.

But as political attitudes changed in the mid-1760s, Howard's position attracted criticism and he was vilified and physically attacked by the Sons of Liberty when he agreed to act as a stamp distributor.[26] Howard was forced to flee to England with his family and his appointment as North Carolina's chief justice less than a year later was recompense for his financial losses in Rhode Island and a reward for political loyalty.

Howard's patent as chief justice was issued in July 1766 and he took office the following year with an annual salary and fees that would have exceeded £1,000 annually.[27] His time in office was dominated by cases prosecuting members of the Regulator Movement and he adjudicated numerous trials between 1768 and 1771, the last of which followed the Battle of Alamance at which six of the Regulators' leaders were executed. Howard was by then a member of the royal council, having been nominated in 1770, and stalwart in his support of Tryon and Martin, the last two royal governors.

Perhaps because of his Rhode Island upbringing, Howard was one of relatively few public officials in the South who were willing to condemn slavery as an institution. In a 1771 statement to a grand jury that had declined to convict a white man for murdering a slave, Howard avowed that slavery is not a natural state and that 'the souls and bodies of negroes are of the same quality with ours - they are our own fellow creatures, though in humbler circumstances, and are capable of the same happiness and misery

---

[26] Joseph Redington (ed), *Calendar of Home Office Papers (George III): 1760-5* (London: HMSO, 1878), pp. 604-16.

[27] *DNCB*: 'I shall have no argument with the Sons of Liberty of Newport; it was they who made me Chief Justice of North Carolina, with a thousand pounds sterling a year.' Cf., also, Redington (ed), *Calendar of Home Office Papers (George III): 1766-9* (London: HMSO, 1879), pp. 56-64.

with us'. His statement was publicised widely and published in the *Cape Fear Mercury* and Rhode Island's *Newport Mercury*.

When fighting with Britain broke out in 1775, Howard chose to remain in North Carolina but withdrew to his plantation on the Neuse River. Two years later when pressed to swear a patriotic oath to the new state of North Carolina he refused and was forced to leave. He fled to the loyalist stronghold of New York and then to England, where he received a pension of £250 per year in recognition of his loyalty. He died in 1781.[28]

William Brimage was equally devoted to Britain.[29] A successful attorney, he had settled in New Bern in 1769 and been appointed judge of the Court of Vice Admiralty at Edenton in 1770 and the following year deputy attorney for New Bern and a judge of the Court of Oyer and Terminer. Montfort knew Brimage through the Royal White Hart and via common social and legal connections. He appointed him provincial grand secretary the same year.

Brimage was extremely competent and, unusually for a North Carolinian attorney, a member of the English Bar Association.[30] The income from his law practice and court fees allowed him to acquire in excess of 10,000 acres, including 5,000 acres in Craven County, and more than 30 slaves.[31] He also remarried and relocated to his new wife, Elizabeth West's estate of Westbrooke (later Brimage's Neck) on the Cashie River in Bertie County.

Brimage made no secret of his loyalist politics and was shunned by many former clients and colleagues when war broke out. He was also arrested and jailed at Edenton in late 1777,[32] but released after only two months

---

[28] The *DNCB* records that his widow and daughter settled in Massachusetts after the war.

[29] William Brimage (d.1793).

[30] De Roulhac Hamilton, 'Southern Members of the Inns of Court', *North Carolina Historical Review*, 10.4 (1933), 279, 281 et al.

[31] State Archives of North Carolina, North Carolina Land Grants database.

[32] *CSRNC*, volume 11, pp. 537-8: Richard Caswell to Robert Smith, 27 July 1777; also, pp. 602-4: Richard Caswell to Cornelius Harnett, 2 September 1777.

when the court ruled the charges against him unproven for lack of evidence. Understandably concerned for his safety and that of his family, Brimage sailed for Bermuda where he was subsequently appointed attorney general. He returned to England in the early 1780s. Haywood gives his date of death as 1783. Other sources as 1793.[33] His wife subsequently returned to North Carolina with their children.

John Burnside, another loyalist, was also a member of the Royal White Hart. A wealthy merchant, he was awarded the position of deputy secretary for the Granville Land Office in February 1775.[34] The role involved collating and overseeing land grants, and in the absence of hostilities with Britain would have been lucrative. But when Burnside arrived in Halifax to secure the proprietary records he encountered opposition from Halifax's committee of safety which made clear their intention to destroy the land registers to frustrate quit-rent collection. Burnside attempted to move the archives to a safe location, hiring transport from James Hepburn,[35] another loyalist, but his efforts failed and - facing arrest - he fled to Virginia. The committee of safety took possession of the Granville land registers and seized Burnside's assets and properties; they were subsequently auctioned.[36]

Other loyalists within the lodge include Thomas Haslen, a doctor and magistrate who left the colony in 1777; and John McKay, if the same officer who fought with the Queen's Rangers.[37]

---

[33] Wills Proved at Prerogative Court of Canterbury, 21 March 1793: William Brimage, Gentleman, of Gray's Inn, Middlesex.

[34] Governor Josiah Martin (1737-1786), last royal governor of North Carolina (1771-75).

[35] James Hepburn (c.1752-1798), a Scottish-born merchant and planter. He was a partner with Joseph Montfort and Robert Nelson in *Hepburn, Nelson and Co*. The venture was dissolved in 1774. He fled to Florida in 1782, where he was appointed attorney general and member of the council, and to the Bahamas in 1784.

[36] North Carolina (Burnside Claim), Series 1, American Loyalist Claims, Exchequer and Audit Department, AO 13/177.

[37] *North Carolina Gazette*, 2 September 1774.

The majority of members of St John's Lodge were nonetheless patriots, most obviously Richard Caswell who in 1777 gave instructions for Brimage to be arrested.[38] Among the remainder, the better known include Joseph Leech,[39] the mayor, a businessman and planter with more than 20,000 acres,[40] who owned properties in New Bern and a tannery, among other interests.

Leech had settled in New Bern in the 1750s and became a leading figure in the town, appointed a justice of the peace, commissioned colonel of the militia, and riding out with Tryon against the Regulators at Alamance. Previously a loyalist assemblyman, Leech's political stance shifted in the 1770s. He served as a delegate to the first, second and third provincial congresses; was a member of the state council for four terms from 1776-79 (and its president in 1778 and 1779), and served again from 1784-86. He also represented Craven County at the Hillsborough and Fayetteville conventions.

Leech supported the creation of the Grand Lodge of North Carolina and put his name forward, unsuccessfully, for the position of grand treasurer. He was also in favour of the establishment of the University of North Carolina and was subsequently a major donor.

Richard Cogdell,[41] another merchant and planter, had been born in Beaufort and moved to New Bern in 1756 in order to expand his trading activities. He became active in local politics as an alderman and represented Carteret County in the assembly until 1767, when he resigned his seat on

---

[38] Members of the lodge who served in the revolutionary cause include Simon Alderson, Nathaniel Alexander, Simon Bright, William Bryan, Richard Caswell, Richard Cogdell, John Craddock, John Davies, William R. Davie, Richard Ellis, Isaac Guion, Solomon Halling, Joseph Leech, William McClure, Cosimo de Medici, Benjamin Williams and John Williams.
[39] Joseph Leech (1720-1803).
[40] State Archives of North Carolina, North Carolina Land Grants database.
[41] Richard Cogdell (1724-1787).

being appointed inspector of commodities for New Bern, a positon he held until 1775 notwithstanding two charges laid against him in 1772 for neglect of office and misfeasance as a justice of the peace. The allegations were tested in court and rejected, albeit on split decisions. He also served as sole judge of the Vice Admiralty Court.

Cogdell was commissioned a lieutenant-colonel in the militia under Leech and subsequently promoted colonel. A firm loyalist until the mid-1770s, he represented Craven County at the first three provincial congresses and chaired the committee of safety at New Bern in 1775 and 1776. Cogdell was appointed to the state council of safety (1777), and held office as New Bern's postmaster and treasurer from 1779-83.

Like many other North Carolina lodges, St John's met initially in its members' homes and in taverns, two of which were owned by lodge members, James Ince and Andrew Mack, respectively. However, in 1794 when the seat of government relocated to Raleigh, the lodge moved its meeting place to Tryon Palace. The location supports the argument that freemasonry had become an integral part of the establishment and a place of association for the local elites. The inference is also bolstered by the value of the lodge's assets, the extent of its charitable contributions, and the high cost of membership and dining.

In subsequent years St John's membership register would include three governors, four chief justices of the North Carolina Supreme Court, six members of Congress, and numerous state legislators and civic leaders.[42] St John's continued to meet at Tryon Palace until the building was destroyed by fire in 1798, when the lodge members agreed to fund a purpose-built masonic temple.[43]

---

[42] Cf., 'Years of light; history of St John's Lodge, no. 3, AF&AM': https://digital.lib.ecu.edu/16929, accessed 12 January 2017.

[43] The lodge voted to purchase lots on Hancock and Johnson Streets on 7 November 1798. The cornerstone was laid on 15 April 1801 and construction was concluded by 1804.

St John's Lodge, Kingston

Kingston or 'King's town' was sited at the centre of a prosperous farming district on the Neuse River around thirty-five miles upstream from New Bern. The town was chartered by the North Carolina legislature in 1762 to mark the accession of George III and intended as the new provincial capital.[44] The bill to establish the town was introduced by Richard Caswell and sanctioned construction at Atkins Bank[45] on land owned by his father-in-law, William Herritage.[46] Two years later Kingston became the administrative seat of Dobbs County and in 1791 of Lenoir County. The town was renamed 'Kinston' in 1784 to disassociate it from its colonial past.

Pridgen's *History of St John's Lodge* argues that it was established in 1760.[47] Citing a previously lost note book supposedly 'used by the Secretary of the Grand Lodge of England down to 1768', Pridgen quotes a reference that 'Benjamin Smith, Esq., Speaker of the house of Assembly [in South Carolina] was appointed Provincial Grand Master of North Carolina, October 14th, 1761, by the Earl of Aberdeen, Grand Master of England', and that in 1760 'Kingston Lodge [was] reported by the Provincial Grand Master of North America to the Grand Secretary of England'.[48]

There are a number of issues with Pridgen's statement. First, the position of provincial grand master of South Carolina was in flux from 1759 through to 1761. Peter Leigh, the incumbent, had died from fever in early

---

[44] *CSRNC*, volume 6, p. 936: Minutes of the Lower House of the North Carolina General Assembly, 2 December 1762.

[45] Robert Atkins of Craven County received a grant of 640 acres from the Lords Proprietors in 1729. He sold it to William Herritage in 1744.

[46] Also written as 'Heritage'. See appendix six.

[47] C.L. Pridgen, *History of St John's Lodge, No. 4, AF&AM, North Carolina, 1760-1923* (Kinton, NC: 1923).

[48] Ibid., p. 4.

1759 and his deputy, James Michie, assumed the chair on an acting basis. Michie might have succeeded permanently but died in 1760, leaving the way open for Benjamin Smith, the senior grand warden and past provincial grand master, to be installed formally in December 1761 as Leigh's successor.[49] But although Smith held a warrant as provincial grand master for both Carolinas he did not hold the title 'Provincial Grand Master of North America'. The only freemason at that time who did was Jeremy Gridley (1702-1767). He was warranted as such in 1755 and continued in office until his death.[50] Nonetheless, Gridley was appointed in respect of New England 'and such other territories where there was no provincial grand master'.[51] He was not responsible for overseeing freemasonry in North Carolina.

Second, Kingston was not chartered as a town until 1762, two years later than the lodge was supposedly established according to Pridgen. And third, the Grand Master of England in 1759 and 1760 was not the Earl of Aberdeen but Sholto Charles Douglas, Lord Aberdour,[52] who held the office until 1761 when he was succeeded by Washington Shirley, the 5th Earl Ferrers.[53] This is a detail that would have been recorded accurately by any grand secretary.

But notwithstanding these inconsistences, the charter issued by Montfort in 1772 was almost certainly to a pre-existing lodge. It was common practice throughout the eighteenth century for lodges to apply for a grand lodge or provincial grand lodge charter post-formation, and not only

---

[49] Cf., *Loyalists & Malcontents*, chapters one – three.

[50] Jeremy Gridley (1702-1767), a lawyer, politician, and attorney general for Massachusetts.

[51] See appendix one.

[52] Charles Douglas, Lord Aberdour, later 15th Earl of Morton (1732-1774).

[53] Washington Shirley, 5th Earl Ferrers, FRS (1722-1778). He inherited the title after the death of his brother, the 4th Earl, the last peer to be tried for murder and hanged in Britain

in the American colonies. It is reasonable to believe that the lodge was established after the construction of the town and that Montfort's warrant was a Moderns' charter for what was possibly a pre-existing Antients lodge.[54]

The early membership records indicate that in common with other North Carolina lodges, St John's Kingston comprised the local elites. They also demonstrate that the lodge centred on the most prominent among these, Richard Caswell.[55]

Born in 1729 in the port town of Joppa in Maryland, Caswell migrated to North Carolina in 1745 with his brother, William. Armed with a letter of recommendation from Thomas Bladen, Maryland's governor, addressed to Gabriel Johnston, Caswell obtained an apprenticeship with the surveyor-general, James Mackilwean,[56] with whom he lodged and whose daughter, Mary, he later married. Two years later Mackilwean ensured that Caswell was appointed deputy surveyor-general for the province. He acquired his first land grant the following year and would eventually obtain more than 11,000 acres across Dobbs, Johnston and Orange counties.[57]

Mackilwean smoothed the way for the Caswell family to obtain other public offices. Caswell's brother became deputy clerk of the Johnston County Court and when he resigned the post to manage the family's plantation, the position went to his father. Caswell took on the role himself from 1749-53, stepping down when he was appointed sheriff of Johnston County.

Mary Caswell died in 1757 and Caswell remarried the following year. Sarah, his second wife, brought additional political and commercial connections. Her father, William Herritage, was a New Bern lawyer who held the

---

[54] As discussed above. *NOCALORE*, 4.3 (1934), 204.

[55] Richard Caswell (1729-1789), planter, soldier and politician, elected governor of the state by the provincial congress in December 1776 and re-elected to annual terms by the general assemblies of 1777, 1778 and 1779.

[56] James Mackilwean (c.1694-c.1767). Born in Ayrshire, Scotland, Mackilwean was taken to North Carolina as a child. He settled in New Bern in around 1738.

[57] State Archives of North Carolina, North Carolina Land Grants database.

pivotal position of clerk to the general assembly. He would be so for over thirty years. Herritage invested his profits in land and slaves, and became extremely wealthy.[58] He encouraged Caswell to study law and used his influence to ensure that Caswell was admitted to the North Carolina Bar in 1759 and a year later appointed to the position of deputy attorney general.

Caswell was also active as a member of the colonial assembly, elected in 1754 and chosen as speaker in 1770 and 1771. He played an important part in drafting legislation, not least concerning education, advancing a proposal to establish a free school in every county and ensuring that a similar undertaking was inserted into the state constitution.

Caswell's politics bridged eastern and westerns interests, at least to a degree. He was speaker when the assembly expelled Herman Husband, then representing Orange County, but when Governor Tryon had Husband arrested and charged with libel and sedition, Caswell was foreman of the grand jury that refused to indict him. Nonetheless, as colonel of the Dobbs militia, Caswell helped organise the defence of New Bern against the Regulators when they threatened to march on the town to free Husband. And he had command of the right wing of Tryon's militia forces at Alamance in May 1771, following which display of loyalty Governor Martin appointed Caswell one of three judges of the Court of Oyer and Terminer.

For the next several years Caswell continued to be considered a firm loyalist but by the mid-1770s his political outlook began to turn. Caswell was one of nine assemblymen who constituted a committee of correspondence and inquiry to coordinate action with other colonies against Britain's five 'Intolerable Acts'.[59] And he took a prominent part in each of North Carolina's

---

[58] William Herritage (1700-1769). Cf., *Will of William Herritage, 8 March 1769*: Grimes, *North Carolina Wills and Inventories*, esp. pp. 142, 239-46. The will provides a revealing portrait of North Carolina's elites. A copy is at appendix six.

[59] The five acts were the Boston Port Act, which closed the port of Boston until the East India Company had received recompense for the 'tea party'; the

five provincial congresses and was selected as a delegate to the first and second continental congresses.

Governor Martin reported Caswell's unwelcome political transformation in a letter to London: 'He has promoted the present Convention with all his might and remains here to superintend its movements and no doubt to inflame it with the extravagant spirit of that daring Assembly at Philadelphia. At New Bern I am credibly informed, he had the insolence to reprehend the Committee of that little Town for suffering me to remove from thence, this man My Lord who at his going to the first Congress and after his return from it, appeared to me to have embarked in the cause with a reluctance that much extenuated his guilt, in my estimation, shows himself now the most active tool of sedition.'[60]

Caswell had crossed a political Rubicon. He led efforts to imprison the governor and royal council, a plan thwarted by Martin seeking safety on board the warship *Cruzier*,[61] and took a lead role in the militia, where he was appointed colonel of the Minutemen. In 1780, he was promoted major general with overall command of North Carolina's patriotic forces.

Caswell was elected governor in 1776, and re-elected in each of the following three years, and served for a second term from 1785-87. He came second to Samuel Johnston in the December 1787 election to become

---

Massachusetts Government Act, which modified the colony's Charter of 1691 and removed many of the rights of self-government; the Administration of Justice Act, which provided that British office holders accused of crimes in a colony could be tried in England; the Quartering Act, which allowed the billeting of British soldiers at colonial expense; and the Quebec Act, extending Quebec's boundaries. Since Quebec did not have representative assemblies, the transfer of land was considered an attempt to reduce colonial representation and cement British authority.

[60] *CSRNC*, volume 10, pp. 230-7: Governor Josiah Martin to William Legge, Earl of Dartmouth, 28 August 1775.

[61] Robert W. Coakley, Stetson Conn, *The War of the American Revolution* (Washington DC: Centre of Military History, U.S. Army, 2004), p. 90.

North Carolina's first grand master of freemasons but succeeded Johnston the following year, remaining in office until his death in November 1789.[62]

Other members of the Caswell family within the lodge include Richard's younger brother, Benjamin, also a planter, merchant, politician and militia officer, who served as captain of the elite North Carolina Light Horse.[63] Winston Caswell was Caswell's second son; Dallam, his third son; and Francis, his nephew.

Members of St John's Lodge, Kingston (Kinston), pre-1800

Thomas Branton	1788 [64]	James Bright	1799
Simon Bright	1789	William Bush	1788
Stephen Cade	1788	Benjamin Caswell	1788
Dallam Caswell	1799	Francis Caswell	1799
Richard Caswell	1788	Winston Caswell	1788
John Coart	1788	Jesse Cobb	1799
James Collier	1799	Probert Collier	1793
Joseph Eliot	1799	John Gatlin	1799
M. Gillies	1789	James Glasgow	1788
Henry Goodman	1788	William Goodman	1789
M. Handy	1788	Frederick Hargett	1788
William M. Herritage	1788	Jacob Lassiter	1789

---

[62] See chapter eleven.

[63] Benjamin Caswell (1737-1791), planter, army officer, merchant, public official and state legislator. Caswell's public service included justice of the peace of Dobbs County, several terms as sheriff of Dobbs (1774-77, 1780-84 and 1787-91), and election to the Commons in 1781. He was a lieutenant then captain in the Dobbs militia; and captain of light horse in the state regiment (1777-9).

[64] The date of membership is the date of first appearance in masonic records. It is not the date of initiation or joining. Data are taken *inter alia* from Parramore, *Launching the Craft*.

John Lovick	1799	William Lovick	1799
Francis McIlwain	1791	Charles Markland	1790
R. I. Powell	1799	William Randall	1788
William Sheppard	1788	Oliver Smith	1789
L. Spalding	pre-1800	James Violeau	1799
Hugh Ward	1789	Robert White	1788
W. Williams	1788		

Several of Caswell's neighbours are also identifiable within the membership, almost all local planters. Many had served with him during the war.

John Coart had estates in Dobbs and Pitt counties, and held land warrants in Tennessee.[65] He was sufficiently close to Caswell to have been made one of his executors[66] and had served with him as Commissary in the New Bern Minutemen and in the assembly, representing Dobbs County in 1779.

Jesse Cobb,[67] originally from Virginia, had married Caswell's sister-in-law, Elizabeth Herritage, in 1772. A merchant and planter, Cobb owned a portfolio of more than 12,800 acres across Dobbs and Caswell counties, together with land in Tennessee.[68] He had served as a captain in the Dobbs County Regiment under Caswell and was one of two county representatives to the 1776 constitutional convention and 1778 general assembly.

---

[65] Coart held over 800 acres of land in Dobbs County and more than 600 acres in neighbouring Pitt County. Cf., for example, NC Land Grants, Patent Book 22 P 296 #4863 22 November 1771; P 343 21 July 1774; P 346 #5022 21 July 1774; Patent Book 25 P 308 #8168 11 March 1775. Pitt County Deed Abstract, DB LP p. 269 (1787). Lenoir County Deeds, 1700-1810: 'Tyndall-Noble Estate Records'.

[66] Richard Caswell's will dated 2 July 1787 in J. Bryan Grimes, *North Carolina Wills and Inventories*, pp. 120-1.

[67] Jesse Cobb (c.1750-1807).

[68] Cobb purchased at least twenty third-party military land warrants in 1793 alone. Cf. State Archives of North Carolina, North Carolina Land Grants database.

Caswell and Cobb worked together as town commissioners, both appointed in 1784 when Kingston was renamed. Their fellow commissioners included both family and neighbours: William Caswell, Isaac Wingate, Richard Caswell, Jr., John Herritage (a brother-in-law), and John Sheppard, all local landowners. Sheppard's land holdings were substantial, with more than 6,700 acres in the immediate area[69] and another 32,000 acres in Tennessee.[70]

William Martin Herritage, another brother-in-law, had an estate on the Neuse and more than 9,000 acres in Craven County. Three of his neighbours were also members of the lodge: two brothers, James and Probert Collier; and Simon Bright. All held properties across Craven County and land warrants in Tennessee. Bright was the leading landowner of the three. He owned *The Hill* and *The Briery* plantations, extending to at least 3,500 acres, as well as property in Bladen, Chatham and Johnston counties.[71] He was also active politically, one of four delegates from Dobbs County, including Caswell, who attended the 1789 Fayetteville convention; he succeeded Caswell as state senator on the latter's death. Bright's younger brother, James, is similarly listed as a member, as is Thomas Branton, the manager of a local corn mill owned by Simon Bright and a middling planter in his own right with some 2,200 acres.

John Gatlin was married to Susannah, Caswell's youngest daughter. He owned in excess of 5,000 acres in adjacent Craven County and served as a town commissioner.

James Glasgow,[72] originally from Maryland and a member of the First Lodge in Pitt County,[73] had studied law at Kingston under David Gordon and was admitted to the Bar in 1764. He received the majority of the *Fairfields*

---

[69] State Archives of North Carolina, North Carolina Land Grants database.
[70] Ibid.
[71] Ibid. Simon Bright (*c*.1757-1802).
[72] James Glasgow (*c*.1735-1819).
[73] He is recorded in the minutes in 1768.

plantation the year afterwards as a gift from his father-in-law, Colonel Abraham Sheppard. Benjamin Sheppard, the colonel's son, a widower, later married Glasgow's sister, Martha.[74] The 'W. Williams' recorded in the membership register is probably Willoughby Williams, one of Glasgow's sons-in-law.

Glasgow acquired additional land over the following years to become one of the wealthiest men in Dobbs County with an estate that would exceed 35,000 acres.[75] Although his fortunes waned as well as waxed, the *DNCB* records that in 1780 Glasgow's taxable estate of lands and slaves was £26,150, 'a figure nearly equalled by six other Dobbs taxpayers but exceeded by only two'.

Like Caswell, Glasgow was active in the Dobbs County militia before the war and served under Tryon at the Battle of Alamance. He was subsequently promoted major and made regimental adjutant. Glasgow worked closely with Caswell to train the Minutemen companies of the New Bern District and fought at the Battle of Moore's Creek Bridge; he was afterwards promoted to colonel.

Glasgow represented Dobbs County at the provincial congress at Hillsborough in 1775 and was elected to the committee of safety for the New Bern District. He became secretary of state in 1776 and was re-elected thereafter until 1797, when he was elected to the United States Senate by the Tennessee legislature. He also served as grand secretary of the Grand Lodge of North Carolina in 1787 when Caswell was deputy grand master, and as senior grand warden the following year when Caswell was grand master; he was deputy grand master from 1790-97 under William R. Davie.

Glasgow's personal, political and masonic reputation suffered egregiously after December 1797 when as secretary of state for North Carolina he was embroiled in allegations of land fraud carried out within his department

---

[74] *DNCB*.

[75] State Archives of North Carolina, North Carolina Land Grants database.

but probably (albeit not certainly) without his knowledge. Unable to present a defence by law, he was found guilty on two of five counts and fined £1,000 on each.[76]

The William Sheppard listed in the lodge membership records was another Caswell brother-in-law. He had been commissioned into the Dobbs County Regiment where he served as an ensign and then captain under his father, and as a major under Glasgow; he was later promoted to colonel.[77] Sheppard owned individually and jointly over 13,000 acres, including around 4,000 acres in Tennessee acquired from third-party grantees.

Frederick Hargett descended from Palatine settlers who had migrated to New Bern at the beginning of the eighteenth century.[78] He fought as a captain in the 8th Regiment of North Carolina Militia having previously served as captain of a company at Moore's Creek Bridge. Following the war, Hargett settled in Jones County, south-east of Kingston. He was an assemblyman for fifteen years and from 1784-94 sat in the state senate where he chaired two influential committees.

Hargett was also one of the original trustees of the University of North Carolina and headed the committee that selected Chapel Hill as the location for the campus. He served as grand treasurer of the Grand Lodge of North Carolina from 1790-93.

William Bush, a planter with an estate at Wheat Swamp, Falling Creek, and land holdings in Craven County and Tennessee,[79] was another who had served under Caswell. He had been commissioned into the 8th North Carolina Regiment before transferring to the 1st, where he served as lieutenant and then captain.

---

[76] Cf., *DNCB* for a summary of the court case.

[77] J.D. Lewis, *NC Patriots 1775-1783: Their Own Words* (Little River, SC: J.D. Lewis, 2012), volume 2, part 1, p. 460.

[78] Frederick Hargett [also Harget] (c.1742-1810), a planter, soldier and politician.

[79] Bush owned more than 2,000 acres in Craven County, over 3,400 acres in Tennessee, and at least 2,000 acres elsewhere.

William Randall, a captain in the North Carolina Regiment, held land in Craven, Dobbs and Jones counties, and in Tennessee. Henry Goodman, promoted to lieutenant-colonel in the Dobbs County Regiment, owned estates across Dobbs, Duplin, Gates and Lenoir counties. And William Goodman, probably his brother, a militia officer, owned more than 7,000 acres, including almost 4,000 acres in Tennessee.

A founding lodge of the Grand Lodge of North Carolina, Kinston was designated No. 4 in 1791. The lodge survived until 1806 when its charter was arrested and the lodge dissolved.[80] In 1903, its charter was re-assigned to lodge No. 96.

DORNOCH LODGE, BUTE COUNTY

Sited above the Fall Line and adjacent to the Roanoke Rapids south of the Virginia border, Bute County was named for the 3rd Earl of Bute.[81] The county was created in 1764 from Granville County and enlarged in 1766 with the incorporation of part of north-west Northampton County. The region was sympathetic to the Regulators and Tryon's instructions to the county militia to take action against them was largely ignored.[82]

As the area became more heavily settled, Bute County was divided along the Shocco Creek, with the northern half renamed Warren County and the southern Franklin County. Bute County itself disappeared as a legal entity, as did its past connection to the former British prime minister.

---

[80] *Proceedings of the Grand Lodge of North Carolina and Tennessee for 1806* (Raleigh, NC: 1807), p. 5.

[81] John Stuart, 3rd Earl of Bute (1713-1792), a Scottish nobleman and prime minister of Britain (1762–1763).

[82] Research Branch, NC Office of Archives and History, 2008: http://www.ncpedia.org/bute-county, accessed 23 July 2017.

Members of Dornoch Lodge, Bute County (1785)

William Brickell   Henry Hill
William Green   John Macon
Durham Hall   William Sewell

The lodge's designation – Dornoch[83] – suggests an association with the small town of that name in the Scottish Highlands, or with migrants from that region, predominantly tenant farmers. There is no town named 'Dornoch' in North Carolina nor elsewhere in North America.

It is not possible to determine whether the six known lodge members are representative of Dornoch Lodge as a whole but all were patriots and each served on the Bute County committee of safety.

William Brickell (d.1811), was commissioned major into the Bute County militia. He served from 1776-79 before transferring to the Franklin County regiment under Benjamin Seawell, where he was promoted to lieutenant-colonel (1780) and then colonel (1780-83).[84] He was one of five county commissioners at the creation of Franklin County (1779) and represented the county in the Commons from 1780-82.[85]

Durham Hall, Henry Hill and William Green were also members of the legislature.[86] Hall, a planter, was elected to the Commons in 1784-87 and 1789. Hill, a captain in the Franklin County Regiment, was a state senator from 1780-82 and again in 1784-87, 1789-91, 1794-96 and 1797-98. And

---

[83] Sometimes written as 'Dornock' or 'Dornach'.

[84] *CSRNC*, volume 17, pp. 858 and 952; also, volume 22, pp. 576-7: William Brickell to Thomas Burke, 25 August 1781. In 1796 he is described as 'General Brickell'.

[85] John Hill Wheeler, *Historical Sketches of North Carolina: From 1584 to 1851* (Philadelphia, PA: Lippincott, Grambo and Co., 1851), p. 149.

[86] Ibid., pp. 149-50.

Green, a former captain in the Bute County militia and then the 1st North Carolina Regiment, served in the Commons alongside Brickell in 1781-82.

John Macon (1755-1828), had been born at *Macon Manor* in the Granville District, later Warren County. His wife, Joanna, whom he married in 1775, was the daughter of William Tabb of Virginia.[87] Macon served as a lieutenant in the Bute County militia and was commissioned a lieutenant then captain in the 7th North Carolina Regiment. He saw action in South Carolina at the battles of Little Lynches Creek, Camden and Guildford Court House, and although captured by the British was later released. He subsequently fought at Valley Forge and was promoted major under William Richardson Davie.

Elected to the Commons to represent Warren County (1779-85), Macon succeeded his brother, Nathaniel, in the state senate from 1786-96. He was a member of the first board of trustees of the University of North Carolina (1789-92), and sat on the commission for the construction of the state capital at Raleigh. Active in grand lodge, Macon was installed as junior grand warden in 1792 and as senior grand warden the following year, both under Davie. In addition to his estates in North Carolina, he held war grants over 1,700 acres in Tennessee, to which he relocated in 1806.

William Sewell [Seawell] was the son of Colonel Benjamin Seawell, colonel of the Franklin County Militia (1779-83) and later sheriff of Franklin County.[88] The family were originally from Virginia and owned a large estate on the south side of the Tar River.

Although the lodge reportedly received a warrant from Montfort in 1773 or 1774,[89] it was subsequently ruled illegal by the Grand Lodge of North Carolina and the lodge ceased. The rationale for this is not known. One reason may have been the proximity of Blandford-Bute Lodge. There

---

[87] 'The Tabb Family', *William and Mary Quarterly*, 13.4 (1905), 270-8.
[88] Franklin County, NC: Deed Book 6, p. 192, 19 March 1789.
[89] Cf., Parramore, *Launching the Craft*, p. 30.

would have been an obvious desire on the part of the Grand Lodge of North Carolina to bring Blandford-Bute into its orbit - the lodge had been constituted by Scottish masons from Virginia – and it is feasible that the chosen method was to combine Dornoch with Blandford-Bute under a new charter.

Offering some support for this argument, the *125th Proceedings of the Grand Lodge of Ancient, Free, and Accepted Masons of North Carolina* note that 'In Warren County, a part of the old county of Bute, were two lodges ... Blandford Lodge and Dornoch Lodge. A visiting brother recorded in the minutes of Unanimity Lodge, at Edenton on February 6, 1777, was: "Henry Machen from Blandford Lodge in Bute County."[90] Dornoch Lodge, of Warren County, sent representatives to the Convention of 1787 which re-organized the Grand Lodge. The Convention held that Dornoch Lodge was not legally constituted (though its delegates were legally made Masons), and chartered a new Lodge, Johnston-Caswell Lodge, No. 10, in Warrenton, which was no doubt made up of former members of both Blandford and Dornoch Lodges.'[91]

ROYAL EDWIN LODGE, WINDSOR

The town of Windsor in Bertie County[92] is located on the upper reaches of the Cashie River which in the 1700s offered a navigable route to the

---

[90] Henry [or Harrison] Macon was the brother of John Macon. He was commissioned in 1776 as a captain in the Franklin County militia and subsequently served under William Brickellin the 2nd NC Regiment of Militia. He was wounded and captured at the battle of Camden, SC. Following his release he served as a captain under Benjamin Seawell.

[91] *Proceedings of the Grand Lodge of Ancient, Free, and Accepted Masons of North Carolina* (Raleigh, NC: 1912), p. 73.

[92] The area is now known loosely as North Carolina's 'Inner Banks' as opposed to the better known 'Outer Banks'.

Albemarle Sound and the Outer Banks. The region had been settled by migrants in the 1720s and was subsequently worked for naval stores and cleared for rice plantations and farming.

Montfort's warrant establishing Royal Edwin is dated 2 July 1772 and made out to 'John Johnston, Thomas Hunter,[93] Samuel Grimes, Peter Clifton and other brethren residing in Bertie County'. Information on the founding members is sparse but all appear to have been relatively substantial farmers or merchants. John Johnston, Samuel Johnston's brother, held land grants over 1,000 acres in Indian Woods and owned land elsewhere.[94] The extent of Samuel Grimes's (*d*.1783) estate is not known but was of sufficient size to allow him to serve as a juror and overseer of the local roads, and he owned slaves.[95] He was awarded military land warrants which were assigned or sold in 1792 to a Samuel Sanford.[96]

Peter Clifton, a Bertie County delegate to the Hillsborough convention,[97] owned land across the Cashie Swamp.[98] And Thomas Hunter (1735-1784), land to the west of Windsor at Rich Square, Scotland Neck and Rocky Mount in Edgecombe County.[99] He had fought as a major in the Edgecombe

---

[93] Thomas Hunter's son, also Thomas, became master of Royal Edwin in 1788. Cf., John Raymond Shute, 'Three Early North Carolina Lodges', *NOCALORE*, 5.2 (1931), 104-11.

[94] State Archives of North Carolina, North Carolina Land Grants database.

[95] Courthouse Records of Bertie County, North Carolina, Section IV. Cf., also, Sandra Lee Almasy, *Bertie County North Carolina Wills, 1781-1797* (Middleton, WI: Kensington Glen Publishing, 1991).

[96] State Archives of North Carolina, North Carolina Land Grants database.

[97] John H. Wheeler, *Historical Sketches of North Carolina from 1584 to 1851* (Genealogical Publishing Co., 2009), p. 31.

[98] State Archives of North Carolina, North Carolina Land Grants database.

[99] *DNCB*.

County Regiment before transferring to the Nash County Regiment, which he would later command as colonel.[100]

Members of Royal Edwin Lodge, No. 5, Windsor, pre-1800

Edward Acree	1798	Silas W. Arnett	1787
Blake Baker	1798	Henry Belote	1775
Hardy Boyce	1798	Willie Brodie	1798
Stephen Buck	1798	Peter Clifton	1772
William J. Dawson	1787	James Granbury	1798
Langley Granbury	1798	Samuel Granbury	1798
William Granbury	1798	Samuel Grimes	1772
Joseph Gurley	1798	Lemuel Hall	1798
Willis Hare	1788	William Higgs	1798
Thomas Hunter	1772	John Johnston	1772
Samuel W. Johnston	1787	Drury Moore	1798
Josiah Moore	1798	James Norfleet	1798
Andrew Oliver	1787	Archibald Parker	1798
Francis Pugh	1795	William Pugh, Jr.	1798
P.R. Rose	1798	Thomas Scholar	1798
H. Taylor	1798	John D. Whyte	1798
		John Wolfenden	1795

Aside from John and Samuel Johnston, who would become governor, a U.S. senator, and grand master of the Grand Lodge of North Carolina, both nephews of Gabriel Johnston, relatively few members of Royal Edwin are readily identifiable. Among the exceptions is Silas Arnett (fl.1783-1806), a lawyer and printer whose New Bern-based firm of

---

[100] *CSRNC*, volume 13, pp. 159-60, 173: Thomas Hunter to Richard Caswell, 11 June and 27 June 1778. Hunter was promoted to lieutenant-colonel in 1777 and full colonel in 1780.

Arnett & Hodge had been elected public printer in December 1785; the firm also published the *State Gazette of North Carolina*.[101] Arnett left the partnership in 1787 and afterwards practiced as an attorney,[102] serving as clerk of the superior court from 1803. He represented Beaufort County at the Fayetteville convention in 1789, voting to approve the ratification of the U.S. Constitution.[103]

Arnett is named as one of three official visitors to Unanimity Lodge Edenton on 11 November 1775. The others comprised John Johnston, the master of Royal Edwin, and Arnett's fellow warden, Andrew Oliver.[104] The same group would represent the lodge at the Tarboro conference.[105]

Johnston fought as a captain in the 2nd Battalion of the North Carolina Militia. He represented the county at the second provincial congress in Hillsborough, at the third, fourth and fifth congresses at Halifax, and was one of the delegates from Bertie County who ratified the Constitution.

Oliver fought as a captain in the Bertie County Regiment under Colonel Peter Dauge,[106] and subsequently represented Bertie in the Commons from 1784-88.

The Granbury family[107] settled in North Carolina in the mid-1750s and owned significant estates across Bertie, Hertford and Northampton counties. The settlement at the crossroads that linked the Roanoke River

---

[101] *DNCB*.

[102] Arnett is first listed in court records as an attorney in 1790.

[103] *CSRNC*, volume 22, pp. 36-53. It was then in force in all states bar North Carolina and Rhode Island.

[104] Johnston, Oliver and Arnett also represented the lodge at the Tarboro Convention.

[105] *DNCB*. The minutes of St John's Lodge in New Bern, which Arnett later joined, record his visit in December 1788 when he was junior grand warden. Members of St John's officiated at Arnett's funeral in May 1806.

[106] Peter Dauge [or Dozier] (1739-1801), a Huguenot whose family had migrated originally to Charleston.

[107] Also written as 'Granbery' or 'Granberry'.

to Winton and the east and western parts of the province was built on land owned by Langley Granbury, the head of the family, and the town that developed was known as Granbury Cross-Roads until the nineteenth century.[108]

William and Francis Pugh were planters and traders. The family had migrated to Nansemond County Virginia and from there to North Carolina. Francis served as a captain in the Bertie County Regiment under Colonel Thomas Pugh, his father, who with John Johnston was a delegate to the fifth provincial congress at Halifax.

William Johnston Dawson (1765-1796), later a congressman, had been born near Edenton in Chowan County, and was the son of Colonel John Dawson, a member of the council, and Penelope Johnston, Governor Johnston's daughter. He was educated in England but nonetheless took a patriotic political stance. Elected a delegate to Hillsborough in 1788, he held a Federalist line, voting to ratify the Constitution.

Dawson was elected to the Commons in 1791 and the same year appointed to the committee that chose Raleigh as the site of the future state capital. In 1793, he was appointed to represent the Eighth Congressional District in the U.S. House of Representatives, serving a single term until 1795.[109] He died a year later and is buried at Eden House.

Joseph Gurley (1751-c.1816), originally from Virginia, a past master of the lodge, was afterwards a founder member of Davie Lodge at Lewiston. He subsequently took orders as an Episcopalian priest.[110]

---

[108] Watson, *Bertie County: A Brief History*, p. 49; J.M. Brown, 'History of Roxobel Township', *Bertie County Historical Society*, 3.1 (1955).

[109] Cf., Watson, *Bertie County: A Brief History*; and Hugh T. Lefler and William S. Powell, *Colonial North Carolina* (New York, NY: Charles Scribner's Sons, 1973).

[110] Cf., *DNCB*; also G. MacLaren Brydon, 'A List of Clergy of the Protestant Episcopal Church Ordained after the American Revolution, Who Served in Virginia between 1785 and 1814, and a List of Virginia Parishes and Their Rectors for the Same Period', *William and Mary Quarterly* 19 (1939).

Royal Edwin had a disproportionately large influence within the Grand Lodge of North Carolina, principally as a function of Samuel Johnston's four terms as grand master. Oliver became senior grand warden in 1788, and Arnett served as junior grand warden in 1788 and senior grand warden the following year.

Royal Edwin's warrant was arrested in 1803 but restored the following year.[111] The lodge ceased in 1822 and its number - 5 - was reassigned in 1857 to Charity Lodge, which remains active today.

ROYAL WILLIAM LODGE, WINTON

Winton in Hertford County is sited on the Chowan River just below its confluence with the Meherrin River, around fifteen miles south of the Virginia border and some forty miles from Edenton and the Albemarle Sound. The Chowan was navigable at Winton and the settlement, originally established as a trading post, was later a regional commercial centre.

Although the area was fairly well settled by the 1740s, a bill to incorporate the town was not passed until 1768. The legislation was sponsored by Benjamin Wynns, who donated 100 acres. The town was named in his honour and became the county seat of government.

Members of Royal William Lodge No. 6, Winton

    Patrick Garvey William P. Little
    Hardy Murfree

---

[111] *Proceedings of the Grand Lodge of Ancient, Free, and Accepted Masons of North Carolina* (Raleigh, NC: 1803), p. 9.

The three delegates recorded in the minutes of the 1787 convention at Tarboro are the only known members of Royal William Lodge.

William Person Little (1765-1829), a land speculator, planter and later horse breeder, had been born in Hertford County. He was adopted by his uncle, General Thomas Person,[112] an anti-Federalist politician and landowner with strong pro-Regulator sentiments. Little inherited a substantial part of Person's vast estate and later founded and built the town of Littleton at *Little Manor* in Warren County.[113] He was elected to the 1788 Hillsborough convention which declined to ratify the Constitution, and was subsequently a member of the state senate for Granville County (1792-98) and Warren County (1804-06), where he also served as a justice of the peace and colonel of the state militia.[114]

Patrick Garvey (*d*.1810), an Irishman from Philadelphia, had been imprisoned briefly during the war on suspicion of illegally trading with the British. The charge was politically motivated. Garvey had worked for Andrew Craigie, the army's apothecary-general, and given evidence against William Shippen, the head of the Army Medical Service, alleging misuse of funds. This was contested and Garvey suffered as a consequence.

Following his release, Garvey relocated to Winton where he became established as a merchant and physician. He was active politically, adopting an ardently Federalist stance in the run-up to North Carolina's constitutional conventions. His opposition to Reverend Lemuel Burkitt, a

---

[112] Thomas Person (1733-1800), had been a land surveyor for the Granville estate and used his insider knowledge and connections to amass vast landholdings that exceeded 82,000 acres. He represented Granville County as an assemblyman and at the provincial congresses, and served as a justice of the peace. During the war he held the rank of brigadier general in the Hillsborough District Militia.

[113] Little's land grants alone exceeded 15,000 acres.

[114] Little also founded a school and in 1822 became the county's first postmaster.

leading anti-Federalist, sparked a riot, and Garvey was encouraged to leave the town.[115] He moved to Murfreesboro in 1789, becoming a partner in a distillery and a justice of the peace, before settling in Jonesborough in Camden County in 1799.

Hardy Murfree (1752-1809), born at his family's estate at *Murfree's Landing*, served as a captain, major, then lieutenant-colonel of the 2nd North Carolina Regiment, and fought at Fort Moultrie, Charleston, and at the battles of Brandywine Creek, Germantown, Monmouth and Stony Point, where he commanded an infantry column in the successful attack on the British position on the Hudson. Following the war, he was appointed an inspector of revenues and Edenton's commissioner for confiscated property.

In 1787, Murfree successfully sponsored a petition to incorporate *Murfree's Landing* as a town – Murfreesboro, a valuable but relatively small part of the immense estates he owned in North Carolina and Tennessee, where he acquired war grants over some 40,000 acres.

Murfree was an original member of The Society of the Cincinnati and a pro-Federalist member of the convention that finally ratified the Constitution. He moved to Tennessee in 1807, dying there two years later. The town of Cannonsburgh was renamed Murfreesboro in his honour in 1811 and chosen as Tennessee's state capital in 1818. It was replaced by Nashville in 1826.

Murfree, Garvey and Little were founder members of American George Lodge No. 17, formed at Murfreesboro in 1789. Murfree was elected master; Garvey, senior warden; and Little, secretary.[116] The lodge's development mirrored that of the town, which came to dominate the area commercially and socially. Its expansion led to the demise of Royal William Lodge, which was removed from the register of the Grand Lodge of North Carolina in 1799.

---

[115] *DNCB*.
[116] *NOCALORE*, VI (1936), 224-5; Parramore, *Launching the Craft*, pp. 66, 111, 229.

Unanimity Lodge, Edenton

Close to the head of the Albemarle Sound on a natural harbour at the mouth of the Chowan River, Edenton, 'the town on Queen Anne's Creek', was established in the early 1700s and incorporated formally in 1722.[117] It was one of North Carolina's first settlements and functioned as the seat of government from 1722-43. The town was also one of the colony's principal ports, albeit that trade was predominantly coastal with local merchants and traders dealing with their counterparts in Boston, Philadelphia, New York and Charleston.

Unanimity Lodge was chartered by Montfort in 1775.[118] Although there is no evidence to indicate the existence of an earlier lodge, this should not be excluded.

The lodge attracted a cross-section of planters, merchants and seamen, but while the membership register is extensive, it appears to include relatively few of the town's more prominent figures, notwithstanding that some were members of lodges elsewhere and might have been expected to join or attend as visitors.[119]

There were exceptions nonetheless, for example, Edward Buncombe (1742-1778), a wealthy Caribbean-born planter who had inherited over 2,500 acres in Tyrrel County on which he built *Buncombe Hall*. And Jasper Charlton, an attorney and the owner of *Charlton House* with some 700 acres in Bertie County. But other attorneys and planters *were* conspicuous in their absence. Whether this was a result of political animosity or social disdain is

---

[117] CSRNC, *Historical Review of the Colonial and State Records of North Carolina*, volume 30, p. 45.

[118] Cf., http://library.digitalnc.org/cdm/ref/collection/ncmemory/id/238010, accessed 11 August 2017.

[119] Parramore, *Launching the Craft*, pp. 36-8. Minutes of Unanimity Lodge No. 7, Edenton, NC: http://library.digitalnc.org/cdm/ref/collection/ncmemory/id/211046, accessed 23 May 2017.

not clear, but the lodge minutes record numerous instances of drunkenness and this may provide one explanation.[120]

Within Edenton's pre-war membership registers are three entries worthy of special mention: Stephen Cabarrus (1754-1808); John Mare (1739-1803); and Cosimo de Medici (*fl.*1767-1789), a captain in the North Carolina Light Dragoons and one of very few Italian officers in the War of Independence.

Cabarrus had been born in Bayonne, France, to a family of merchants, bankers and ship owners. He arrived in Edenton in 1776 and within a year had married Jeanne Bodley, the French widow of Joshua Bodley.[121] She had inherited the *Pembroke* plantation and Cabarrus bought the adjacent farm, the first of what would be many land purchases. By 1778, he owned around 1,980 acres and 60 slaves - with his estate valued at over £15,200.

Cabarrus was elected to the assembly to represent Edenton and later Chowan County. He was chosen as speaker in 1789, served as a Federalist delegate at the Hillsborough and Fayetteville conventions, and remained an active politician until 1805.

Carbarrus was also Unanimity's delegate to the Tarboro Convention in December 1787. Two years later he was appointed to the first board of trustees of the University of North Carolina, serving from 1789-92, the year that Cabarrus County was named for him.

John Mare, the portrait painter and later merchant and politician, migrated to Edenton from New York in the late 1770s.[122] He had visited before and is recorded as attending the lodge in 1776 and again in 1777.[123]

---

[120] Minutes of Unanimity Lodge No. 7: 20 July 1778; 3 August 1779; and 27 December 1781, *et al.*

[121] Joshua Bodley (1705-1775), Lord Granville's former attorney and land agent in North Carolina. He had married while living in Brittany.

[122] Helen Burr Smith & Elizabeth V. Moore, 'John Mare: A Composite Portrait', *North Carolina Historical Review*, **44**.1 (1967), 18-52.

[123] Ibid.

Mare was a New York freemason, a member of Master's Lodge No. 2 in Albany and St John's Lodge No. 2 in New York.[124] It is possible that his membership was linked to his work for Sir John Johnson, the provincial grand master of New York. Mare had painted Johnson's portrait in 1772 and may have hoped for other commissions.[125] Indeed, at least one unsigned contemporary portrait has been attributed to Mare because of its masonic content.[126]

Mare supported the patriotic cause and participated in local Edenton politics. After the war he became the town's postmaster (1783-86), coroner (1786-88), and treasurer, and a town commissioner and justice of the peace.

Samuel Johnston appointed him to his council in 1787 and in 1789 he was elected to represent Edenton at the Fayetteville convention, voting for ratification. He also took part in the discussions that preceded the establishment of a new grand lodge for North Carolina.

Mare was elected master of Unanimity Lodge in 1779 and became the fulcrum on which the lodge pivoted. The lodge failed two decades later, five months after Mare declined reappointment as master.[127]

Mare's masonic career mirrored his commercial success and decline. He built an import-export business with the West Indies and acquired a portfolio of properties, but Mare's financial standing declined in the 1790s and he was forced to mortgage and sell. He was also sued for outstanding debts.[128]

---

[124] Constituted in 1757 by the Grand Lodge of England (Moderns) by George Harison, fourth Provincial Grand Master in New York. The lodge is now St John's Lodge No. 1.

[125] The same practice had been evident in London since the 1720s.

[126] *DNCB*.

[127] Smith & Moore, 'John Mare', 41.

[128] Ibid., 45-7.

Mare's money problems became so serious after 1800 that he did not list his taxes and at his death was virtually destitute.[129]

Cosimo de Medici is known to have been a member of three lodges: Unanimity in Edenton; St John's in New Bern; and Washington No. 15 in Beaufort County.[130] Commissioned a lieutenant in the 3rd company of light horse in 1776, he was promoted captain of an independent company of light horse the following year.[131]

De Medici's military service was marred by accusations of poor leadership and fraud. He was indicted for 'rarely attending to any public duty', handling his men with 'indifference and inhumanity', and misappropriating military funds.[132] Unusually, de Medici was permitted to resign in 1779 rather than face court martial.[133] He remained in North Carolina until 1789.[134]

Edenton was by-passed by the British and the lodge continued to meet throughout the war years. It was unusual in this respect. Halifax, Wilmington and most other significant towns in North Carolina were occupied, even if temporarily, and active recruitment for the militia and Continental Army periodically stripped most areas of their men.

Unanimity Lodge ceased working in 1791 and was dissolved in 1799. The lodge number remains in use having been assigned in 1857 to lodge No. 193. There were several reasons for Unanimity's decline, including the westward move in the state's population, a shift that led to the failure of several formerly significant lodges. Another was the shrinking use of

---

[129] Ibid.

[130] DNCB.

[131] CSRNC, volume 11, pp. 367, 370-1: James Moore to Richard Caswell, 22 January 1777 and Robert Howe to Richard Caswell, 31 January 1777.

[132] CSRNC, volume 11, p. 409: Richard Caswell to Robert Howe, 7 March 1777.

[133] CSRNC, volume 14, p. 111: Benjamin Lincoln to Richard Caswell, 6 June 1779.

[134] CSRNC, volume 21, pp. 193-436: Minutes of the North Carolina House of Commons, 2 November - 22 December 1789.

Edenton as a port and the negative impact this had on the town's economy. But there was also a third factor - the schism between patriots and loyalists within North Carolina's merchant community, a particularly acute dynamic in Edenton.[135]

---

[135] The *Report on Land Grants of Confiscated Property, 1787-1788*, North Carolina Historical Commission, provides a list of loyalists whose assets were subject to confiscation and sale. Cf., also, Robert O. DeMond, *The Loyalists in North Carolina During the Revolution* (Genealogical Publishing Co., 2009).

Chapter Eight

'Over the Hills and Far Away'

The Irish in Pennsylvania and North Carolina

May the road rise up to meet you.
May the wind be always at your back
May the sun shine warm upon your face ...
May God hold you in the palm of His hand. [1]

An estimated 250 - 300,000 Irish migrated to North America in the eighteenth century.[2] They included Anglicans, Catholics and Quakers, but most, more than three-quarters, were Ulster Presbyterians, described as

---

[1] Traditional Irish blessing.

[2] Some source suggest *c*.400,000. Cf., among many relevant books and journal articles, Kerby A. Miller *et al*, *Irish Immigration in the Land of Canaan: Letters and Memoirs from Colonial and Revolutionary America, 1675-1815* (Oxford: OUP, 2013), esp. 656-9; Marianne S. Wokeck, *Trade in Strangers: The Beginnings of Mass Migration to North America* (University Park, PA: Penn State University Press, 1999); Wokeck, 'Irish Immigration to the Delaware Valley before the American Revolution', *Proceedings of the Royal Irish Academy*, 96C 5 (1996), 103-35; Wokeck, 'German and Irish Immigration to Colonial Philadelphia', *Proceedings of the American Philosophical Society*, 133.2 (1989), 128-43; R. J. Dickson, *Ulster Emigration to Colonial America, 1718-1785* (London: Ulster Historical Foundation, 1966); Aaron Fogleman, 'Migrations to the Thirteen British North American Colonies, 1700-1775: New Estimates', *Journal of Interdisciplinary History*, 22.4 (1992), 691-709; Patrick Fitzgerald, 'The Scotch-Irish & the Eighteenth-Century Irish Diaspora', *History Ireland*, 7.3 (1999), 37-41; T.W. Moody, 'Irish and Scotch-Irish in Eighteenth-Century America', *Studies: An Irish Quarterly Review*, 35.137 (1946), 85-90; Francis G. James, 'Irish Colonial Trade in the Eighteenth Century', *William and Mary Quarterly*, 20.4 (1963), 574-84.

Scotch-Irish or Scots-Irish, to differentiate them from the Catholic Southern Irish who dominated nineteenth-century migration.

The Scots-Irish were the descendants of Lowland Scots who had been encouraged to colonise the Plantation of Ulster in the seventeenth century, a process that began under James I in the early 1600s and continued through to William and Mary in the 1690s. As Presbyterians, they were subject to Ireland's Penal Laws which restricted full legal rights to Anglicans - members of the Church of Ireland. But despite what is often claimed, their departure from Ireland was not due solely or even mainly to religious and political discrimination, nor was it a function of the famines that racked the country decade by decade, although all these factors played a role. The main driver was the financial hardship caused by high land rents and Britain's anti-Irish trade legislation, and the pull of better economic prospects elsewhere.[3]

Although the number of eighteenth-century Irish migrants appears modest when compared to the four million or more who arrived in America in the nineteenth and twentieth centuries, it was nonetheless a significant portion – over 10% - of the total white settler population that stood at around 2.2 million in 1780.[4] And the Irish were not spread evenly across the colonies. They tended to gravitate towards specific regions, especially Pennsylvania and the Carolina Piedmont, where they comprised up to half, and sometimes more, of the white settler population.

Until the eighteenth century and aside from the Navigation Acts of 1663, few laws had regulated Ireland's foreign trade and domestic markets

---

[3] Excellent overviews are provided by Miller, *Irish Immigration in the Land of Canaan*; Thomas M. Truxes, 'Ireland, New York, and the Eighteenth-Century Atlantic World', *American Journal of Irish Studies*, 8 (2011), 9-40; and R.C. Nash, 'Irish Atlantic Trade in the Seventeenth and Eighteenth Centuries', *William and Mary Quarterly*, 42.3 (1985), 329-56.

[4] *Colonial and Pre-Federal Statistics*, Series Z 1-19, 20-3. The data is imperfect and confuses Scotch and Ulster migrants. 'Free State' migrants are also likely to be labelled incorrectly.

more onerously than those of England and no duties were levied that affected Ireland alone. The introduction of the Wool Act in 1699 and the anti-free trade legislation that followed changed everything. Ireland's exports lost unrestricted access to world markets and the tariffs, excise duties and compulsory routing of exports through British ports, made Irish agricultural and manufactured products uncompetitive.[5]

The impact fell particularly harshly on Ireland's middling and lower middling tenant farmers, tradesmen and artisans,[6] and by the end of the century almost half of Ulster's Presbyterians had chosen to leave. Some migrated to England but a more formidable number travelled west across the Atlantic. Those with agricultural leases and businesses that had value sold up and used the proceeds to fund their fares to America and acquire land.[7] Those that could not travelled as indentured labourers, working for up to five years to pay-off their debts.[8] They sailed from Belfast, Londonderry, Dublin, as well as Ireland's minor ports, for Charleston, New York, Baltimore and Boston, but especially Philadelphia, the first port of call for over half of Irish migrants.

Pennsylvania was both a destination in itself and a distribution point for further settlement. Ireland's links to the province dated back to William Penn, the colony's founder, who had extensive estates in Ireland, including Shanagarry.[9] But more effective drivers were the letters from friends

---

[5] Cf. Curtis Nettels, 'The Menace of Colonial Manufacturing 1690-1720', *New England Quarterly*, 4.2 (1931), 230-69, esp. 235-8.

[6] Ibid.

[7] Wokeck, *Trade in Strangers: The Beginnings of Mass Migration to North America*; Wokeck, 'Irish Immigration to the Delaware Valley before the American Revolution', *Proceedings of the Royal Irish Academy*; also 'Irish Immigration to the Delaware Valley before the American Revolution'.

[8] Cf., Miller, *Irish Immigration in the Land of Canaan*. Also, Patrick Griggin, *The People with No Name: Ireland's Ulster-Scots, America's Scots Irish and the Creation of a British Transatlantic World* (Princeton, NJ: Princeton University Press, 2001).

[9] Shanagarry was granted by Charles II to Admiral Sir William Penn in exchange for Macroom, a town near Cork, and its castle, which Penn had received from Cromwell.

and relatives containing encouraging first-hand accounts of life in America, and the glowing advertising commissioned by land speculators and shipping agents.[10] There would be taxes and hardships, but the former were lower than those levied at home and the latter manageable. And unlike Ireland, America had inexpensive land from which decent profits could be earned and plentiful food grown, and relative political and religious autonomy.

In the second half of the eighteenth century the number of migrants leaving Ulster became so considerable that Ireland's linen industry was considered under threat of collapse and the exodus of agricultural tenants rendered some estates unviable.[11] And although migration slowed during the war years from 1775-83, it accelerated afterwards, with over 10,000 departures in 1784 alone, a number that rose further in the following years.[12]

THE LONDON IRISH

London also attracted Irish exiles, some of whom used the city as a staging post before leaving for America. Estimates vary but in the 1750s the figure would have been in the low tens of thousands. At the end of the century when census data became available London's Irish population was measured at only 40,000, but this excludes second and third generation Irish who had been born in the capital and who then numbered around 100,000, some 10% of London's million-strong population.

In earlier centuries Irish migration to England had been seasonal and based on the harvest. But in the eighteenth century the pattern changed,

---

[10] Miller, *Irish Immigration in the Land of Canaan*.

[11] Wokeck, *Trade in Strangers: The Beginnings of Mass Migration to North America* and 'Irish Immigration to the Delaware Valley before the American Revolution'.

[12] Miller, *Irish Immigration in the Land of Canaan*, p. 34. In the nineteenth century the vast majority of Irish incomers were from the South of Ireland, driven by famine as well as hope for a better future. The influx was so large that 'Irish American' became synonymous with Irish Catholic.

with the pull of economic opportunity inspiring many to seek permanent work. It was Irish labour that helped build Britain's emerging infrastructure, its docks, mines, canals and bridges. Irishmen and women plied the streets as pedlars and hawkers, and worked as domestic servants. And many thousands served in the army and navy, up to a third of the lower ranks.

Although London's Irish migrants were dispersed across the capital, many congregated in the slums of St Giles – known as 'Little Dublin', and St Martin's – 'Porridge Island',[13] and in the crowded alleys, courts and lanes to the east of the City of London where Rosemary Lane and the Ratcliffe Highway stretched from the Tower to Wapping and the docks. For the majority with limited education and narrow skills, life was tough with irregular and poorly-paid work. And even though waged labour became more common in the second half of the eighteenth century, conditions were sweated with workers relying on parish funds and charity to supplement their earnings. But despite these barriers, a minority successfully climbed the social and economic ladder. The number of Irish-owned businesses expanded, as did those who entered the professions. Many prospered and broke free from poverty, and it was from this stratum of aspirational London-Irish society that Antients freemasonry was born.[14]

ANTIENTS FREEMASONRY

There is a reason that Irish migrants formed and joined Antients' lodges: they were largely excluded from English freemasonry. The split between Irish and English freemasonry was real, not contrived,[15] and in 1758 the

---

[13] 'Porridge Island' was a reference to the many take-away shops that fed those too poor to have access to a kitchen or who could not afford cooking equipment. It was the case then – as it is now – that cheap take-out shops proliferated in deprived areas where the cost of labour and premises was low.

[14] Cf., *Schism*, esp. chapters two and three.

[15] Ibid., esp. chapter one.

Grand Lodge of Ireland ceased fraternal relations with the Grand Lodge of England, pejoratively tagged as 'Moderns', and recognised the Antients Grand Lodge as the only legitimate masonic authority in England.

The schism between English, Irish and Antients freemasonry had little to do with ritual. Although there were differences, most obviously the Royal Arch, these were exaggerated intentionally by both sides as were disputes over the role of deacons and the transposition of key words in the degree ceremonies.[16] Indeed, Moderns and Antients' ritual had far more in common than was admitted, something attested to at the time.[17]

The real areas of conflict were religious and social. Religious, because the Grand Lodge of England was viewed by some as having secularised freemasonry and moved away from spirituality. And social, because many English freemasons wanted freemasonry to remain a relatively elitist organisation.

Almost without exception, eighteenth-century England disdained Ireland, and English freemasonry followed suit. Expatriate Irish freemasons in London were disparaged and many who asked to join a London lodge were refused. There were several reasons, including an unfounded belief in the feckless nature of the Irish and a general contempt for a country

---

[16] In the eighteenth century masonic ritual took slightly different forms in England, Ireland and Scotland. Lodge practice also varied on a regional basis and could differ from lodge to lodge. This was mainly a result of freemasonry's oral tradition but it was also the case that individual lodges could determine the nature of the ritual they adopted. There was in addition a financial incentive to promote and sometimes invent 'higher' degree ceremonies since extra fees could be levied. This may have been a motive behind the spread of the Royal Arch, which appeared on the masonic scene in Ireland and England only in the 1730s and 1740s.

[17] Anonymous, *Hiram: or the Grand Master Key* (London: W. Griffin, 1766), 2nd edn, a contemporary study that compares the two forms of ritual, makes clear that the contradictions were few.

viewed as an economic and political backwater.[18] But the greater and more proximate concern was the threat the Irish were deemed to pose to London freemasonry's charitable funds.

The position was made clear at the top of the organisation with the Moderns' grand secretary, Samuel Spencer, reportedly telling an Irish supplicant that 'your being an Antient Mason, you are not entitled to any of our charity. The ancient masons have a lodge at the Five Bells in the Strand and their secretary's name is Dermott.[19] Our society is neither arch, royal arch or ancient so that you have no right to partake of our charity'.[20]

Spencer expanded his arguments against Antients freemasonry and Laurence Dermott, the Antients' grand secretary, in a pamphlet - *A Defence of Freemasonry*.[21] His description of a 'three-hour lecture' by 'a red hot Hibernian' drips with sarcasm, as does his account of the initiation of a sedan chairman who, too poor to pay his lodge fee in full, pays half in cash and half via an IOU. The pamphlet denigrates the Antients' 'customs and ceremonies' and disparages their members as a 'disgrace to society' with 'scarcely a coat or shirt to their backs', commonly to be found in ale houses 'hooting and hollooing'.[22]

Spencer's view of Irish and Antients freemasons was a caricature. The Antients' membership records and minutes indicate that its members shared

---

[18] Anti-Catholic feeling also ran high, notwithstanding that many émigré London Irish were Protestants.

[19] Laurence Dermott (1720-1791), the Antients' grand secretary (1752-70) and deputy grand master (1771-77, 1783-87).

[20] Henry Sadler, *Masonic Facts and Fictions* (1887); reprinted Kessinger Publishing, 2003.

[21] Anon., *A Defence of Free-Masonry as Practiced in the Regular Lodges, both Foreign and Domestic under the Constitution of the English Grand Master* (London: Printed for the Author and sold by W. Flexney, near Gray's Inn Gate, Holborn, 1765).

[22] Cf., Ric Berman, 'Headnotes' in Róbert Péter (ed), *British Freemasonry, 1717-1813*, volume 4: *Debates*, pp. 129-50.

a common desire for social and financial betterment.[23] And this was equally true on the other side of the Atlantic where Antients freemasonry captured the new American zeitgeist.

ANTIENTS FREEMASONS

The early registers of the Antients Grand Lodge from the 1750s contain details of thousands of members.[24] More than a quarter were skilled artisans, including gold and silversmiths, clock and watch-makers, printers and book-binders; and almost the same number were in professional occupations, including apothecaries and attorneys, or were merchant-traders. Others are more difficult to categorise but many who are listed in apparently low-end livings and described as tailors, weavers, hat-makers, painters and wig-makers were not employees but employers defined by their business.

Antients freemasonry was not for the poorest. Membership and dining fees, and the obligatory charitable contributions, were set at levels too onerous for most working men and those who could not find the money were obliged to resign or were expelled for non-payment.[25]

But for those who could afford to join there were multiple reasons to remain. The lodge provided an exclusive space for fraternal association, a spiritual experience, and opportunities for self-improvement.

One of the most important factors for the aspirational Irish and the lower middling writ large was the benefit of belonging to a proto-friendly

---

[23] Cf., *Schism*, esp. chapter three.

[24] *Registers of the Grand Lodge of the Antients, 1751-1813*: UGLE Library and Museum of Freemasonry: GBR 1991 ANT 3/1/10. Cf., also, J. R. Dashwood (ed.), *Early Records of the Grand Lodge of England according to the Old Institutions* (London: Quatuor Coronati Lodge No. 2076, 1958), published as *Quatuor Coronatorum Antigrapha*, vol. XI; and *Schism*, esp. chapter three.

[25] Cf. for example, Minute Books and Treasurer's Book of Lodge No. 4 (Antients); and Minute Books of No. 6 (Antients); No. 20 (Antients) and No. 55 (Antients); all at UGLE Library & Museum.

society that offered opportunities for networking on a local, national and even international scale.

Membership of a lodge provided access to a community of other Antients' lodges, not only in Britain and Ireland but also America, the Caribbean and elsewhere, with a masonic membership certificate attesting to the holder's financial and masonic respectability.[26]

THE ANTIENTS GRAND LODGE

The five Irish-led lodges that founded the Antients Grand Lodge in London in 1751[27] were joined by another four within twelve months and a further thirty within five years, by which point the number of members recorded in the registers exceeded a thousand.[28] Two decades later the Antients had over 200 lodges across London, provincial England and overseas, a figure that excludes lodges warranted by Pennsylvania and other overseas grand lodges, and lodges that lacked the formality of an Antients' warrant.

Membership growth was underpinned partly by the decision of a prominent Anglo Irish aristocrat, the Earl of Blessington, to accept the titular role

---

[26] 'Received honourably, as he has paid all his dues in our lodge'. Cf., Minutes of Lodge No. 20 for 2 September 1754. Quoted in *Schism*, pp. 63-4.

[27] The Antients Grand Lodge came into being following a meeting at the Turk's Head tavern in Greek Street on 17 July 1751. The meeting was attended by about eighty masons from five lodges: the Turk's Head; The Cripple, Little Britain; The Cannon, Water Lane, Fleet Street; The Plaisterers' Arms, Gray's Inn Lane; and The Globe, Bridges Street, Covent Garden. The new grand lodge referred to itself as a Grand Committee until 27 December 1753.

[28] *Registers of the Grand Lodge of the Antients, 1751-1813*. Associated records include registers of returns: GBR 1991 ANT 3/2.

of grand master,[29] and by the publication of *Ahiman Rezon*,[30] the Antients' book of constitutions.

Dermott, as grand secretary, used *Ahiman Rezon* to position Antients freemasonry as a body that would 'keep the ancient landmarks in view', and in describing the rival Grand Lodge of England as 'Moderns', a word that was designed to be and was derogatory, he raised doubts as to their masonic legitimacy. Dermott reinforced his points with humour and irony, and satirised traditional masonic historiography. His literary style was deliberately at odds with the more precious approach of the Moderns' chroniclers and his conversational tone reflected the Antients greater accessibility.

Although *Ahiman Rezon* borrowed heavily from Spratt,[31] which was itself a plagiarised version of Anderson's *Constitutions*,[32] the book was immensely popular in Britain, Ireland and North America.

Six editions were published in England during Dermott's lifetime and at least another six in the two decades to 1813.[33] Over the same period more than twenty editions were printed in Ireland while in North America *Ahiman Rezon* circulated widely and would provide the basis for the constitutions of most state grand lodges.[34]

---

[29] William Stewart, 1st Earl of Blessington (1709-1769); GM of the Grand Lodge of Ireland (1738-39); GM of the Antients (1756-60).

[30] Laurence Dermott, *Ahiman Rezon* (London, 1756).

[31] Laurence Spratt, *New Book of Constitutions* (Dublin, 1751). Spratt was grand secretary of the Grand Lodge of Ireland.

[32] James Anderson, *New Book of Constitutions* (London, 1738).

[33] A second edition was published in 1764; a third in 1778; and a fourth, fifth and sixth in 1779, 1780 and 1782, respectively. Other editions were published in 1795, 1797, 1800, 1801, 1807 and 1813. There were also many plagiarised versions, copyright being impossible to enforce effectively.

[34] The Grand Lodge of Pennsylvania published an edition in 1783 dedicated to George Washington, and other states followed suit. The Grand Lodge of Virginia issued *Constitutions and Regulations ... containing the New Ahiman Rezon* in 1791; Maryland published a version in 1797; and New York, Georgia, South Carolina

FREEMASONRY ON THE AMERICAN FRONTIER

A minority of Irish and Scottish migrants were already freemasons when they arrived in America. Others were initiated into freemasonry afterwards. And as they moved west to settle the back-country of Pennsylvania and Virginia, and south-west along the wagon trails to the Piedmont, they carried their freemasonry with them.

The chartering of Antients, Irish and Scottish lodges in the middle and southern colonies is documented from the late 1750s. The provincial grand lodge of Pennsylvania was highly active, warranting lodges not only in Pennsylvania but also Virginia, Delaware, Maryland, New Jersey, and North and South Carolina.[35] Other lodges were chartered by the Grand Lodge of Scotland and Mother Kilwinning Lodge, the latter warranting at least two lodges in Virginia. And many American lodges operated without a formal charter.

Irish, Scottish and Antients freemasonry were also transported to America by the British military, many of whose regiments were deployed to Ireland before crossing the Atlantic and granted travelling warrants by the Grand Lodge of Ireland.[36] Others regiments received warrants directly

---

and North Carolina produced bespoke editions in the early nineteenth century. North Carolina's edition of *Ahiman Rezon* was printed in New Bern in 1805 by order of the Grand Lodge of North Carolina and Tennessee. New York published its own edition the same year.

[35] Norris S. Barratt & Julius F. Sachse, *Freemasonry in Pennsylvania, 1727-1907* (Philadelphia, PA: Grand Lodge of Philadelphia, 1908); also Charles E. Meyer, *Masonic Lodges in Pennsylvania from 1730-1880* in *History of the Grand Lodge of Pennsylvania* (Philadelphia, PA: Library Committee of the Grand Lodge of Pennsylvania, 1877). Ibid, pp. x-xi; and Julius F. Sachse, *Old Masonic Lodges of Pennsylvania, Moderns and Ancients, 1730-1800* (Philadelphia, PA: Grand Lodge of Philadelphia, 1912).

[36] The officer commanding British forces in America, Jeffrey Amherst, had at least nineteen regimental lodges under his command all but two of which held Irish, Antients or Scottish warrants.

from the Antients Grand Lodge in London, which was keen to encourage America's 'right worshipful and very worthy gentlemen' to join its version of the Craft.[37]

In North Carolina, Antients and Irish lodges mark the path of Scots-Irish migration from the 1750s onwards. Old Cone at Salisbury and Phalanx at Charlotte were established on the Upper Road of the Great Wagon Trail. Dornoch and Blandford-Bute at Warrenton, and Union at Fayetteville, were located on the Fall Line Road. Caswell Brotherhood Lodge was founded between the Upper Road and an offshoot of the Great Valley Road. Other lodges mark new settlements on the western frontier, for example, Independence Lodge at Pittsboro in Chatham County, and Rutherford Fellowship Lodge in Rutherford County.

Once planted, Antients freemasonry flourished across the Piedmont, providing a social and spiritual forum and a means of 'polite' fraternal association. Membership encompassed aspirational farmers and planters; store-keepers and tavern-owners; and local merchants.

This was also the case elsewhere, including South Carolina. In his *History of Freemasonry*, Mackey comments on how Antients freemasonry dominated post-war South Carolina,[38] describing the organisation as 'very popular' and '[embracing] many of the intelligent and influential citizens of the state'. The Grand Lodge of the State of South Carolina, Ancient York Masons, was established four years after the war and by 1791 had thirty-five lodges on its roster.[39] Just nine years later in 1800, there were fifty-two Antients lodges in the state, with others chartered in Georgia and Florida.

Pennsylvania may not have instigated the roll-out of Antients freemasonry across the middle and southern colonies but it expedited the process.

---

[37] Dermott, *Ahiman Rezon* (London, 1764), 2nd edn.

[38] Albert G. Mackey, *History of Freemasonry in South Carolina* (Columbia, SC: South Carolinian Steam Press, 1861), p. 53.

[39] Ibid., pp. 69-73.

Philadelphia's lodge No. 4[40] had applied for recognition to the Antients Grand Lodge in London in June 1758 and the relevant minutes record that their petition was presented to the grand master's lodge, No. 1, at the Five Bells Tavern in September 1759.[41]

Barratt & Sachse in *Freemasonry in Pennsylvania* offer a slightly different chronology, stating that lodge No. 4 received its provincial grand warrant from London in January 1759.[42] The implication is that Dermott issued the warrant in advance of obtaining formal approval.

But the more important detail is that lodge No. 4 was unlike other Pennsylvania lodges. It had been constituted 'for seafaring men, artisans and tradesmen' and stood apart from Philadelphia's more elite lodges.[43]

The Antients changed the social demographics of American freemasonry. Unlike Moderns freemasonry which restricted membership principally to the more prominent men in society and was in part an advertisement for their social as well as financial and political standing, the Antients included those who had lesser social distinction and lower financial status.

Although America's Antient lodges were still relatively exclusive, they proved to be more flexible than their Moderns counterparts, sourcing members from a broader social spectrum and adopting Irish and London Irish mores.[44] The gulf between the Moderns and Antients grew and in Pennsylvania reached an extreme position such that when Benjamin Franklin, a former

---

[40] No. 4, then a Moderns lodge, had received its warrant on 24 June 1757.

[41] Dashwood, *Early Records of the Grand Lodge of England according to the Old Institutions*, p. 114.

[42] Barratt & Sachse, *Freemasonry in Pennsylvania, 1727-1907*, volume I, Preface, pp. viii-ix.

[43] Ibid. Cf., also, Bullock, 'The Revolutionary Transformation of American Freemasonry, 1752-1792'; and Bullock, *Revolutionary Brotherhood: Freemasonry and the Transformation of the American social order, 1730-1840* (Chapel Hill, NC: University of North Carolina Press, 1996).

[44] Many elements of Antients and Irish masonic ritual remain present in American freemasonry today.

Moderns provincial grand master, returned from Europe in 1785 he was not permitted to enter a Pennsylvania lodge without converting formally to become an Antient freemason.[45] He did not do so and his funeral in 1790 was not attended by Philadelphia's freemasons who were now entirely Antient; indeed, they would not mark his death formally until its second centenary.

But what may be more remarkable is that in post-war North Carolina, unlike many if not most of the thirteen new American states, there was no apparent antagonism or schism between Antients and Moderns freemasonry. When letters were sent out inviting the state's lodges to convene to establish a grand lodge and elect a grand master, all lodges were invited without distinction and all agreed to submit to its jurisdiction.

There is no obvious explanation. It remains to be explored whether this was a function of Joseph Montfort's probable links to Irish freemasonry, or the desire to avoid a repeat of the Regulator conflict that had divided east and west - or a product of both these and other factors.

---

[45] Bullock, 'The Revolutionary Transformation of American Freemasonry, 1752-1792'.

Chapter Nine

Governor Tryon and the Battle of the Alamance

The Regulator Movement

The scarcity and rising price of land along the eastern seaboard and inland coastal plain[1] encouraged tens of thousands of first, second and third generation migrants to move south and west into the Piedmont, the majority travelling overland from Pennsylvania and Maryland through Virginia. And what began as a trickle of incomers in the 1740s rose to a torrent in the second half of the eighteenth century. August Spangenberg, a Moravian bishop, chronicled the extent of migration as early as 1753,[2] noting that 'even in this year more than 400 families with horses, wagons and cattle have migrated'.

As settlement expanded, the Piedmont became marked by family farms strung out along its numerous rivers and creeks with their 'abundance of good wood ... meadow land and pasture'.[3] There were large and small

---

[1] Land prices may have been the principal driver but other influences behind western and southern migration included soil depletion, Quaker reluctance to defend Pennsylvania's western frontier, and a clash of religions. Cf., Robert W. Ramsey, *Carolina Cradle: Settlement of the Northwest Carolina Frontier, 1747-1762* (Chapel Hill, NC: UNCP, 1964).

[2] August Spangenberg, *The Moravian Diaries* (1752) in Andreas Lixl (ed), *Memories of Carolinian Immigrants: Autobiographies, Diaries, and Letters from Colonial Times to the Present* (Manham, MD: University Press of America, 2009), pp. 29-39.

[3] By the 1760s the Moravians had become a potent influence in Rowan, Mecklenburg and Cabarrus counties and within three decades accounted for around a quarter of settlers in those counties. But where the first generation of migrants were content with communal farming the second generation began to break away, with the proportion of those expelled or leaving the church accounting for around a quarter of the Moravian community after 1770.

farms, but no vast plantations as on the coastal plain. And although the assembly legislated a number of towns into being, many were launched with 'neither houses nor inhabitants [and] are towns only by Act of Assembly'.[4] William Few in 1764 commented that Hillsborough and Salisbury were villages of no more than thirty or forty inhabitants with a handful of stores and two or three ordinary taverns.[5] But size did not always reflect significance and both towns developed rapidly into commercial and social centres for the growing populations within their hinterlands.

Although the Piedmont was predominantly agricultural it was not a subsistence-based backwater nor was it cut-off from trade. Trails and tracks provided connections to towns east of the Fall Line and from there via the Tar, Neuse and South rivers to the Pamlico Sound or Cape Fear, and to the Atlantic coast. And although most east-west roads were impassable by wagon in poor weather they were used, and over time became an extensive network.

Nonetheless, North Carolina's geography dictated that the Piedmont's principal trading connections would be with South Carolina and Virginia rather than with the province's east coast. Access to overseas markets was more efficient and less costly via the navigable rivers that flowed south-east to Georgetown and Charleston, and along the wagon roads that ran north and south.

Although the Piedmont could in theory trade with almost every town from Philadelphia to Savannah, by the mid-1760s Charleston had become the region's most important commercial hub, its merchants offering competitive prices for exports and lower costs for imported products on better credit terms than their counterparts in Virginia, let alone Wilmington, Edenton and New Bern. Henry Laurens, among others, ventured as far as

---

[4] Spangenberg, *The Moravian Diaries*, pp. 29-39.
[5] Quoted in Harry Roy Merrens, *Colonial North Carolina in the Eighteenth Century* (Chapel Hill, NC: UNCP, 1964), p. 163.

Wachovia to secure trade and provided the additional incentive of a regular postal service alongside his factoring and merchant businesses.[6] Commerce between the Piedmont and South Carolina became a matter of routine and with wagons travelling around twenty miles per day, a 250-mile journey from Rowan County to Charleston could be completed in less than two weeks and the round trip in little more than a month.[7]

A network of stores and taverns across the Piedmont functioned as collection points for agricultural produce, furs and deerskins. The trade was vast and, as noted, the Moravians' Bethabara store alone accounted for more than 6% of the deerskins exported from Charleston in the 1760s.[8] The stores also provided an outlet for locally-made goods and imported manufactures, wine and spirits. Sales were commonly on credit or barter, an arrangement that eased the currency shortage, with store-keepers and merchants in effect providing a banking service.

As the Piedmont became more heavily settled, the region's under-representation in the provincial assembly became obvious. Pressure developed to secure the same rights to proportionate representation as in the east, and for the legislature, a body dominated by eastern commercial and social interests, to be obliged to consider the Piedmont's requirements. Regarded as particularly inequitable was the system of provincial taxation that levied the same rate on land on the frontier, several weeks by road or river from the coast, as on more accessible and fertile plantations on the coastal plain.

---

[6] Henry Laurens to John Ettwein, 19 January 1761 in Henry Laurens and Philip M. Hamer, *The Papers of Henry Laurens* (Columbia, SC: South Carolina Historical Society, 1972), volume 3, p. 56. Cf., also, *Records of the Moravians in North Carolina* (Raleigh, NC, 1922-69).

[7] Daniel B. Thorp, 'Doing Business in the Backcountry: Retail Trade in Colonial Rowan County, North Carolina', *William and Mary Quarterly*, 48.3 (1991), 387-408.

[8] Ibid., p. 392.

The Regulator Movement that developed lobbied for greater western autonomy and control over the region's own affairs. It was led by farmers and traders - entrepreneurs motivated by the prospect of developing land and accumulating wealth. Many had travelled to the Piedmont from Ireland to escape absentee landlords and legislators whose primary interests were not their own. Greater self-determination was a means to an end. It was a method to achieve lower and more equitable taxes, and public investments that would be of benefit to the west, not those such as Tryon Palace which brought zero advantage at a high cost. The movement also had a religious component, being led principally by dissenting and evangelical Protestants for whom private and public morality were paramount and intertwined.

The Regulators championed the interests of the Piedmont. They did not rail against royal government *per se*, nor pitch for notionally self-sufficient localism, nor were they engaged in a 'Marxist class struggle' against an exploitative merchant class. If anything, the movement had three main thrusts: economic self-interest; moral outrage at the corruption of North Carolina's east-coast legislators and their appointees; and a mission for religious self-determination.

The movement's leaders were generally affluent up-country farmers such as Herman Husband, Rednap Howell and James Hunter. Such men not only had the most to gain commercially and in financial terms, but had been excluded from provincial politics and, when elected, been treated with disdain.[9] The parallels with Ireland are self-evident.

Husband, a sometime Presbyterian and later a Quaker convert, was seized in May 1768 by Edmund Fanning and jailed at Hillsborough as a rebel organiser - albeit that Fanning was forced to release him when faced with mass public protests.[10] Husband was elected to the assembly the following

---

[9] For example, *CSRNC*, volume 8, pp. 268-70: Minutes of the North Carolina Governor's Council, 20 December 1770: the expulsion from the assembly and arrest of Herman Husband.

[10] Edmund Fanning (1739-1818), a New York-born, North Carolina lawyer, land speculator and colonial official.

year to represent Orange County but was expelled in the 1770 session for alleged libel and sedition. Tryon, who viewed the Regulators as an existential threat, ordered his arrest again in January 1771.[11]

With so many within the eastern establishment (including their representatives in the Piedmont) members of masonic lodges, Husband argued that freemasonry was an anti-democratic weapon used by the elites against the Piedmont: 'It seems that Fanning, and others of the Officers had impressed the minds of the People, in general with a belief, That such was the union of Brotherhood, founded in Masonry, that extended itself into all parts of the County, that it would be vain for the Planters, or common People, to make any attempt, by an election, either to turn the present Officers out, or to chuse others, from amongst themselves.'[12] 'And this accounts for what was said before of F[anning]'s influence with the Governor. It shows also how very careful the civil Officers were to make the Law a Secret; and this may account for what the People say of a Mason Club, whose system is Secrecy.'[13]

From their perspective, indeed, from most perspectives, the Piedmont's farmers and traders' grievances were unanswerable. They faced a tax and legal system that was biased against them and operated by eastern-appointed officials who enforced the law to their own advantage. Effective challenge through the ballot box was impossible while the Piedmont remained under-represented in the legislature. Nor was redress available through the courts, which were dominated by eastern appointees. And with fines and fees levied upon them, the common assessment was that their efforts in clearing

---

[11] Although he was jailed at New Bern, Husband was released when the charge of libel was dropped.

[12] Herman Husband, 'A Fan for Fanning' in William K. Boyd (ed), *Some Eighteenth Century Tracts Concerning North Carolina* (Raleigh, NC: North Carolina Historical Commission, 1927), p. 353. I am grateful to Jonathan Underwood for pointing out this reference.

[13] Ibid., p. 359.

and farming would be for nought if the land was then open to seizure and exploitation by a cabal of eastern lawyers, merchants and placemen.[14]

Other grievances compounded the economic pain. Before 1748, taxes and other official payments could be settled in rated commodities or via promissory notes issued by the warehouses in which rated commodities were stored.[15] After 1748 the use of commodities was withdrawn and in 1768 promissory notes were terminated, with payments accepted only in specie, bills of credit or proclamation money.

The decision caused dissent across North Carolina but especially in the Piedmont, where the argument was not limited to *how* taxes should be paid but extended to *whether* they should be paid and how they should be assessed.

Husband argued that the Piedmont's taxes were too high relative to those paid by those in the east and should be proportionate to profit and payable in rated produce: 'the public taxes is an unequal burden on the poor of this province, by reason the poorest man is taxed as high as the richest. Allowing the taxes to be all necessary, yet there ought to be some regard had to the strength of the beast; for all asses are not equally strong. We ought to be taxed accordingly to the profits of each man's estate. And as we have no trade to circulate money, this tax ought to be paid in country produce'.[16]

---

[14] Cf., James P. Whittenburg, 'Planters, Merchants, and Lawyers: Social Change and the Origins of the North Carolina Regulation', *William and Mary Quarterly*, 34.2 (1977), 215-38, for an overview of the opposing arguments. Also, A. Roger Ekirch, *'Poor Carolina': Politics and Society in Colonial North Carolina, 1729-1776* (Chapel Hill, NC: UNCP, 2011), new edition.

[15] A 1740 law had rated products used to pay taxes and settle debts.

[16] Herman Husband, *An Impartial Relation of the First Rise and Cause of the Recent Differences in Publick Affairs, in the Progress of the So Much Talked of Regulation in North Carolina* (1770).

Although the same problems were present across the American frontier, their impact in the Piedmont was disproportionately large.[17] Between 1750 and 1780, North Carolina's white population increased by almost 130,000 from around 52,000 to 180,000, the vast majority of whom had settled above the Fall Line.[18]

Others Regulator leaders, such as George Sims,[19] protested against the 'malpractices of the Officers of our County Court, and the abuses which we suffer by those empowered to manage our public affairs'.[20] Sims attacked the excessive fees charged by lawyers, court officials and sheriffs that could dwarf the value of legal claims, and the inequity that forced those claimants unable to pay into penury, with their estates sold at auction at a fraction of intrinsic value to satisfy their debts. The Regulators' manifesto was clear:

> That we will pay no Taxes until we are satisfied they are agreeable to Law and Applied to the purposes therein mentioned unless we cannot help and are forced.
>
> That we will pay no Officer any more fees than the Law allows unless we are obliged to it and then to shew a dislike to it & bear open testimony against it.
>
> That we will attend our Meetings of Conference as often as we conveniently can or is necessary in order to consult our representatives on the amendment of such Laws as may be found grievous or unnecessary and to choose more suitable men than we have heretofore done for Burgesses and Vestry men and to Petition His Excellency our Governor the Hon.

---

[17] Cf., D. Andrew Johnson, 'The Regulation Reconsidered: Shared Grievances in the Colonial Carolinas, *South Carolina Historical Magazine*, 114.2 (2013), 132-54.

[18] Colonial and Pre-Federal Statistics, Series Z 1-19.

[19] George Sims (1728-1808), a schoolmaster, farmer and later Regulator leader. He was descended from a relatively wealthy Virginia planter family and by the 1780s owned over 1,000 acres and six slaves. Cf., *DNCB*.

[20] George Sims, *An Address to the People of Granville County* (1765).

the Council and the Worshipful House of representatives His Majesty in Parliament &c. for redress of such Grievances as in the course of this undertaking may occur and to inform one another & to learn, know and enjoy all the Privileges & Liberties that are allowed us and were settled on us by our worthy Ancestors the founders of the present Constitution in order to preserve it in its ancient Foundation that it may stand firm & unshaken.

That we will contribute to Collections for defraying necessary expenses attending the work according to our abilities.

That in Cases of differences in Judgment we will submit to the Majority of our Body.[21]

WILLIAM TRYON

North Carolina was in political turmoil when William Tryon (1729-1788), was appointed governor, and his time in office is defined largely by his uncompromising response to the Regulator Movement.

Tryon has been characterised as a loyal public servant who, when faced with the fall-out from the Stamp Act crisis, defended the crown's prerogative to tax but, at the same time, sought a compromise and to lessen discontent by offering to pay personally many of the duties the act imposed. But Tryon could be inflexible to the point of arrogance where his authority was questioned and when convinced of his righteousness. It is this which explains his insistence on deploying the militia with lethal force against the

---

[21] *CSRNC*, volume 7, pp. 671-2: Regulators' Advertisement No. 4, January 1768. Cf., also, William K. Boyd (ed), *Some Eighteenth Century Tracts Concerning North Carolina* (Raleigh, NC: North Carolina Historical Commission, 1927); William S. Powell, James K. Huhta, and Thomas J. Farnham (eds), *The Regulators in North Carolina: A Documentary History, 1759-1776* (Raleigh, NC: Department of State Archives, 1971).

Regulators, notwithstanding that he was encouraged to do so by many within North Carolina's east-coast establishment.

Like his predecessors, Tryon, a prosperous army officer, became governor of North Carolina as a result of patronage and connections. His father, Charles,[22] owned an estate at Bulwick Hall in Northampton and was a former High Sheriff of Northamptonshire,[23] and his mother, Lady Mary Shirley, was the daughter of the 1st Earl Ferrers[24] by his second wife, Selina Finch.[25] Following their marriage they moved to Norbury Park, a vast wooded estate in Surrey inherited by Lady Mary.

Family influence allowed Tryon to obtain a commission in 1751 as a lieutenant in the 1st Foot Guards, a prestigious regiment.[26] He acquired a captaincy the same year and by 1758 held the rank of lieutenant-colonel. His marriage a year earlier to the daughter of a former East India Company merchant and governor of Bombay, William Wake,[27] brought a £30,000 dowry and what would be a useful connection to Wills Hill, Earl of Hillsborough (1718-1793), president of the Board of Trade from 1763-65 and again in 1766-67, and secretary of state for the colonies, a new department of state, from 1768-72.[28] It was Hillsborough's support that underpinned Tryon's appointment in 1764 as deputy governor to an ailing Arthur Dobbs, his

---

[22] Charles Tryon (1702-1763).

[23] *London Gazette*, 10 January 1737.

[24] Robert Shirley, 1st Earl Ferrers (1650-1717).

[25] Selina Finch Shirley (1681-1762).

[26] A commission was not just a matter of paying. It also required the right social connections.

[27] *The India List and India Office List* (London: Harrison, 1819), p. 126.

[28] Wills Hill, known as Viscount Hillsborough (1742-93), Earl of Hillsborough (1751-89), and 1st Marquess of Downshire (1789-93). Cf., Peter Marshall, *ODNB*, online edn, January 2008.

confirmation as Dobbs' successor the following year, and his subsequent appointment as governor of New York.[29]

Tryon followed in his predecessors' steps in North Carolina by supporting settlement of the interior and seeking to improve the collection of quit-rents. A definitive boundary between North and South Carolina was agreed, internal administration upgraded, and Tryon toured widely to improve his knowledge of the province's geography and his understanding of its colonists.

He was also adamant that measures be explored to improve North Carolina's trade and standing. But mixed in with what can be viewed as a relatively progressive approach to office was a sense of prerogative and entitlement instilled by Tryon's aristocratic upbringing. It was evident in the design and commission of his proposed new gubernatorial residence and office, a building known as 'Tryon Palace', self-described as 'a Governor's House [which] will exceed for magnificence and architecture any edifice on the continent'.[30]

Tryon had started to plan the building before he left England and convinced John Hawks,[31] a master builder and architect, to accompany him to North Carolina to work on the project. Despite some opposition, the legislature was persuaded to allocate £15,000 for design and construction; work began in 1767 and the structure was completed four years later.

---

[29] *CSRNC*, volume 6, p. 1055: William Tryon to Wills Hill, Marquis of Downshire, 16 October 1764.

[30] Tryon to the Earl of Shelburne, 23 February 1767, in William S. Powell, *The Correspondence of William Tryon* (Raleigh, NC: Division of Archives and History, 1980), volume I, p. 432; also, Jeanne L. Barnes, *Deconstructing Tryon Palace* (Wilmington, NC: MA thesis, 2005): https://libres.uncg.edu/ir/uncw/f/barnesj2005-1.pdf, accessed 10 October 2017.

[31] John Hawks (c.1731-1790). Hawks had trained with Stiff Leadbetter, a fashionable English architect with a string of aristocratic clients known best for his Palladian works.

While arguably a source of pride for some within the east coast establishment – 'a public ornament and credit to the Colony, as well as an honor to British America'[32] – construction was viewed less positively elsewhere and not only in the Piedmont, where taxes were raised by 8s per head to finance the costs.

An open letter criticising Tryon printed in the *Virginia Gazette* would have mirrored the thoughts of many in North Carolina – 'regardless of every moral as well as legal obligation, [you] changed the plan of a province-house for that of a palace, worthy the residence of a prince of the blood, and augmented the expense to fifteen thousand pounds. Here, Sir, you betrayed your trust, disgracefully to the governor and dishonorably to the man … You reduced the next Assembly … to the unjust alternative of granting ten thousand pounds more or sinking the five thousand they had already granted. They chose the former. It was most pleasing to the governor but directly contrary to the sense of their constituents'.[33]

Dissent in North Carolina's western counties was more direct: 'we want no such House, nor will we pay for it'.[34] Complaints against inequitable and excessive taxation were already being voiced, and a construction levy to be paid regardless of income or wealth did nothing but aggravate existing tensions.

Western sentiment against Tryon was exacerbated further by his support for building new Anglican churches across the Piedmont and his promotion of the Society for the Propagation of Christian Knowledge, whose

---

[32] *CSRNC*, volume 8, pp. 282-302: Minutes of the Upper House of the North Carolina General Assembly, 5-31 December 1770.
[33] *CSRNC*, volume 8, pp. 718-27: 'Atticus' to Tryon, 7 November 1771. [Attributed to Maurice Moore.]
[34] Quoted in William S. Powell, *North Carolina through Four Centuries* (Chapel Hill, NC: UNCP, 1989), p. 148.

missionaries were regarded as unnecessary and intrusive.[35] The promotion of Anglicanism was seen as an affront to the dissenting and evangelical faiths that dominated the west, and to the Regulator Movement's leaders who shared those faiths.

That the movement took off shortly after the Great Awakening was not a coincidence. Many in the Piedmont drew a link between religious liberty and its civil counterpart, and opposition to the influence of the Anglican Church was not restricted to the additional taxes levied to finance it but included a call for greater religious autonomy.[36]

Notwithstanding the growing percentage of North Carolina's population that was living west of the Fall Line and the political legitimacy of the demand for proportionate representation, the Regulators were positioned by the east-coast establishment as rebels seeking to undermine the authority of the legislature and the governor, and thus the crown:

> Men who call themselves regulators [have] sapped its whole foundation, brought its courts of Justice to their own control, leaped the strong barrier of private property, and audaciously violated the laws of God and man.[37] In short, all civil government in Orange County is relaxed, the courts of justice totally stopped, and everything reduced to the power and control of a set of men who call themselves regulators; but are in fact

---

[35] The Anglican establishment had pursued a narrow policy of religious recognition to the extent that Presbyterian marriages were not legal in North Carolina until 1766. Tryon later reversed his stance, supporting the Moravians and encouraging the establishment of Queen's College in Mecklenberg County, a Presbyterian school.

[36] Cf., A. Roger Ekirch, '"A New Government of Liberty": Herman Husband's Vision of Backcountry North Carolina, 1755', *William and Mary Quarterly*, 34.4 (1977), 632-46, for an exposition of this viewpoint; also Arthur Palmer Hudson, 'Songs of the North Carolina Regulators', *William and Mary Quarterly*, 4.4 (1947), 470-85.

[37] *Virginia Gazette*, 25 October 1770, dated New Bern, 5 October 1770.

no other than a desperate and cruel banditi, actuated by principles that no laws can restrain, no honour or conscience bind.[38]

In New Bern, the movement was deemed an insurrection and was to be treated as such. The legislature passed Samuel Johnston's Riot Act, which made any gathering of ten or more unlawful when ordered to disperse by a justice or sheriff. The penalty for a failure to comply would be death.[39] The act was signed by Richard Caswell as speaker of the assembly in January 1771, and by James Hasell and William Tryon as president of the council and governor, respectively.

The proximate background to the legislation was an attack on Edmund Fanning and his colleagues in Hillsborough the previous September, a protest whose particulars were publicised widely to bolster anti-Regulator sentiment: 'When they had fully glutted their revenge on the lawyers, and particularly Colonel Fanning, to shew their opinion of courts of justice they took from his chains a negro that had been executed some time, and placed him at the lawyer's bar, and filled the Judge's seat with human excrement, in derision and contempt of the characters that fill those respectable places.'[40]

But a letter from the New Bern District Court of Oyer and Terminer two months after the act had been signed into law made clear that Regulator opposition had not been dented:

> Whereas a number of unthinking and deluded People, inhabitants of the county of Orange and of the neighbouring counties in this Province, under the influence and direction of several Wicked, Seditious, Evil Designing and disaffected Persons have assumed to themselves the Title of Regulators and in open Defiance of the Law of the Land, in great Numbers, under Arms, assembled together, violently resisted insulted

---

[38] Ibid.
[39] The Act was passed into law on 15 January 1771.
[40] *Virginia Gazette*, 25 October 1770.

and beat the sheriffs and other officers in the execution of their Office and expressly refused to pay their shares of the Public Taxes laid by the General Assembly of the Province for the support of Government, and at the last superior Court of Justice held for the District of Hillsborough in the month of September last, assembled together, in a riotous and tumultuous manner, barbarously insulted and broke up that Court, cruelly beating and wounding the Officers thereof, destroying and pillaging the Houses of such Persons who were obnoxious to their Ringleaders and have lately assembled themselves in great numbers armed and arrayed in warlike manner and publickly avowing their intention of Marching to Newbern and of carrying into execution by Force their hostile measures.

We, the Grand Jury of the district of Newbern being thoroughly sensible that actions and attempts so execrable and mischievous (if permitted) are plain usurpations of the Power of the Legislature, substituting in its place armed and lawless Force, and thereby leaving as a prey to the stronger the lives, liberties and properties of our weaker fellow subjects, and that honest industry can have an existence only no longer than property, which is the Fruits of it, is secured by fixed and established Laws. And we being fully and perfectly sensible of the great happiness and liberty which the subjects of this Province do enjoy under his Majesty's gentle and benign Administration thereof and that such flagitious crimes, in proportion to the success of them, must necessarily be subversive of the invaluable Blessings, and introductive of Anarchy and Confusion, Do therefore present all such wicked, seditious, evil, designing and disaffected Persons, who under the Title of Regulators have hitherto perpetrated or attempted to perpetrate or may hereafter attempt to perpetrate such enormous crimes or Offences, as being enemies to his Majesty's Person and Government, and to the liberty, happiness and tranquillity of his good and faithful subjects of the Province.[41]

---

[41] *CSRNC*, volume 8, pp. 528-32: Minutes of the New Bern District Court of Oyer and Terminer, 11-16 March 1771.

The missive provoked an immediate response from Tryon, who ordered the provincial militia to muster and march against the Regulators. The first militia company assembled at New Bern in the third week of April. Other companies joined subsequently and by early May Tryon had more than 1,000 men under his command.

Tryon's militia troops left Hillsborough for Salisbury on 11 May with the intention of joining forces with General Hugh Waddell, who was gathering companies from the south and west of the province.[42] Tryon paused at Alamance Creek on route, where more than 2,000 Regulators had gathered at a plantation owned by Michael Holt.[43] On 16 May Tryon ordered his forces to move into position against the Regulators and issued a demand that they disperse. The ultimatum was ignored and battle commenced an hour later.

The Regulators' numerical superiority was insufficient to overcome Tryon's better-trained militia, which included artillery - two field cannons and four swivel guns. And although nine militiamen were killed and sixty-one wounded, Regulator casualties were substantially higher, with upwards of 300 killed and wounded. Fifteen prisoners were taken, one of whom was hanged on the battlefield, and in the trials that followed another twelve were found guilty of treason, six of whom were executed. The movement's principal leaders - Herman Husband, Rednap Howell, James Hunter and William Butler - escaped capture, were outlawed, and all bar Hunter fled the colony.

---

[42] Hugh Waddell (1734-1773), merchant, planter, militia officer and political official, born in County Down, Ireland and a friend of Arthur Dobbs. Much of Waddell's militia was drawn from the Piedmont and shared pro-Regulator sentiments. This explains Waddell's decision to decline to engage a Regulator force while on route to join Tryon and his subsequent retreat to Salisbury.

[43] Michael Holt (1723-1799), a farmer, one of the justices of the peace in Orange County and a captain in the militia. He had been one of several local officials attacked during the rioting in Hillsborough.

The Battle of Alamance effectively ended Regulator resistance. However, the nature of the battle and the numbers killed and wounded led to condemnation of Tryon, even in the east: 'All your duty could possibly require of you on this occasion, if it required anything at all, was to direct a prosecution against the offenders. You should have carefully avoided becoming a party in the dispute. But, Sir, your genius could not lie still; you enlisted yourself a volunteer in this service and entered into a negotiation with the Regulators, which at once disgraced you and encouraged them. They despised the governor who had degraded his own character by taking part in a private quarrel, and insulted the man whom they considered as personally their enemy. The terms of accommodation your Excellency had offered them were treated with contempt. What they were, I never knew; they could not have related to public offences; these belong to another jurisdiction. All hopes of settling the mighty contest by treaty ceasing, you prepared to decide it by means more agreeable to your martial disposition, an appeal to the sword.'[44]

Tryon left North Carolina for the greater prize of governor of New York within days of the victory. His successor, Josiah Martin,[45] continued and extended Tryon's policy of offering pardons to those willing to swear an oath of allegiance and within two months over 6,000 Regulators had accepted, including Hunter. Nonetheless, having completed a tour of the Piedmont, Martin's reports to London made clear that many of the Regulators' grievances had been and remained valid:

---

[44] 'Atticus' to Tryon, 7 November 1771.

[45] Josiah Martin (1737-1786), last royal governor of North Carolina. Born in Dublin, Ireland, to a wealthy Anglo-Irish family with large estates in the Caribbean and North America, he benefited from the protection and patronage of his older half-brother, Samuel Martin (1714-1788), MP for Camelford (1747-68) then Hastings (1768-74), agent for Montserrat, 1742-49, and for Nevis, 1744-50; secretary to the Chancellor of the Exchequer, 1754-55; secretary of the Treasury, 1756-57 and 1758-63; and treasurer to the Princess of Wales, 1757-72. Lord Hillsborough was a close friend.

I now see most clearly that they have been provoked by insolence and cruel advantages taken of the peoples ignorance by mercenary tricking attorneys, clerks, and other little officers who have practiced upon them every sort of rapine and extortion by which having brought upon themselves their just resentment they engaged government in their defence by artful misrepresentations that the vengeance the wretched people in folly and madness aimed at their heads was directed against the constitution and by this stratagem they threw an odium upon the injured people that by degrees begat a prejudice which precluded a full discovery of their grievances.

Thus My Lord, as far as I am able to discern, the resentment of government was craftily worked up against the oppressed, and the protection which the oppressors treacherously acquired where the injured and ignorant people expected to find it drove them to acts of desperation and confederated them in violences which as your Lordship knows induced bloodshed and I verily believe necessarily.

Enquiries of this sort My Lord I am sensible are invidious nor would anything but a sense of duty have drawn from me these opinions of the principles of the past troubles of this country.[46]

It is not known whether Tryon was initiated into freemasonry while in England. The masonic records that cover the relevant period are sparse at best. And other than when he attended the dinner hosted by St John's Lodge at New Bern to celebrate the feast of St John the Baptist, there is little indication of Tryon's involvement with freemasonry in North Carolina other than the masonic connection with Edmund Fanning complained of by Herman Husband.[47]

---

[46] *CSRNC*, volume 9, pp. 329-33: Josiah Martin to Wills Hill, Marquis of Downshire, 30 August 1772.

[47] *North Carolina Magazine or Universal Intelligencer*, 21-28 December 1764.

If correct, this is intriguing and throws a light on eighteenth-century colonial governance. However, a counter argument would be that few colonial governors appear to have been willing to meet 'on the level' with those they governed, even when they had previously been involved with freemasonry at a senior level. One of the more obvious examples is that of James Wright, the provincial grand master for South Carolina before becoming governor of Georgia. Wright is not recorded as having attended the Lodge at Savannah, notwithstanding that more than half his royal council and many, if not most, of his senior officials were freemasons.

Regardless, several members of Tryon's family *were* freemasons, including his first cousin, the Hon. Robert Shirley (1723-1787), a member of the King's Arms Lodge in the Strand in London. Shirley was a grand steward in 1745-46 and served as senior grand warden from 1747-51.[48] That Tryon Palace was used as a meeting place for St John's Lodge at New Bern is not significant. Tryon had left the colony by the time that occurred.

---

[48] Cf., *Schism*, pp. 157, 201-2.

CHAPTER TEN

IRISH, ANTIENTS AND OTHER EARLY NORTH CAROLINA LODGES

OLD CONE LODGE, SALISBURY

Situated along the Great Wagon Road where it met the Upper or Western Great Road, and close to the Yadkin River, Salisbury was almost certainly named not for the English cathedral city but after the town in Maryland from where a number of mainly Irish settlers originated.[1]

The settlement was a stopping point on the trails running south and a trading post with burgeoning links to the interior. In 1753 it was chosen to be the administrative centre of the newly created Rowan County. It was incorporated as a town two years later,[2] a deed from Lord Granville conveying the land on which construction would take place.[3]

The Great Wagon Road and Upper Road provided the principal routes along which settlers arrived in Rowan County. Settlement was first in the corridor between the trails, with subsequent migrants moving along the Yadkin River and west to the Catawba River, and then along the Catawba and Yadkin valleys toward the Blue Ridge Mountains. Most incomers bought and cleared land for family farms and small plantations, but a minority opened stores, workshops and taverns, and prospered from the growing population and the steady stream of travellers heading south and west.

---

[1] *CSRNC*, volume 4, xxi-xxii: preface.

[2] The court house at Salisbury served Rowan, Orange and Anson counties. Cf., *CSRNC*, volume 5, pp. 260-1: Minutes of the Lower House of the North Carolina General Assembly, 12-31 December 1754.

[3] Jethro Rumple, *A History of Rowan County, North Carolina* (Salisbury, NC: J.J. Bruner, 1881), p. 76.

Known Members of Old Cone Lodge, Salisbury, pre-1800
1775-95 [4]

William Temple Coles[5] John Armstrong
James Craig Alexander Dobbin
David Caldwell Montfort Stokes
John Steele

1795-97 [6]

(in the order in which they are first named in the minutes)

Samuel Dayton[7] William Lee Alexander
John H. Petchey Hugh Cunningham
William Cupples Michael Troy
Owen Mailey William Hampton
David Miller George Miller
Thomas Carson Hudson Hughes

---

[4] It is likely but not proven that Captain John Stokes (1756-1790), Montfort's younger brother, was a member of the lodge. He does not appear in the minutes but John and Montfort were fellow members of the Royal White Hart, both recorded in 1783, and there is no reason to believe that John would not have attended Old Cone.

[5] Also written as 'Cole'. Cf., *CSRNC*, volume 7, pp. 460-1: William Tryon to John Stuart, 20 May 1767: 'William Temple Cole the messenger is a very trusty person and may be safely charged with your intelligence'.

[6] Members of the lodge after 1800 include Joseph Pearson, John Farris, David Brannon, Hugh Newman, Henry Freeland, John Fulton, David Caldwell, Sr., Edwin J. Osborne, Nathan Chaffin, Jr., Jess Pearson, Benjamin Toris, David Woodson, Jacob Fisher, Charles C. McKenzie and Thomas Holmes. Some may also have been members earlier. Cf., *NOCALORE*, 6 (1936), 24.

[7] Dayton died in 1796. The lodge met in February that year to discuss his burial arrangements.

David Caldwell	Andrew Caldwell
David Cowan	Robert Torrance
Hugh Newnan	Samuel Cummins
Thomas Clarke	John Harris
Douglas Haydon[8]	Henry Pennington
James Williams	Thomas Hudson
Jesse Haydon	John McClelland
Isaac Jones	Barnabus Dunn
Conrad Brem	Robert Williams, Jr.
Anderson Hunt[9]	Adlai Osborne
David Brannon	Hugh Campbell[10]
Joseph Clarke	Hugh Newman
Barnabas Dunn	James Farris
Henry Freeland	

Parramore suggests that Old Cone was the 'missing' eighth lodge chartered by Montfort.[11] Patterson takes a similar view but states that the lodge was warranted in 1774 by 'Joseph Stokes', a confusing combination of Joseph Montfort and Montfort Stokes.[12] Both are probably incorrect. Salisbury too far inland to have been constituted by Montfort and the available evidence suggests that Old Cone was an Irish or Antients lodge established by Irish Protestant settlers in or before the early 1770s.

The earliest known member of the lodge is William Temple Coles (d.1775), born in Aungier Street, Dublin, one of the grandest pre-Georgian

---

[8] Also written as 'Hayden'.
[9] Hunt's death was reported on 20 August 1796. He received a Masonic burial.
[10] Master of the lodge, 1801-05.
[11] Parramore, *Launching the Craft*, p. 33.
[12] Daniel W. Patterson, *The True Image: Gravestone Art and the Culture of Scotch Irish Settlers in the Pennsylvania and Carolina Backcountry* (Chapel Hill, NC: UNCP, 2012), 159-60.

thoroughfares in the city.[13] Coles, a tavern owner in Salisbury, had been a town commissioner and magistrate.[14] He was also sheriff of Rowan County.[15] His will, written in 1775 with probate granted two years later, includes a request that he receive masonic burial rites and a legacy gifting a half-acre lot in the centre of Salisbury as a burial ground, half of which was for the exclusive use of 'the Society of Free Masons'.[16]

There are no records to indicate that Old Cone was chartered by any of the home grand lodges, nor by Pennsylvania, nor by Montfort. It was the lack of a warrant that probably underlay its petition to the Grand Lodge of North Carolina on 20 November 1788 requesting formal recognition. The petition was granted and Old Cone chartered and given warrant No. 9 in order of precedence. At that date James Craig was master of the lodge and Alexander Dobbin its senior warden. John Armstrong, the junior warden, had served as the lodge's delegate at Tarboro. Thereafter from 1790-95, Old Cone was represented at grand lodge by David Caldwell, John Steele and Montfort Stokes.[17]

Old Cone's members include many of Rowan County's more prominent figures, most of whom were Scots-Irish from Pennsylvania's Lancaster County.

---

[13] Rowan County Records, *Will Book A*, p. 221, cited in *NOCALORE*, 6 (1936), 9, where Aungier is incorrectly spelled as 'Angier'. Aungier Street was an affluent residential street lined by prominent houses beyond the city walls which bisected medieval Dublin and linked St Patrick's Cathedral with St Stephen's Green.

[14] Coles was a loyalist (*CSRNC*, volume 10, pp. 673-4: Memorandum from John Ross Dunn), however, his son served as an officer in the Salisbury District Minutemen and subsequently in the 4th North Carolina Regiment.

[15] *CSRNC*, volume 9, pp. 188-9: Minutes of the Lower House of the North Carolina General Assembly, 16 December 1771; volume 10, pp. 673-4: Memorandum from John Ross Dunn concerning his imprisonment, 27 July 1776. Also, volume 9, pp. 298, 447-591; volume 10, pp. 136-225.

[16] Rumple, *A History of Rowan County, North Carolina*, pp. 84-5.

[17] The information is reproduced in *NOCALORE*, 6 (1936), 12-3.

Although there were several 'John Armstrongs', the lodge's representative at Tarboro was probably the John Armstrong who with his brother, Martin, had been a leading figure in the Regulator Movement and a major landowner in the region. They were Irish Presbyterians and had migrated to Salisbury in the 1750s via Virginia. They were also land speculators, an activity assisted by Martin's inside track as county surveyor, surveyor of the boundary between Rowan and Surry, and for the county town of Richmond.[18]

In 1782 the brothers gained greater influence with Martin appointed surveyor of the bounty lands in Tennessee and placed in charge of the land office in Nashville, while John was made entry-taker for eastern Tennessee.[19] The opportunities for land fraud were considerable and probably taken, but the Armstrongs were not indicted and put on trial. Instead in 1797 James Glasgow, the secretary of state, was accused of misdemeanours in office. As noted, he was arraigned before a petite jury, found guilty on two counts, and fined £1,000 on each.[20]

John Armstrong eventually acquired around 1,100 acres in Surry County, over 580 acres in Rowan County, and additional land elsewhere, including 700 acres bought at public auction from Henry Eustace McCulloh's estate.[21]

The Armstrong brothers adopted a patriotic stance during the war and were commissioned into the militia. John, a captain in the 2nd North Carolina Regiment and then major in the 4th North Carolina Regiment, subsequently served in the North Carolina Light Infantry and the Surry County Regiment

---

[18] Cf., Charles D. Rodenbough, *Governor Alexander Martin: Biography of a North Carolina Revolutionary War Statesman* (Jefferson, NC: McFarland & Co., 2011), esp. p. 40, 46-7, 50, 85, 97, 178.

[19] Cf., *DNCB*, 'Martin Armstrong (*c.*1739–1808)'.

[20] Kemp P. Battle, 'The Trial of James Glasgow', *The North Carolina Booklet*, 3.1 (1903), 5-11; also, North Carolina State Archives, Raleigh: North Carolina Court of Conference Minutes, book 7; North Carolina Secretary of State documents, 743-56; *DNCB*, 'James Glasgow (*c.*1735-1819)'.

[21] State Archives of North Carolina, North Carolina Land Grants database.

as lieutenant-colonel. He later commanded the 3rd North Carolina Regiment as full colonel.[22] Martin was stripped of his military command in 1781 for insubordination but nonetheless finished the war as brigadier general of the 8th Brigade of North Carolina Militia. He afterwards held a string of local offices including justice of the peace, tax collector and sheriff, and in 1783 was elected a state senator for Surry.

James Craig, the first master of the lodge under its GLNC charter, had been a lieutenant then captain in the Rowan County Regiment, part of the 6th North Carolina Regiment.[23] The Craig family, Scots-Irish, had migrated from County Monaghan in Ulster and settled temporarily in Lancaster County before moving south in around 1750.[24] Craig held around 450 acres of land in his own right on the south side of the Yadkin River and another 500 acres jointly with his brother, David. He served as county sheriff in the 1780s.[25]

Alexander Dobbin (d.1792), a merchant and sometime tanner and leather worker,[26] joined the county committee of safety in 1774.[27] He was commissioned lieutenant-colonel in the 1st Rowan County Regiment two years later. The family were originally from Carrickfergus in County Antrim

---

[22] *CSRNC*, volume 10, pp. 592-4: Minutes of the Rowan County Committee of Safety, 7-8 May 1776. Also, J.D. Lewis, *NC Patriots 1775-1783: Their Own Words* (Little River, SC: J.D. Lewis), volume I.

[23] Lewis, *NC Patriots 1775-1783: Their Own Words*, pp. 50, 71, 94, 835.

[24] Rumple, *A History of Rowan County*, pp. 326-9. Also, Marion Stark Craig, *The American Ancestry of Marion Stark Craig* (Little Rock, AR: Craig, 1985); and http://www.electricscotland.com/history/world/bios/craig_david.htm, accessed 12 October 2017.

[25] *CSRNC*, volume 22, p. 558: Alexander Martin to Thomas Burke, 10 August 1781.

[26] Johanna Miller Lewis, *Artisans in the North Carolina Backcountry* (Lexington, KY: University Press of Kentucky, 1995), pp. 53, 147. His name is also given as 'Dobbins'.

[27] *CSRNC*, volume 10, pp. 592-4: Minutes of the Rowan County Committee of Safety, 7-8 May 1776, *et al.*

and had settled in Pennsylvania before moving to Rowan County in around 1750. Dobbin owned 1,700 acres at the junction of Withrow's Creek and Second Creek, close to the South Yadkin River, alongside land elsewhere in Rowan County and more than 300 acres in Surry County.[28] Unlike the majority of incomers, he was Episcopalian.[29] His will, dated 19 July 1798, left an extensive estate to his wife and six children.[30]

David Caldwell (1725-1824), had been born in Lancaster County to Scots-Irish parents.[31] Intent on becoming a Presbyterian minister, Caldwell studied at the College of New Jersey, now Princeton, graduating in 1761, and after teaching for a year was licensed by the New Brunswick Presbytery and ordained in 1765. He was one of the first Presbyterian preachers in the Piedmont and two years later opened 'Caldwell's Log College', which soon gained a reputation for scholastic excellence.[32] In 1768, the following year, he took on the additional role of minister of the churches at Alamance and Buffalo, established by the Irish-Presbyterian Nottingham Colony.

Caldwell also studied medicine, becoming a self-taught physician, and farmed. His estate included 780 acres in Guilford County and 2,300 acres in Rowan County.[33] He was a leading moderate within the Regulator Movement

---

[28] Ibid.

[29] Rumple, *A History of Rowan County*, p. 414. Also, Robert W. Ramsey, *Carolina Cradle, Settlement of the Northwest Carolina Frontier 1747-1762* (Chapel Hill, NC: UNCP, 1964), pp. 37, 44, 56, 67, 122, 159-160.

[30] www.accessgenealogy.com/north-carolina/caswell-county-north-carolina-wills-1777-1799.htm, accessed 26 October 2017.

[31] Cf., Eli Washington Caruthers, *A Sketch of the Life and Character of the Rev. David Caldwell* (Greensboro, NC: Swaim & Sherwood, 1842).

[32] Ibid. 'Five of his scholars became governors of different states; many more members of Congress [and] a much greater number became lawyers, judges, physicians, and ministers of the gospel.' Cf., also, Edwin Mims (ed), *The South in the Building of the Nation: History of the Literary and Intellectual Life of the Southern States* (Gretna, LA: Pelican, 2002), esp. pp. 168-9.

[33] State Archives of North Carolina, North Carolina Land Grants database.

and prior to the Battle of Alamance had attempted vainly to persuade Tryon to negotiate.

Caldwell took a patriotic stance when war broke out and became a member of the committee of safety for Rowan County.[34] He was commissioned a captain in the 1st Rowan County Regiment in 1775 and promoted to major in 1780. The following year he was promoted again, to lieutenant-colonel, and joined the newly formed 2nd Rowan County Regiment.[35] Unusually for a serving minister, Caldwell represented Guilford County at the Halifax provincial congress and at the Hillsborough convention, where he was part of the anti-Federalist majority that refused to ratify the Constitution.

Andrew Caldwell, David's younger brother named for their father, achieved success as a farmer and in politics, representing the county in the assembly. His son, David Franklin Caldwell (1791-1867), married Fannie Alexander, the daughter of another lodge member, William Lee Alexander (1765-1806), originally from Mecklenburg County Virginia and one of the first families to settle in Rowan County.[36]

John Steele (1764-1815), had been born in Salisbury, the son of William Steele (d.1773) and Elizabeth Gillespie, both Ulster Presbyterians from Pennsylvania. They had married in 1763, each for the second time.[37] The family's store and tavern was inherited from Elizabeth's first husband and provided the foundations for their commercial success, although they also

---

[34] *CSRNC*, volume 10, pp. 252-4: Minutes of the Rowan County Committee of Safety, 20 - 25 September 1775.

[35] Caldwell took part in the Cherokee Expedition (1776), and fought at the battles of Briar Creek, Ramseur's Mill, Colson's Mill, Cowan's Ford, Tarrant's Tavern and Guilford Court House.

[36] Rumple, *A History of Rowan County*, p. 81.

[37] Elizabeth's first husband, Robert, was killed by Cherokees in 1760. Their daughter, Margaret, married the teacher and preacher Samuel Eusebius McCorkle, who was also from Lancaster County, PA.

held investments in property lots around the town.[38] It developed into one of the principal businesses in the county, providing an outlet for local manufactures and a distribution and collection point for farmers.[39] The profits made John Steele wealthy, which he consolidated by marrying Mary Nessfield, the step-daughter of Robert Cochran, a prosperous merchant and mill owner, and a town commissioner for Campbellton.

Steele became tax assessor for the Salisbury District at the age of twenty and was appointed to a string of local offices that included county court justice. He was also active politically, elected to the Commons in November 1787 and representing Salisbury as a Federalist member of the Hillsborough and Fayetteville conventions.

Steele was a member of the first and second Congresses in 1790 and in 1792, but in December 1792 failed to gain election to the Senate, defeated by Alexander Martin, a leading anti-Federalist and supporter of states' rights.[40] He returned to the North Carolina Commons where he represented Salisbury from 1793-95. From 1796-1802 he served as Comptroller of the Treasury in Washington.

Colonel Adlai Osborne (1744-1814), had been commissioned lieutenant-colonel of the Salisbury District Minutemen and subsequently promoted colonel of the 2nd Rowan County Regiment. A lawyer and clerk of the county court, Osborne was a trustee of the University of North Carolina from which his four sons would graduate.[41]

William Alexander (*c*.1759-1832), another member of the county committee of safety, was probably the officer of that name who served as a captain in the 1st Rowan County Regiment.

---

[38] Lewis, *Artisans in the North Carolina Backcountry*, pp. 44, 54, 59, 62-6, 71-2, 94, 104-9 *et al*. Cf., also, DNCB.

[39] Ibid.

[40] Alexander Martin (1740-1807). Cf., DNCB.

[41] His sons were Alexander Osborne, graduated 1798; Edwin J., 1798; Adlai L., 1802; and Spruce M., 1805.

Although not listed, Joseph Dickson (1745-1825), born in Chester County, Pennsylvania, was also a member of Old Cone.[42] His family moved to Rowan County in around 1755 where he continued his schooling and then studied law. Admitted to the North Carolina Bar, Dickson opened a law practice in Salisbury and later inherited the family's cotton and tobacco farm.

Dickson was commissioned a captain in the Continental Army and subsequently promoted major with command of the Lincoln County Men under Colonel Charles McDowell.[43] He fought against Cornwallis and was promoted to colonel and subsequently brigadier general in the militia. Following the war, Dickson became clerk of the Lincoln County Court. He served until his election to the state senate, where he sat for four terms from 1788-95.

Dickson was nominated to the legislative commission that established the University of North Carolina and named a trustee in the 1789 bill that founded the university. In 1799, he was elected on a Federalist ticket to the United States House of Representatives, serving in the sixth session from 1799-1801.[44]

Dickson moved to Tennessee in 1803, settling in Davidson, now Rutherford County, where he became a planter, although he continued to practice as an attorney. In addition to his membership of Old Cone, he was a member of Phalanx Lodge No. 31, Old Cone's sister lodge at Charlotte, and a founder member of Murfreesboro Lodge.

Elected master in 1790, Montfort Stokes would remain in the chair until 1798. The son of Sarah and David Montfort Stokes, Joseph Montfort's sister and brother-in-law, respectively, he had grown up in Halifax County and been held prisoner by the British in New York for much of the war. He afterwards settled in Salisbury, studying law under his brother,

---

[42] Al Tate, *History of Friendship Lodge No. 388, Boiling Springs, NC*: www.friendship388.org/history; also, 'North Carolina Masons in the Revolutionary War' at www.ncgenweb.us/halifax/misc/masons-nc.htm, both accessed 22 May 2017.

[43] Charles McDowell (1743-1815), born in Winchester, VA. He was later commissioned brigadier general.

[44] *DNCB*.

John,[45] whose influence helped Stokes obtain the position of assistant clerk at the state senate from 1786-90.

Stokes was promoted to clerk in 1791 and retained the role for the next 18 years. He declined the offer of a seat in the U.S. Senate in 1804[46] but accepted a commission as major general of state militia. Stokes served as deputy grand master for North Carolina from 1802-07, and as a trustee of the University of North Carolina from 1805-38.

At the end of 1796, Stokes proposed that the lodge reduce the number of its meetings:

> The Worshipful Master brought forward the following regulations which were agreed to, viz. That whereas the small number of members remaining in the Old Cone Lodge renders the duties required by the Constitution and the rules of the Craft extremely laborious and expensive —
>
> Resolved, that in future the quarterly meetings except those in March and September shall be dispensed with until it shall be otherwise ordered by this Lodge. And that the quarterly dues from each member shall be suspended until otherwise ordered Providing always that the foregoing

---

[45] John Stokes was commissioned into the 6th Virginia Continental Regiment and promoted to captain. He was seriously wounded at the Battle of the Waxhaws in 1780 – his right hand was severed – and took no further part in the war, returning to Halifax to study law. Stokes moved to Rowan County in 1784 where he practiced as an attorney, and to Montgomery County in 1786. He was elected a state senator in 1786 and commissioned lieutenant-colonel of the Salisbury District Militia. Stokes was elected to the Commons and named a trustee of the University of North Carolina in 1789, the same year he attended the constitutional convention at Fayetteville on a Federalist ticket. Appointed by Washington as the first federal judge for the district of North Carolina in 1790 he died later the same year on the return journey from New Bern. Stokes was buried in Fayetteville in a masonic ceremony. Stokes County, created in 1789, was named in his honour.

[46] He was however asked to complete James Turner's term in the U.S. Senate following his resignation in 1816 and was reappointed for a second term.

regulation shall not affect the meetings on the festivals nor prevent the Master from calling a Lodge at any time that may be thought beneficial to the Craft or to discharge the duties thereby required Providing also that when a Lodge is called at the request of any particular person the expenses thereof shall be defrayed by such person. But when met on either of the Festivals or on the regular meetings in March and September the expenses shall be discharged by the Treasurer out of the funds of the Lodge as heretofore.

The resolution was agreed and signed by a roll call of the lodge's members: Montfort Stokes, Thomas Carsen, Willian Alexander, Hudson Hughes, Isaac Jones, William Cupples, Barnabus Dunn, Conrad Brem, David Miller, William Hampton, Owen Mailey, John Henry Petchey, George Miller, Hugh Cunningham, Robert Williams Jr., Robert Torrance, Michael Troy, John McClelland, Douglas Hayden, Henry Pennington, Thomas Hudson, James Williams, Jesse Hayden, Thomas Clarke.

Although the lodge met often during 1795, the variety of activities – including the admission of members to the Royal Arch, and the number of visitors,[47] seem to jar with the sentiment behind Montfort's resolution. Nonetheless, there had been a decline in membership and those that remained hoped to secure the lodge's future with a less onerous schedule.[48] In the longer term they were unsuccessful; the lodge warrant was surrendered in 1811.

---

[47] Two visitors were recorded on 25 March: John Ford and an A. Younge. A single visitor, Samuel Warren, attended on 24 June. Five visitors attended the meeting on 5 August: Charles and Anderson Hunt, Robert Leinster, Hugh Carson and Thomas Clarke. Visitors were also present at both September lodge meetings.

[48] A copy of the minutes covering the twelve-month period from November 1795 to November 1796 was deposited with the GLNC and provides details of the lodge's proceedings, members and visitors.

Phalanx Lodge, Charlotte

Forty-four miles to the south of Salisbury,[49] Charlotte was little more than a trading post and crossroads in the early 1750s but developed rapidly over the next two decades, a reflection of the growing number of settlers and the increasing importance of the Piedmont as North Carolina's economic engine.

Mecklenburg County was created in 1762 to accommodate Scots-Irish and German migrants arriving via the Great Wagon Road, and Charlotte, chartered in 1768 and built on land obtained by John Selwyn from Henry McCulloh, became the county seat.[50] Following the war, the discovery of gold nearby led to an inrush of prospectors, providing a further boost to the town.

The history of Phalanx Lodge holds that it was formed in 1779 under a warrant, No. 20, from the Grand Lodge of Pennsylvania issued to the 4th North Carolina Regiment.[51] When Pennsylvania revoked its regimental warrants in 1784, the lodge ostensibly turned to the Grand Lodge of the State of South Carolina, Ancient York Masons, in Charleston, where it obtained a replacement charter. It appears in 1787 as Phalanx Lodge No. 7.

The link to the 4th North Carolina Regiment has been queried[52] and there is an alternative explanation for the lodge's origins: that it was originally established without a lodge charter by Scots-Irish settlers. Phalanx Lodge thereafter moved to regularise its status and approached the Grand Lodge of the State of South Carolina, Ancient York Masons. This is credible.

---

[49] Phalanx Lodge, No. 31. The lodge was re-chartered in 1827, possibly due to the loss of its earlier warrant.

[50] The county was named after Charlotte of Mecklenburg-Strelitz, the British queen.

[51] The 4th North Carolina Regiment took part in the defence of Charleston in 1780 where the majority of those serving were captured and made prisoners of war.

[52] Parramore, *Launching the Craft*, p. 147.

Charlotte had a close trading relationship with Charleston and strong social connections with South Carolina. Indeed, Mackey notes that Philanthropic Lodge No. 78 of Yorkville in adjacent York County 'was organized on the recommendation of Phalanx Lodge No. 7, at Charlotte, NC', with the warrant issued by the Antients Grand Lodge in Charleston on 3 May 1794.[53]

A decade after the grant of its South Carolina charter and accepting that it might be more appropriate to hold a North Carolina warrant, Phalanx was re-chartered in December 1797 as lodge No. 31 under the Grand Lodge of North Carolina.

Although the earliest members of the lodge are not known, those in office in the late 1790s are recorded in the lodge returns to the GLNC. They include William Polk (1758-1834),[54] a Scots-Irish Federalist politician, who in 1799 was elected grand master of North Carolina; Samuel Lowrie (1763-1863), the lodge secretary, a judge of the superior court; and Nathaniel Alexander (1756-1808), the junior warden, a Jeffersonian politician and state governor from 1805-7.[55] The master of the lodge at its re-chartering was General Robert Smith (d.1805). Joseph Dickson served as senior warden.

The lodge charter was forfeited in 1839 but restored the same year. The lodge remains active today.

Old Cone and Phalanx lodges were within a day's ride of each other and jointly sponsored other lodges on the frontier, most notably Stokes Lodge No. 32 at Concord in Cabarrus County, chartered in 1797 and roughly midway between Salisbury and Charlotte. Montfort Stokes acted as the consecrating master and Robert Smith as consecrating junior warden.[56] The initial membership was twenty-eight. The lodge surrendered its warrant in 1811,

---

[53] Mackey, *History of Freemasonry in South Carolina*, p. 541.

[54] He was initiated into Phoenix Lodge, Fayetteville, in 1789.

[55] In 1806 Alexander was installed as grand marshal of the GLNC.

[56] Neither were on the membership roster. Martin Shrive served as master from November 1797: cf., Minutes of Concord Lodge, 15 August 1797, GLNC Archives.

was restored in 1828, ceased again in 1840, restored again a decade later, and ceased for three years in 1884. It has remained active since. Other lodges were formed further west; many survived, others lasted less than a decade.

THE FIRST LODGE IN PITT COUNTY

Although the part of North Carolina that became Pitt County was settled from the late seventeenth century, the number of migrants increased dramatically following the Tuscarora War of 1711.

Pitt County was formed in 1760. It was named for William Pitt the Elder, secretary of state for the Southern Department, and created from part of Beaufort County, itself fashioned from Bath County. The region was economically productive, with naval stores, lumber and agricultural commodities shipped or rafted down the Tar and Pamlico rivers to the Pamlico Sound.

Unrelated to Montfort and pre-dating all but a few of North Carolina's lodges, the lodge at Crown Point in Pitt County was founded in the early 1760s. The minutes of St John's Lodge Massachusetts confirm that an application for a warrant was made in 1764 and the fee of £2 16s remitted the ensuing year and recorded as received on 10 December 1765.[57] The following October, Crown Point is listed as twenty-eighth in order of precedence among the lodges attending St John's quarterly communication.[58]

In September 1767, Thomas Cooper, Crown Point's master, attended St John's. He delivered a report detailing the names of the officers elected at Crown Point's first post-charter meeting who had served through to 24 June 1767 and the names of those who had signed the by-laws:[59]

---

[57] *Proceedings of Masonry. St John's Grand Lodge, 1733-1792* (Boston, MA: Grand Lodge of Massachusetts, 1895), p. 95.

[58] Ibid., p. 108, 24 October 1766.

[59] Ibid., pp. 116-7.

Officers and Members of the Lodge at Crown Point, Pitt County

Mr Thomas Cooper, Master
Peter Blinn, Senior Warden
Colonel John Simpson, Junior Warden
Captain Richard Evans, Esq., Treasurer
James Hall, Esq., Secretary
Mr Thomas Hardy, Steward
Mr James Hill, Steward
Mr Richard Richardson, Tyler

Dr William Pratt	Mr George Miller
Mr John Leslie	Captain Nathaniel Blinn
Mr Peter Richardson	Mr James Glasgow
Mr Robert Newell	Mr Peter Johnson
M William Brown	Mr Bolen Hall
Mr John Barber	Mr William Kelley
Mr Robert Bignell	Mr George Evans
Mr Livingston Lockhart	Mr William McClellan
Colonel Thomas Hall	

At the next meeting of St John's in October, Henry Price, the grand master, appointed Cooper deputy grand master of North Carolina. The rationale is as stated below, albeit that there is no evidence that Cooper warranted any lodges.

> Now therefore Know Ye, That by Virtue of the Power and Authority committed to us, by the Right Honorable and Right Worshipful Anthony, Lord Viscount Montague, Grand Master of Masons, Do hereby Nominate, Appoint, and Authorise, our said Right Worshipful Brother Thomas Cooper to be our Deputy Grand Master within the Province of North Carolina aforesaid, and do Impower him to Congregate all the Brethren, that at present reside (or may hereafter Reside) in said Province, into one

or more Lodges as he may think fit, and in such Place or Places within the same, as shall most redound to the general benefit of Masonry.[60]

The lodge in Pitt County is reputed to have met in the upper long room of the Crown Point Inn, a way-station on the road from Halifax to New Bern, close to present day Greenville.[61] The area was developing rapidly. The Pitt County tax returns for 1765 indicate 750 taxable white men and 429 black slaves, male and female; the numbers had risen to 798 and 470, respectively, a year later,[62] an indication of what was a dynamic community with a total population of around 2,600.

The officers of the lodge include several leading local figures. Cooper, the master, was a merchant, which explains his presence and contacts in Boston; and Peter Blinn, the senior warden, a planter and assemblyman, representing Bath in 1767.[63] A lay reader, he later took holy orders. And John Simpson (1728-1788), the junior warden, was another merchant and planter, owning more than 7,000 acres across the county.[64] Simpson served as a justice of the peace and as colonel of the Pitt County Militia.[65]

---

[60] Ibid., p. 129.

[61] Cf., also, *115th Proceedings of the Grand Lodge of Ancient, Free, and Accepted Masons of North Carolina* (1902), pp. 13-16.

[62] Henry T. King, *Sketches of Pitt County. A Brief History of the County, 1704-1910* (Raleigh, NC: Edwards & Broughton, 1911), p. 46. The figures can be compared with the tax returns for adjacent Beaufort County which gave 411 whites and 476 blacks.

[63] Francis Hodges Cooper, *Some Colonial History of Beaufort County, North Carolina* (Chapel Hill, NC: UNCP, 1916).

[64] State Archives of North Carolina, North Carolina Land Grants database, Pitt County.

[65] Simpson was temporarily promoted to brigadier general during the War of Independence.

Captain Richard Evans (1735-c.1774), the treasurer, another planter and assemblyman,[66] owned the land – some 100 acres - on which Martinboro (renamed Greenville in 1786) was later founded. James Hall, the secretary, served as clerk for Edgecombe County;[67] and Thomas Hardy,[68] the senior steward, was a planter on Swift Creek Swamp.[69] James Glasgow is referred to above. He owned around 2,700 acres in Pitt County, principally on the north side of the Tar.[70]

George Washington stopped at Crown Point Inn on 19 April 1791 when on his southern tour.[71] The business was then owned by Shadrach Allen (d.1812), a local planter[72] who had ended the war as a colonel.[73] Pitt County was by then in relative decline compared with other parts of the state, with the immediate commercial centre of gravity having moved north-west to the new county seat. The lodge at Crown Point had effectively disappeared, and although another lodge was formed at Greenville in 1792, it failed to survive.[74]

UNION LODGE, LATER PHOENIX LODGE NO. 8, FAYETTEVILLE

Fayetteville was the product of an amalgamation of the adjoining settlements of Cross Creek and Campbellton, the latter chartered in 1762 and named

---

[66] Evans represented Pitt County in the assembly in 1769.

[67] *CSRNC*, volume 9, p. 298: List of public officials in North Carolina counties, 1772.

[68] Also 'Hardee'.

[69] State Archives of North Carolina, North Carolina Land Grants database, Pitt County.

[70] Ibid. Also, *DNCB*.

[71] Warren L. Bingham, *George Washington's 1791 Southern Tour* (Charleston, SC: The History Press, 2016).

[72] State Archives of North Carolina, North Carolina Land Grants database.

[73] Allan was also one of Pitt County's representatives in the Commons and had been nominated to the Hillsborough convention.

[74] Union Lodge, warranted 6 December 1792.

for Joseph Montfort's brother-in-law. Cross Creek had been settled from the 1730s but its population increased significantly from the mid-1740s as Gabriel Johnston encouraged numbers of Highland Scots to migrate to the area, not least by offering a ten-year tax exemption.

The incomers were mainly farmers who raised livestock and produced grain, naval stores and lumber. Their success spurred regional growth and led to further investment in the town and its infrastructure. The settlement became an entrepôt, providing a link from the interior to the coast via the Cape Fear River, and to towns north and south along the Fall Line Road.

The area was a centre of Scottish loyalist resistance and its post-war merger with Campbellton in 1783, and the renaming of the joint township in honour of the Marquis de Lafayette, was a means of dealing with this legacy. By then Fayetteville had become one of the most important commercial centres in the state and its largest inland town, and had garnered a political influence to match.

In 1789 the general assembly convened at Fayetteville and in that session chartered the University of North Carolina, ceded land to form Tennessee, and ratified the U.S. Constitution. Fayetteville remained the state capital until 1794, when it was transferred to Raleigh.

The unnumbered Union Lodge at Cross Creek was not chartered by any of the home grand lodges of Scotland, Ireland or England, Modern or Antient, and it has been suggested that the lodge may have had links to Unity Lodge, No. 18 in Pennsylvania's grand register.[75]

Unity was the regimental lodge for the 17th Regiment of Foot which had been warranted by the Grand Lodge of Ireland in 1743.[76] The regiment served in Ireland from 1748-57 and was posted to Nova Scotia at the outbreak of the Seven Years' War. It was then billeted in the West Indies from 1761-67,

---

[75] Charles E. Meyer, *List of Lodges of Pennsylvania from 1730 to 1880, 'Moderns' and 'Antients'*, in *The Grand Lodge of Pennsylvania, Its Early History and Constitutions* (Philadelphia, PA: Grand Lodge of Pennsylvania, 1877).

[76] Warrant No. 136, issued to brethren in the 17th Foot, 24 June 1743.

before returning to Britain from where it was posted to America to fight in the War of Independence where it was one of only a few regiments present in North Carolina in 1780-81.[77] But such a relationship is tenuous at best.

The name of the lodge and shared Scottish antecedents make it more likely that Union was a daughter lodge or unchartered off-shoot of Union Kilwinning of Charleston, No. 98 on the register of the Grand Lodge of Scotland. It is reasonable to speculate that Union's members would have had regular contact with traders and merchants in Charleston, and especially their fellow Scots.

Union Kilwinning's Scottish loyalist links are clear.[78] Its members include John Deas, the master of the lodge and later provincial grand master for South Carolina (Moderns), a partner with his brother, David, in the successful slave trading house of *David & John Deas*.

There are no extant records of the members of Union Lodge before the 1780s and the first reference to freemasonry at Fayetteville appears only in 1784 in correspondence with North Carolina's governor, Alexander Martin, a fellow freemason, in response to a letter from the master of the lodge. By this time the loyalists had been defeated and many had left Cross Creek for refuge in Canada.

> To the Right Worshipful the Master, the Gentlemen Wardens and Gentlemen of the most ancient and Honorable Fraternity of Free and Accepted Masons, who constitute the lodge at FayetteVille:
>
> With singular pleasure I accept your congratulations on my arrival at this place more especially when I am told my presence hath contributed to your felicity.

---

[77] The 17th Foot had its warrant captured and returned in 1779 by General Samuel Parsons (1737-1789), a fellow freemason.

[78] Union Kilwinning Lodge, No. 4, was chartered in May 1755. Among the founders were Samuel Bowman, D. Campbell, John Cooper, Robert Wells, William Michie, John Bassnet and John Stewart. Other Scottish surnames on the membership roll in the 1750s included a Gordon, Rowand, Macaulay and Bailie. Cf., *The Free Masons Pocket Companion* (Edinburgh: Auld & Smellie, 1765), p. 265.

To heal the wounds of a late, cruel and intestine War, to repair, and smooth its ravages too deeply marked in this part of the State, and to reconcile a number of our late revolted Citizens to our happy Government to inoffensive for prosecution, and over whom the act of pardon and oblivion hath cast a veil, are the principal objects of my visit; and if I am so fortunate as to accomplish this desirable end, I shall be discharging the high trust reposed in me by my Country, and answering the great purposes of the Legislature.

The favorable opinion you entertain of me, in the chief magistracy of the State cannot but be flattering and acceptable; in return to those friendly sentiments I can only wish, that my public conduct may be equal to the expectations of my fellow Citizens in general, and to those of your ancient and honorable Society in particular.

To cultivate the arts of peace and diffuse its blessings round the State by a due execution of the Laws, by extending trade, by promoting unanimity and good order & affording protection to all ranks worthy of it are the first objects of my administration; and your concurrence and assistance in these salutary measures, afford me the highest satisfaction.

Rest assured that while I have the honor to preside in the Government of the State, or in the private walk of life, that the Town of Fayette Ville and the Interest of its Inhabitants shall receive my warmest support and your ancient and honorable fraternity my particular countenance.

I return you my grateful acknowledgments for your friendly wishes in my Administration, at the same time accept Right Worshipful my hearty thanks for the polite and handsome address, in which you have conveyed to me the Sense of the Fraternity.

Alexander Martin

Union sought a dispensation at the meeting of the Grand Lodge of North Carolina at Fayetteville on 17 November 1788, just under a year after it participated in creating the new grand lodge.[79] It was agreed that it would

---

[79] See appendix seven.

receive a new name - Phoenix - and on 25 June 1791 after a wider renumbering the lodge obtained a new charter and was assigned No. 8 in order of precedence. The change of name and new warrant drew a line under Union's past loyalist associations.

Two years later in 1793, the lodge received a deed for a property lot in Fayetteville.[80] The cornerstone for what would be a purpose-built masonic hall was laid on 25 June the same year. The building at St John's Square at Mason and Arch was removed in 1849 and rebuilt on the original foundations in 1858. The site remains in use and Phoenix Lodge continues to be active today.

BLANDFORD-BUTE LODGE, BUTE COUNTY, LATER WARREN COUNTY

Named for John Stuart, 3rd Earl of Bute, Britain's prime minister from 1762-63, Bute County was formed from part of Granville County in 1764. Located to the immediate south of the Virginia border, the county was sub-divided into Franklin and Warren counties in 1779.

Migration to this area of North Carolina began in the late seventeenth century with traders and merchants sourcing furs and pelts from the Haliwa, Tuscarora, and Saponi tribes, and selling them to merchant factors in Virginia. More permanent settlements came in the eighteenth century with naval stores and lumber production, and land clearance, which opened up the area to agriculture and tobacco plantations. The resulting output was exported along the wagon trails and trading paths running north into Virginia, and via the Roanoke and Tar rivers that flowed east to the Albemarle and Pamlico Sounds, respectively.

In his paper in *NOCALORE*, Allen quotes the earliest lodge minute book. It details a meeting in 1766 at 'Buffaloe',[81] or Buffalo Race Path, subsequently the

---

[80] Cumberland County Deeds, Office of the Register of Deeds, Cumberland County Courthouse, Fayetteville: Book 13, p. 6, and Book 21, p. 395.

[81] J. Edward Allen, 'How Blandford-Bute Lodge was Formed', *NOCALORE*, 6 (1936), 162-78.

site of the Bute County court house. The land on which the building was constructed was donated by Jethro Sumner,[82] a member, steward[83] and later treasurer of the lodge, which until the 1770s was known colloquially as the 'Lodge at Buffaloe'.[84]

There were four initiates at the lodge's first minuted meeting on 29 April 1766 - William Martin, John Smith, Paul Patrick and Allen Groves. A further three joined two weeks later on 12 May - John Gordon, William Tabb and James Burk.[85] Eight months on in December 1766, membership stood at over thirty, and by the following December it approached fifty, including five members of the Hill family.[86]

Officers and Members of Blandford-Bute Lodge, Bute County (December 1766)

William Park, Master *
Benjamin Hill, Senior Warden *
Thomas Bell, Junior Warden *
Robert Turnbull, Secretary
Jethro Sumner, Treasurer *

Thomas Machen *	Allan Groves
Paul Patrick	William Martin
William Moore	Lewis Parham

---

[82] Jethro Sumner (1733-1785), a Virginia-born planter, tavern owner and store keeper, and revolutionary soldier. He was a justice of the peace and later sheriff. At his death he owned over 20,000 acres and 34 slaves.

[83] In Antients, Irish and Scottish lodges the 'steward' was often the charity steward.

[84] I am grateful to Jonathan Underwood for this information.

[85] Cf., *Transcript of the Blandford-Bute Minutes*, 1776-1779: MSS-6323, Wilson Library, UNC, Chapel Hill, NC.

[86] Henry Hill, Ben Hill, Thomas Hill and Green Hill, the sons of Green Hill, Sr.

William Tabb *	Thomas Bell *
Robert Turnbull	Lewis Parham
Allen Groves	James Burk[87]
Solomon Alston *	Benjamin Tucker
John Smith	John Christmas *
John Gordon	Thomas Hill *
William Gilbreath *	William Johnson *
Thomas Sherwood	James Ransom[88] *
Patewells Milner[89] *	John Norwood *
Edward Jones *	John Scott

*= member of the Committee of Safety

The lodge's founders had migrated to Bute County from Virginia where they were members of Blandford Lodge in Prince George County just north of Petersburg.[90] That lodge, now No. 3 in the register of the Grand Lodge of Virginia, was then No. 82 on the register of the Grand Lodge of Scotland having been warranted on 9 September 1757.[91] The lodge would have been established at least a year earlier.

William Park, the master, provides a direct connection to Scotland. A successful planter, he was also a partner in and factor for *Dinwiddie Crawford & Co.*,[92] a Glasgow-based merchant house specialising in importing tobacco

---

[87] Also written as 'Burke'.

[88] 'James Ransom (Fishing Creek) having been voted in at a former Lodge is Initiated and rece'd as a member thereof accordingly.' Fishing Creek was located in what became Warren County. There is no information on the former lodge.

[89] A possible relation of James Milner.

[90] Allen, 'How Blandford-Bute Lodge was Formed', 163.

[91] *The Free Masons Pocket Companion* (Glasgow: Joseph Galbraith, 1765), p. 195.

[92] Mecklenburg County, Virginia Deeds, 1771-1776, volume 2, p. 63.

and exporting manufactured goods.[93] Although Park was a member of the Bute County committee of safety, as were over half the lodge members,[94] *Dinwiddie Crawford*'s assets were seized and forfeited after the war.[95]

The resolutions passed by the lodge at its St John's Day meeting on 24 June 1766 followed standard eighteenth-century lodge practice.[96] The reference to Virginia currency was not unusual in lodges close to the Virginia border given that trade was more likely to be with Virginia than with North Carolina's east coast.

> The following rules being read are agreed to be Entered in the Rule Book as follows:
>
> Rule First, that every Member shall duly attend the Lodge in Course or give a sufficient reason for his absence or pay the sum of two shillings & six pence for each non-performance.
>
> Secondly, that no member shall profanely Swear in the Lodge under no less penalty than two shillings & six pence for the first offence & five shillings each after.
>
> Thirdly, that there shall no member indecently behave such as whispering or laughing in the Lodge under the above penalty.
>
> Fourthly, that no member shall disclose the proceedings of the Lodge to any Masons, and not to them without they intend to become Members or should give such reasons as they should think they should.
>
> Fifthly, that no member shall speak in the Lodge without rising & addressing himself to the Master.

---

[93] John Richard Alden, *Robert Dinwiddie: Servant of the Crown* (Charlottesville, VA: Colonial Williamsburg Foundation, 1973), p. 116.

[94] *Bute County Committee of Safety Minutes, 1775–1776* (Warrenton, NC: Warren County Bicentennial Committee, 1977).

[95] Cf., John Haywood, *A manual of the laws of North Carolina, arranged under distinct heads* (Raleigh, NC: J. Gales, 1819), p. 124.

[96] Cf., *Schism*, 61-71.

Sixthly, that every Member shall pay for his quarterly payment six shillings & eight pence proclamation money to the treasurer that shall be appointed by the Lodge.

Seventhly, that no member shall reflect, or laugh, at any Rules proposed by any member without, in the Lodge, and then to make their objections in a manner becoming any Mason.

Resolved, that this Lodge from this time take the title or name of Blandford-Bute Lodge.

Resolved, that no person be Initiated in this lodge Except he pay the money down for his Initiation or give one of the Members of the Lodge for his Security to wit, 4-4-6 Pounds Virginia Currency.

Resolved, that whoever is appointed Tyler of this Lodge shall receive the sum of five shillings Virginia Currency each night, except as such time that there is new members initiated which shall be five shillings Virginia Currency, each new member, and on failure of such new Member being made the said Tyler is to be paid by the Treasurer for his said attendance.[97]

The by-laws follow a pattern used in many Scottish, Irish and Antients lodges which operated as proto mutual benefit clubs. The fees levied provided for benevolent distributions, with individual payments recorded in the treasurer's account book. Regular attendance was also expected and logged in the secretary's register. As in lodges elsewhere, promotion ceremonies were funded by those being advanced: 'resolved that the Members Initiated & Raised as members of this Lodge pay the night's expenses & those having been raised twice to pay two parts'.[98]

With its members serving in the Pitt County and North Carolina militias,[99] no lodge meetings took place during the war but on 6 April 1782 four

---

[97] Allen, 'How Blandford-Bute Lodge was Formed', 166-7.
[98] Ibid., 175.
[99] Cf., 'Revolutionary War Soldiers for NC and SC' at http://www.carolana.com, accessed 11 April 2017.

members met to reconstitute and reopen the lodge. William Johnson, one of the earliest settlers, presided as master supported by General Sumner and Edward Jones as senior and junior wardens, respectively, and John Scott, who served as secretary and tyler.[100] Inquorate, they 'resolved, that a summons be issued to all the late members of our lodge to repair to our room at this place the first Saturday in May next, by 10 o'clock'. Only six members were present at the 4 May meeting and it was agreed to adjourn the lodge until 18 May and relocate to Warrenton.

Incorporated in 1779, the town had become the principal commercial and social centre for the county and many local planters and merchants maintained a residence there. The 18 May meeting had nine attendees[101] and, now quorate, the lodge was opened and a James Johnson initiated, possibly the master's son.

Within two months lodge membership had risen to seventeen and in the following months it increased further as the lodge hosted a stream of visitors from within and without the county. Indeed, the lodge's popularity was such that meetings were held as often as weekly to accommodate the flow of new applicants.

On 14 September, the lodge convened as a 'lodge of Arch and Royal Arch Masons' and seven members - Edward Jones, Benjamin Kimbell, John Macon, James Johnson, Thomas Armstrong, John Withers and William Wortham - were exalted. It is the first recorded occasion on which the Royal Arch degree was conferred in North Carolina and confirms that the lodge was working either Scottish, Irish or Antients ritual.[102] A second Royal Arch meeting was held the following year on 17 November at which Rodham Atkins, a member of the lodge, and a visitor, Nathaniel Christmas, were exalted.

---

[100] Blandford-Bute Minutes, 6 April 1782.

[101] William Johnson, master; Jethro Sumner, deputy master; Edward Jones, senior warden; Thomas Turner, junior warden; John Scott, secretary; James Burk, tyler; and four others, Messrs - Jenkins, - Devany, George Tassie and John Withers.

[102] Blandford-Bute Minutes.

On 12 December 1788, twelve months after the Tarboro convention at which it had participated, Blandford-Bute was dissolved and immediately reconstituted under a new warrant from the Grand Lodge of North Carolina. A new name was adopted - Johnston-Caswell – and the lodge granted No. 10 on the grand register.

Johnston-Caswell Lodge evolved into a mother lodge for lodges across the backcountry and although the warrant was surrendered four times in the nineteenth century it was restored on each occasion.[103] Johnston-Caswell Lodge remains active today.

---

[103] Surrendered 1827, 1858, 1880 and 1882; restored 1832, 1865, 1882 and 1902. Unlike Blandford-Bute, the records of other frontier lodges working in the 1760s and 1770s have not survived. One lodge is believed to have operated in Anson County adjacent to the border with South Carolina. It may have been the lodge which Major James Auld (c.1725-c.1782) joined after he left the Royal White Hart Lodge and Halifax, but virtually nothing is known of its origins and since it did not participate in the foundation of the GLNC it may have ceased working by the early 1780s.

Chapter Eleven

Revolution and Beyond

Towards a new Grand Lodge

Despite the prominence of many North Carolina patriots within the organisation, freemasonry resumed relatively slowly following the war. Social and economic dislocation offers one explanation. Another is that lodges in the east continued to operate under the nominal authority of the Grand Lodge of England, which may have had limited attraction for men who had spent the past decade opposing the British. But a third factor was the absence of any central force to drive and coordinate freemasonry in the state.

Before the war, North Carolina freemasonry had operated without a province-wide governance structure. Lodges in the Piedmont were either independent or looked nominally to grand lodges elsewhere, and Montfort's remit as North Carolina's provincial grand master in practice extended no further than the colony's north-eastern corner and within the coastal plain. His appointment was effectively from March 1772,[1] and Montfort's growing incapacity from 1774, and death in March 1776, allowed insufficient time for his influence to develop. Moreover, during the war years there was no obvious or effective successor.

James Milner, whom Montfort had appointed deputy grand master, had been killed in a riding accident in December 1772 and his replacement, Cornelius Harnett Jr., a leading figure in the Sons of Liberty and in the patriotic resistance to the British, was occupied fully by the war and dead by 1781. Additionally, William Brimage, Montfort's provincial grand secretary, the third most senior figure in the province, was an ardent loyalist who fled North Carolina shortly after hostilities commenced. The names of

---

[1] The month that he presented his deputation to the Royal White Hart.

Montfort's other grand officers, if any, are not known, and there are no extant records of any provincial grand lodge or provincial grand officers after Montfort's death.

The impetus for creating a state-wide governing body for freemasonry was not driven by those whose authority had been vested by the Grand Lodge of England but from lodges in the Piedmont. At Blandford-Bute in May 1782 Jethro Sumner put forward a proposal that other lodges be contacted to establish whether a grand master was to be chosen for the United States and whether in the interim the grand master of the Grand Lodge of Virginia (a body established in 1778) could charter lodges in North Carolina. There was apparently no response and frustration may have spurred Sumner to apply his energies to other causes, not least the founding of the North Carolina Chapter of the Society of the Cincinnati.

The following year in November 1786 the general assembly met at Fayetteville. The legislators, generally the most prominent men in their respective communities, included many freemasons,[2] and what may have been a series of informal conversations regarding developments elsewhere in America led to a consensus supporting the creation of a grand lodge for North Carolina. The proposal was raised formally at Union Lodge on 1 January the following year by Colonel James Emmett, a past master.[3] The lodge responded by constituting a committee of Alexander Martin, Henry Hill and John Macon, the latter two members of Dornoch Lodge, to compose a letter to the state's lodges.[4] It noted that North Carolina freemasonry had been 'deprived of its head by the death of our late Respectable and

---

[2] For example Richard Caswell, James Glasgow, John Stokes, Alexander Martin, Henry Montfort, John Macon, Dixon Marshall, John Simpson and Augustine Willis, among others.

[3] Emmett had fought under Sumner in the 3rd North Carolina regiment and subsequently in the Cumberland County militia.

[4] Macon and Martin were both founding trustees of the University of North Carolina.

worthy Provincial Grand Master' and proposed that the lodges convene to elect a replacement, with each lodge delegating one or more members to meet at Fayetteville on 24 June.

But while some lodges received the letter others did not or did so only belatedly, leaving little or no time to respond.[5] Moreover, with the invitation stating that the new grand master would be invested 'by the Continental Grand Master', a non-existent position, some invitees may have been unwilling to participate.

Only six delegates representing three lodges attended Fayetteville the following June,[6] and with a majority of North Carolina's lodges unrepresented it was agreed that a second convention should be arranged. Accordingly, St John's New Bern issued a new invitation to meet at Tarboro, where the legislature would convene. The town was closer to the more-populated northern half of the state and at the centre of a rough circle sixty miles in diameter on the circumference of which were six masonic lodges - Kinston, New Bern, Edenton, Murfreesboro, Windsor and Winton.

Representatives from ten lodges were present at Tarboro in December 1787. John Mare and Stephen Cabarrus represented Unanimity Lodge; Benjamin Manchester and Abner Neale, St John's New Bern; and John Johnston, Andrew Oliver and Silas Arnett, Royal Edwin. John Geddy, Samuel MacDougall and William Muir had been delegated by the Royal White Hart. Royal William was represented by Patrick Garvey, William Person Little and Hardy Murfree. Union by James Portersfield. Blandford-Bute by William Johnston and Edward Jones; and St John's Kinston by Richard Caswell, James Glasgow and William Randall. Old Cone sent a single delegate, John Armstrong; and John Macon and Henry Hill represented Dornoch,

---

[5] Warrenton, 8 June; Edenton, 12 June.

[6] John Craddock and Benjamin Manchester represented St John's, New Bern; Edward Jones, Warrenton; and William Brickell, Dornoch Lodge. James White and Duncan Ochiltree attended from Union, Fayetteville. Edenton, Kinston, Rockingham, Salisbury, Wilmington, Windsor and Winton were not represented.

although neither would be allowed to vote.[7] St John's Wilmington was not represented.

John Mare was elected to preside. Procedural rules were agreed and nominations for the vacant grand offices tabled. Three names were put forward for grand master: Samuel Johnston, Richard Caswell and Richard Ellis, none of whom were present. John Mare and John Williams were nominated as prospective deputy grand masters; Charles Johnson and Gooderum Davis for the position of senior grand warden; William Gilmour, James Glasgow and Joseph Leech to be grand treasurer; and Montford Stokes, Richard Freear and Benjamin Manchester for the role of grand secretary.[8]

Johnston, on the verge of becoming state governor, received five votes and Caswell three. He was elected grand master and Caswell appointed his deputy. The other offices went to members of St John's New Bern and St John's Kinston, with Richard Ellis and Michael Payne appointed senior and junior grand wardens, respectively; Abner Neal, grand treasurer; and James Glasgow, grand secretary. Parramore suggests that 'the critical factor in the selection of officers appears to have been proximity to the seat of state government, then at New Bern'.[9]

The Grand Lodge of North Carolina was established formally on 12 December 1787, the constitution having been drawn up by Caswell, following which the grand officers were installed and a six-man committee appointed to draft the regulations that would govern its operation.[10] The committee's report was adopted in July 1788 when the grand lodge reconvened at Hillsborough,

---

[7] Possibly because the lodge was so close to Blandford-Bute Lodge. It was later specified that other than with specific authorisation lodges could not be established within ten miles of one another.

[8] *Draft Minutes of the Convention to Establish the Grand Lodge of North Carolina*: http://library.digitalnc.org.

[9] Paramore, *Launching the Craft*, p. 96.

[10] *Draft Proceeding Minutes of the Grand Lodge of North Carolina*: http://library.digitalnc.org.

alongside a meeting of North Carolina's legislature. Member lodges were directed to provide a copy of their by-laws and regulations, inform grand lodge annually of the names of their members and the dates and location of meetings, and provide an annual summary of their proceedings.[11]

Eighteen months later in order to forestall arguments over precedence, North Carolina's lodges were instructed to send a copy of their charters to grand lodge so that primacy could be determined. The grand lodge also set out the quantum of annual dues and charitable contributions that were to be paid.[12]

By 1791, eighteen lodges were recorded on North Carolina's grand register in the following order of precedence:

Lodge Number	Name	Current Status	Original Ritual
No. 1	St John's Lodge, Wilmington	Active	Moderns
No. 2	Royal White Hart Lodge, Halifax	Active	Moderns
No. 3	St John's Lodge, New Bern	Active	Moderns
No. 4	St John's Lodge, Kinston	Active	Antients[13]
No. 5	Royal Edwin Lodge now Charity Lodge, Windsor	Active	Moderns
No. 6	Royal William Lodge, Winton	Extinct	Moderns
No. 7	Unanimity Lodge, Edenton	Extinct	Not known
No. 8	Phoenix Lodge formerly Union Lodge, Fayetteville	Active	Antients/ Scottish
No. 9	Old Cone Lodge, Salisbury	Extinct	Antients/ Irish
No. 10	Johnston-Caswell Lodge, formerly Blandford-Bute Lodge, Warrenton	Active	Antients/ Scottish

---

[11] *Proceedings of the Grand Lodge of North Carolina*, 9-12 December 1787.
[12] *Proceedings of the Grand Lodge of North Carolina*, 24 July 1789.
[13] The GLNC ascribes Moderns ritual to Kinston.

No. 11	Caswell Brotherhood Lodge, Caswell County	Extinct	Antients
No. 12	Independence Lodge, Chatham County	Extinct	Antients
No. 13	St John's Lodge, Duplin County	Extinct	Not known
No. 14	Rutherford Fellowship Lodge, Rutherford County	Extinct	Antients
No. 15	Washington Lodge, Beaufort County	Extinct	Not known
No. 16	Tammany Lodge, Martin County	Extinct	Not known
No. 17	American George Lodge, Hertford County	Active	Moderns
No. 18	King Solomon's Lodge, Jones County	Extinct	Not known

Six of the nine lodges that voted to form the Grand Lodge of North Carolina had been constituted as Moderns lodges but their representatives at Tarboro were implicit converts to Antients freemasonry.[14] The adoption of the name 'Ancient York Masons' in the nineteenth century and the use of Irish *qua* Antients ritual in the eighteenth, consigned North Carolina's Moderns to the past.[15]

The rationale was understandable. Both in the run-up to war and during the years of conflict with Britain, prominent Moderns' freemasons had been called-out as loyalists, not least in Halifax, New Bern and Edenton, with a number forced to flee the province. Elsewhere in America from

---

[14] *Draft Minutes of the Convention to Establish the Grand Lodge of North Carolina*: library.digitalnc.org. Although Dornoch Lodge was not considered to be legally constituted, its representatives – John Macon and Henry Hill - were recognised.

[15] The Grand Lodge of North Carolina was renamed the Grand Lodge of Ancient York Masons of North Carolina in 1821. In 1858 the name was altered to the 'Grand Lodge of Free and Accepted Masons of North Carolina' and in 1867 to the 'Grand Lodge of Ancient, Free, and Accepted Masons of North Carolina'.

Massachusetts to South Carolina and Georgia, Antients freemasonry had become synonymous with resistance and patriotism and the Moderns with loyalism.[16] But it would be wrong to oversimplify that division. Among North Carolina's more fervent loyalists were the Highland Scots at Cross Creek, and many Moderns lodges had considerably more patriots than loyalists.

Unlike South Carolina where animosity between the Moderns and Antients persisted into the nineteenth century, Antients freemasonry in North Carolina absorbed its Moderns counterpart with apparent ease. The letters despatched in 1787 by Union Lodge at Fayetteville, and later the same year by St John's at New Bern, inviting North Carolina's lodges to convene to nominate a grand master and create a new grand lodge, were circulated to all 'regularly constituted lodges' without discrimination.

American society had shifted towards accessibility and democracy, with Antients freemasonry part of that process before and during the war. America's military lodges operated under the Antients' banner. Massachusetts and Pennsylvania, the dominant provincial grand lodges in eighteenth-century America, had been proselytising Antients freemasonry with increasing effect since the 1760s. And George Washington, the nation's founding father, commander-in-chief, and its first president, had been initiated into Antients freemasonry, as had many of his patriot colleagues.[17]

---

[16] The Antients' St Andrew's Lodge in Boston and the provincial grand lodge of Massachusetts contained numerous revolutionary figures. They included Joseph Warren, the first provincial grand master; Paul Revere, a grand officer from 1769, deputy grand master (1784, 1791-2), and later grand master (1794-97); William Palfrey, grand secretary; Thomas Crafts, grand treasurer; and, among others, William Molyneux, John Hancock, Edward Proctor, Caleb Hopkins and Thomas Urann. Georgia's freemasons included Oliver Bowen, Samuel Elbert, John Habersham, Joseph Habersham, John Houstoun, Sir Patrick Houstoun, Noble W. Jones, Benjamin Lloyd, William O'Bryan, Mordecai Sheftall, William Stephens, Samuel Stirk and George Walton.

[17] George Washington was initiated an Antients freemason on 4 November 1752 at Fredericksburg, Virginia.

Following the war, freemasonry was placed on a moral pedestal as an organisation that could rise above political and religious division. Membership and promotion to office would be 'grounded upon real worth and personal merit only',[18] and the movement was positioned as a path to self-knowledge and self-improvement:

> It is well known that our Order was at first composed of scientific and ingenious men who assembled to improve the arts and sciences and cultivate a pure and sublime system of morality. Knowledge at that time was restricted to a chosen few but when the invention of printing had opened the means of instruction to all ranks of people, then the generous cultivators of Masonry communicated with cheerfulness to the world those secrets of the arts and sciences which had been transmitted and improved from the foundation of the institutions then our Fraternity bent their principal attention to the cultivation of morality. And Masonry may now be defined as a moral institution, intended to promote individual and social happiness.[19]

> Our institution asserts, in language not to be misunderstood, the natural equality of mankind. It declares that all brethren are upon a level, and it throws open its hospitable doors to all men of all nations. It admits of no rank, except the priority of merit, and its only aristocracy is the nobility of virtue.[20]

---

[18] 1723 *Constitutions*, p. 51.

[19] From an address by De Witt Clinton, before Holland Lodge, the evening of his installation, 24 December 1793, reprinted in *The Craftsman*, 1866. Cf., also, Nancy Beadie, 'Encouraging Useful Knowledge…' in Benjamin Justice (ed), *The Founding Fathers and "The Great Contest"*, pp. 94-6.

[20] Ibid.

From the 1780s until the late 1820s when the Morgan Affair changed public perceptions and catalysed an anti-masonic movement,[21] freemasonry was woven into the American political fabric and the masonic commitment to be a 'good man and true' held up as a sacred component of the post-revolutionary ideal. The evidence is not only in the masonic treatises and pamphlets published at the time but in the names of North Carolina's lodges themselves: Royal Edwin was renamed Davie Lodge; Royal William renamed American George; and Union reborn as Phoenix. Newer lodges were given correspondingly patriotic tags including Independence (No. 12), Washington (No. 15), Eagle (No. 19), Democratic (No. 21), Columbian (No. 28), Freeland (No. 33), Unanimity (No. 34), Federal (No. 42) and Liberty (No. 45).

Freemasonry's reputation was high across America, reinforced by a roll-call of members that included iconic figures at both state and national level within the legislature, judiciary and armed forces.

North Carolina was no exception with freemasonry's standing epitomised by the social and political status of its members and officers, and especially its first three grand masters: Samuel Johnston, Richard Caswell and William R. Davie.

THE FIRST GRAND MASTERS

SAMUEL JOHNSTON

Born in Dundee in Scotland, Samuel Johnston (1733-1816) moved to North Carolina with his family in or around 1735. His father, John, was Gabriel Johnston's elder brother and the family expected to benefit from their connection to the governor. They acquired an estate in Onslow

---

[21] Named for William Morgan (1774-1826), whose disappearance in 1826 led to accusations of abduction and murder against New York freemasons and spurred a powerful anti-masonic movement in the United States that persisted until the mid-nineteenth century.

From Roanoke to Raleigh

Samuel Johnson (1733-1816)
Repainted from an original by Jacques Busbee, *c.*1905.
From the Collection of the Grand Lodge of North Carolina

County[22] and Samuel was later sent to Yale, although he left before graduating and in 1753 moved to Edenton to study law under Thomas Barker.[23] Johnston was admitted to the Bar in 1756 and elected to the assembly three years later, representing Edenton and Chowan counties until 1775.

Family connections smoothed Johnston's path to a succession of well-paid offices, including clerk of the Court of Oyer and Terminer and clerk of the Superior Court of Chowan County, a position of some value since it required a £2,000 bond, albeit that this was paid in proclamation money.[24] By 1765 Johnston had amassed sufficient wealth to acquire the 540-acre *Hayes* plantation[25] and five years later purchased the lucrative position of deputy naval officer for the province.[26]

Johnston was a prominent member of the east coast establishment and one of the leaders of the anti-Regulator majority in the assembly. He was also trusted by the British, not least by Josiah Martin, who wrote servilely to Johnston in February 1772 that with respect to 'any person, or thing, your word, or recommendation, will be my sufficient warrant'.[27] In October that year, Martin offered Johnston a seat on the royal council: 'I wish to know whether you will permit me to name you to the King, if it be agreeable to

---

[22] The *Poplar Spring* plantation on the principal road between New Bern and Wilmington.

[23] Thomas Barker (1713-1789), merchant, planter, attorney and later politician.

[24] *CSRNC*, volume 7, pp. 716-7: Bond from Samuel Johnston for performance as Clerk of the Edenton District Superior Court, 25 April 1768.

[25] Cf., for example, *CSRNC*, volume 8, pp. 43-4: Alexander Elmsley to Samuel Johnston, 26 May 1769; pp. 257-8: Samuel Johnston to Alexander Elmsley, 7 November 1770; and volume 9, pp. 12-3, Alexander Elmsley to Samuel Johnston, 27 July 1771.

[26] *CSRNC*, volume 10, pp. 332-3: Samuel Johnston to Josiah Martin, 16 November 1775: 'an honest purchase for which I have punctually paid an annual sum, which I shall continue to pay till the expiration of the Term'.

[27] *CSRNC*, volume 9, pp. 236-7: Josiah Martin to Samuel Johnston, 6 February 1772.

you, I shall be much flattered by an opportunity of making so honorable an acquisition to the Council of this Province'.[28] Johnston declined, but the governor's opinion of him continued to be favourable during the run-up to war and the two remained close personally until at least 1774.[29] This despite Johnston joining the standing committee of correspondence and enquiry in December 1773 to coordinate North Carolina's response to Britain's Intolerable Acts.

Johnston was elected to the first and second provincial congresses, and convened the third and was elected its president. He was subsequently made treasurer of the northern district and the following month joined the council of safety. The fourth provincial congress met in April 1776 and Johnston was once again elected president. And from the end of May when Josiah Martin fled the colony, until October, when Harnett became chair of the provincial council, Johnston headed the provincial government.

Although he failed to be elected to the fifth provincial congress, Johnston was appointed to the commission tasked with reviewing which royal statutes should be retained. In 1779 he returned to the legislature as a state senator from Chowan County, and the following year served as a delegate to the continental congress. He was re-elected in 1781 but resigned to return to North Carolina. He was re-elected to the state senate in 1783 and 1784.

Johnston was elected governor unanimously at Tarboro in December 1787, although he was not a member of the legislature at the time, and in July 1788 elected president of the Hillsborough convention, notwithstanding that he was a leading Federalist. He was also re-elected governor. The following year Johnston presided over the Fayetteville convention and became governor for a third time.

---

[28] *CSRNC*, volume 9, pp. 342-3: Josiah Martin to Samuel Johnston, 4 October 1772.

[29] *CSRNC*, volume 9, p. 693: Josiah Martin to Samuel Johnston, 16 October 1773. Also, volume 9, pp. 968-9: Samuel Johnston to William Hooper, 5 April 1774. Johnston was only removed as deputy naval officer in 1775.

Johnston served as North Carolina's first grand master from December 1787 until November the following year, when he resigned on being elected North Carolina's first U.S. senator. Richard Caswell succeeded him as grand master but died in November 1789, and Johnston accepted the nomination to replace him. He was installed that month and thereafter re-elected annually until withdrawing in 1792.

In common with many other freemasons, Johnston actively supported the founding of the University of North Carolina and in 1789 was the first trustee to be selected. He died at Edenton in 1816 and is buried in the family graveyard at the *Hayes* plantation.

RICHARD CASWELL

Caswell, an assemblyman and delegate to the provincial and continental congresses, chaired the committee that drafted North Carolina's constitution. Like Johnston, he had been close to the loyalist establishment until the early 1770s when he underwent a political epiphany. Indeed, Governor Martin was sufficiently shocked at the change to describe Caswell on his return from a meeting of the continental congress as an active 'tool of sedition'.

The provincial congress elected Caswell governor in December 1776, and he was re-elected in each of the following three years, the maximum number of terms that the state constitution permitted. On leaving office in April 1780, he was immediately elected major general and placed in command of the state militia. Ill health forced a temporary step-down six months later but Caswell returned to active service after less than a month. He was subsequently given the role of state controller-general, serving for three years, and in 1785 was elected governor once again, serving a further three terms.

Caswell followed a Federalist line, a view that put him at odds with his Dobbs County electors and denied him a seat at the Hillsborough convention. He succeeded Johnston as grand master in 1788 but was in office for barely a year before his death. He was at the time speaker of the state senate.

Richard Caswell (1729-1789)
Repainted from an original by Jacques Busbee, *c.*1905.
From the Collection of the Grand Lodge of North Carolina

A state funeral was held at Fayetteville, and Caswell's body subsequently taken to Kinston where he was interred in the family cemetery at the *Red House* plantation.

WILLIAM R. DAVIE [30]

William Davie's marriage to Sarah, the daughter of Allen Jones, his wealthy, politically-connected former commanding officer, and his law practice in Halifax, place him at the heart of the eastern establishment. But Davie's background as a Piedmont-raised member of the predominantly Scots-Irish Presbyterian community gave him a complexity and accessibility that was not shared by many of his political contemporaries. Davie was a committed Federalist, an intellectual elitist, and a war hero. He was also a successful attorney, planter and slave-owner whose commercial interests were reflected in his activities as a legislator. And he was the driving force behind the establishment of the University of North Carolina, the first public university in America.

Born in Cumberland in 1756 to Scottish parents on the English side of the Scottish-English border, Davie was brought to America in 1764 as an eight-year old when his family migrated to the Waxhaws, an area straddling the North-South Carolina border. His maternal uncle, William Richardson, a charismatic Presbyterian minister and missionary, had a parish that stretched from Charlotte to Camden in South Carolina along the main wagon trail from Salisbury to Charleston. The region was dominated by Ulster-Irish migrants, whose numbers rose rapidly following the Treaty of Paris in 1763 which brought the Seven Years' War to a close.[31]

---

[30] William Richardson Davie (1756-1820).

[31] With the ending of hostilities between Britain's American colonies and the French and their Native American proxies, the Piedmont became a less dangerous and more hospitable place, and settlement expanded accordingly.

William Richardson Davie (1756-1820)
Repainted from an original by Jacques Busbee, c.1905.
From the Collection of the Grand Lodge of North Carolina

The Richardson and Davie families were middling rather than affluent, and in addition to his house and town lot, William Richardson acquired a 150-acre land holding in 1760 and a second estate five years later.[32] Davie's father, Archibald, owned two adjacent lots of 200 acres and 150 acres, respectively.[33]

William Richardson died in 1771.[34] Without a family of his own he bequeathed his estate to his sister's children. Although not vast, it included slaves, farm animals and general goods, in addition to land holdings.[35] The legacy allowed Davie to enrol at the College of New Jersey, later Princeton, in 1774. He graduated in 1776 and obtained a clerkship in Salisbury to study law with Spruce Macay, another New Jersey graduate who would become North Carolina's attorney general two years later.[36]

Although fighting in New England at Lexington and Concord had broken out in 1775, the first major clash in the South occurred in June 1776 and centred on British efforts to take Charleston. Davie joined the militia to defend the city but his company returned without having engaged. Back in Salisbury, Davie persuaded Captain Robert Bartley[37] to raise a company of light horse.

This gave Davie the chance to become Bartley's deputy and obtain a commission as a lieutenant. Davie took full command three months later

---

[32] South Carolina Archives: S 111001, volume 9, p. 264.

[33] South Carolina Archives: S 213184, volume 9, pp. 24, 279.

[34] There is an argument over whether he committed suicide or was murdered. Cf., Blackwell P. Robinson, *William R. Davie* (Chapel Hill, NC: UNCP, 1957), pp. 19-22.

[35] Ibid.

[36] Spruce Macay (1755-1808); he was also law tutor to Andrew Jackson. Cf., *DNCB*.

[37] Of the 1st Rowan County Regiment and Rowan County Regiment; originally from Lancaster County, PA.

when Bartley was forced to step down.[38] He saw action at the Battle of Stono Ferry in June 1779, where he was wounded, and recuperated at Charleston, then Salisbury, where he resumed his law studies, receiving his certificate to practice in November.

Davie returned to fighting in 1780. He was promoted to major under Robert Irwin, and then colonel. In the last year of the war, Davie served as commissary-general under Nathanael Greene (1742-1786), the commander of the Southern Continental Army and a trusted friend of George Washington.

When hostilities ended in 1782, Davie moved east to Halifax to open a law practice.[39] His in-laws eased Davie into polite society and local and state politics, where he worked closely with Samuel Johnston and James Iredell against the anti-Federalist pro-Jeffersonian faction led by his uncle, his father-in-law's younger brother, Willie Jones (1741-1801), a member of the Royal White Hart Lodge and Joseph Montfort's son-in-law.[40]

---

[38] J.D. Lewis, *NC Patriots 1775-1783: Their Own Words, Volume 2, Part 2* (Little Rive, SC: published privately, 2012), p. 235, states that Bartley was court-martialled for intemperance. Other sources corroborate.

[39] His father-in-law, Allen Jones (1739-1807), was a member of the committee of safety for Halifax (1775); vice-president of the provincial congress (1776); speaker of the North Carolina senate (1778); a delegate to the continental congress (1779-80); a member of the North Carolina council of state (1782) and state senator (1783, 1784 and 1787).

[40] Willie Jones returned to North Carolina in the mid-1760s and entered politics in 1767, elected to represent Halifax County. He aligned with the eastern establishment and was close to Tryon, serving as his aide-de-camp at the Battle of Alamance and commanding a raid on Herman Husband's farm. But despite his planter background Jones became one of the main opponents of British rule in the colony. He was elected to all five provincial congresses and at the last was nominated to the committee tasked with drafting a new state constitution. Jones represented Halifax Town in the Commons (1777-78) and then Halifax County (1779-80). He also served in the continental congress and was a state senator (1782-92). Jones was an active supporter of UNC and served on the committee that founded the new state capital, Raleigh. He died there in 1801. A Deist, Jones

Willie Jones was an unlikely radical. Educated at Eton in England,[41] his father had been Robert 'Robin' Jones (1718-1766), formerly Lord Granville's agent in North Carolina and the attorney general for the province, who used his offices to accumulate one of the largest land holdings on the Roanoke River. His listings in the North Carolina Land Grant archives comprise thirty-four entries in Granville County alone and total in excess of 35,000 acres.[42]

Having inherited a share in his father's estate, Willie Jones, like his brother, was one of the wealthiest planters in the province with substantial plantations and more than 120 slaves. A firm loyalist until the mid-1770s, his conversion to the patriotic cause was rapid and absolute, and he became a leading states' rights radical, heading the political charge towards independence and advocating greater democracy.

Halifax had prospered in the pre-war period and this continued after Independence. The economy expanded and the town's wealthy elites emulated the mores of their Virginia and South Carolina neighbours with elegant Palladian homes and expensive entertainments. Halifax also became the temporary seat of the North Carolina legislature and with his path to political office smoothed by his wife's family, Davie was elected to the lower house in 1784. He also thrived professionally, building a successful law practice and investing his profits in land and slaves.

Although he played a supporting rather than leading role at the Philadelphia convention, Davie was central to the debates at Hillsborough and Fayetteville regarding the ratification of the Constitution, and to the introduction of a bill to charter a public university in the state - the University

---

instructed that his grave be unmarked and that 'my family and my friends are not to mourn'. Cf., Samuel Eliot Morison, 'The Willie Jones - John Paul Jones Tradition', *William and Mary Quarterly*, 16.2 (1959), 198-206, esp. 202.

[41] Eton College, then as now one of England's leading and most prestigious schools. Jones was thereafter despatched on a 'grand tour' of Europe.

[42] State Archives of North Carolina, North Carolina Land Grants database.

of North Carolina. The legislation was contentious and Davie's ability to co-opt political adversaries, including Willie Jones, demonstrated not only pragmatism but an ability and willingness to work across the political divide.

Despite his in-laws being active members of the Royal White Hart Lodge, Davie was initiated into freemasonry only in 1791 and in New Bern rather than Halifax. James Glasgow, then DGM, presided as master.[43] Within the year Davie had been nominated and elected grand master of North Carolina in succession to Samuel Johnston. The move was probably at Johnston's instigation and Davie's nomination was unopposed:

> Tuesday 11th December AD 1792 AL 5792
> Resolved that the following Brethren be put in nomination as Grand Officers for the ensuing year, to wit:
>
> Wm. R. Davie as Grand Master.
>
> Friday 14th December AD 1792 AL 5792
>
> J. Macon, Secy.[44]

Davie was not present at his installation on 30 December 1792 but presided a year later at the subsequent annual communication. There is no indication that he had previously been a master of a lodge other than the Grand Lodge of North Carolina.[45] The rapidity of Davie's masonic ascent and his unconventional initiation, passing and raising, about which little is known, suggest the intervention of senior figures within the state.[46] Davie was re-elected annually thereafter until 1799, when he was succeeded by William Polk.

---

[43] Minutes of the St John's Lodge, New Bern, 24 December 1791.

[44] GLNC Minutes.

[45] He does not appear in the minutes of the Royal White Hart Lodge until 24 June 1795.

[46] If there are parallels they are with the election of noble grand masters in England.

Although Johnston was a prominent political figure within the state, as grand master of freemasons he had made relatively modest progress. In the three years to December 1792, when he withdrew from office, only five lodges were warranted in North Carolina: Eagle Lodge, at Hillsborough in Orange County, whose warrant was granted on 9 January 1792; and Union, Raleigh, Democratic and Laurel Hill, whose warrants were granted in the eight-day period from 6 - 14 December. In contrast, during Davie's seven years in office, twenty-two new lodges were chartered or received a dispensation to continue working.

Lodge	*Location*	*Date of Warrant or Dispensation*
Union	Greenville, Pitt County	6 December 1792
Raleigh	Tarboro, Edgecombe County	11 December 1792
Democratic	Raleigh, Wake County	14 December 1792
Laurel Hill	Laurel Hill, Richmond County	14 December 1792
Malta	Germantown, Stokes County	18 January 1792 (disp.)
		14 December 1793
Hiram	Williamsboro, Granville County	15 April 1793 (disp.)
		17 December 1793
Pansophia	Carthage, Moore County	25 December 1793
Davie-Glasgow	Glasgow County	20 January 1795
Statesville	Statesville, Iredell County	25 January 1795
Columbian	Wayne County	26 November 1789 (disp.)
		9 December 1796
St Tammany	Nashville, Tennessee	17 December 1796
St Tammany	Wilmington, New Hanover County	2 December 1797
Phalanx	Charlotte, Mecklenburg County	2 December 1797

Stokes	Concord, Cabarrus County	17 December 1796 (disp.)
		2 December 1797
Freeland	Forks of the Yadkin, Rowan County	17 December 1706 (disp.)
		2 December 1797
Shallowford	Huntsville, Surry County	20 January 1795 (disp.)
		disp. cont'd 1796/7
Unanimity	Rockford, Surry County	2 December 1797
Beaufort	Beaufort, Carteret County	5 December 1797 (disp.)
		disp. cont'd 1798
St John's	Morganton, Burke County	17 December 1797 (disp.)
		disp. cont'd 1798
Sandy Run	Sandy Run, Bertie County	24 November 1798 (disp.)
		disp. revoked 1799
Jerusalem	Straights, Carteret County	9 December 1798
Friendship	Fort Barnwell, Craven County	4 December 1799
William R. Davie	Lexington, Davidson County	9 December 1798 (disp.), 6 December 1799
Rising Sun	Morganton, Burke County	16 December 1799
Davie	Ahoskie, Bertie County	16 December 1799
Hiram	Raleigh, Wake County	16 December 1799

Davie's call to become grand master in preference to freemasons of longer standing suggests he had an appeal across geographic lines. And it reflects an appreciation of his administrative skills and willingness to work on both sides of the aisle, something evident in the foundation of UNC.

The composition of the board of trustees and of the university's major donors underscores the extent of Davie's influence between 1789 and 1795, and how freemasonry became a unifying force within the state, bringing together politicians from east and west, and from both sides of Federalist-Jeffersonian rift.

Davie was elected state governor in 1798, standing on a Federalist ticket, and resigned as grand master thereafter. One year into his term, President Adams appointed him one of three envoys to Paris to negotiate an end to the undeclared naval war with France following publicity given to the 'XYZ Affair' - a demand by France for the continuation of debt repayment.[47]

When Davie returned to North Carolina in 1800 having agreed the Treaty of Mortefontaine, the political consensus in North Carolina had changed and Jeffersonian policies were in the ascendant. Davie failed to be elected to Congress and thereafter disengaged from politics. He sold his properties in Halifax and retired to his estate, *Tivoli*, in the Waxhaws. He was 49. Davie spent the following years farming, growing cotton and corn. He is buried in the Old Waxhaw Presbyterian Churchyard.

---

[47] Following the French Revolution, the United States refused to continue debt repayment on the grounds that it had been owed to the previous regime. When America sought to negotiate, France's representatives demanded a $250,000 bribe before substantive negotiations could commence. Plus ça change, plus c'est la même chose – nothing changes.

Chapter Twelve

A Masonic Education?

The University of North Carolina

Throughout the eighteenth century until the outbreak of hostilities with Britain, a minority of wealthy Carolina families sent their sons to university in England and Scotland, or to London's Inns of Court to read Law. War and post-war acrimony temporarily shut off those avenues and the drive to establish a university in North Carolina was viewed cynically by some as a means to provide a substitute education for the sons of the elites but funded by North Carolina's ordinary taxpayers.

Political opposition to the proposal to establish a public state university made much of its potential as an engine of privilege and a means to foster a permanent ruling class. And there were additional and specific concerns among the western counties, whose representatives in the legislature argued or suspected that the cost of construction and ongoing operating expenses would mean a poll tax that would not only reopen Regulator divisions but impact disproportionately those least likely to benefit.[1]

Such apprehensions were not unreasonable, not least since university donors gained not only kudos but a right to educate a son free from tuition fees. But this interpretation overly disparages the altruism of many of the founders for whom the university was a statement of intent to provide a tertiary education for those unable to afford a private eastern university, let alone Oxford or Cambridge, but of sufficient intellect. It was also a mechanism to reconcile political differences within the state and a masonic project. The university's curriculum would be designed to mirror the Enlightenment

---

[1] Cf., for example, Thomas Tyson's comments in: *CSRNC*, volume 21, p. 430: Minutes of the North Carolina House of Commons, North Carolina. General Assembly, 2 November - 22 December 1789.

philosophical mores that eighteenth-century freemasonry had embraced. And the institution would be led and governed by freemasons.[2]

A 20,000-acre gift of land warrants from Benjamin Smith, later governor of North Carolina, a nephew of the former provincial grand master for South and North Carolina and a member of St John's Lodge Wilmington, was the first major donation to support the university.[3] Others followed. And reflecting importance of freemasons and freemasonry in post-war civil and political society in North Carolina, more than two-thirds of the initial trustees who stewarded the construction and governed the development of the university were members of North Carolina's masonic lodges.[4]

Having obtained in-principle approval from the legislature, Davie's next step was to secure funding. On 21 December 1789 the legislature was persuaded to pass an act to endow the university with *escheat* assets - property that would revert to the state where the owner died without legal heirs. This raised the prospect of a potentially vast endowment that included Tennessee land given as a bounty for past military service. But although those tracts might eventually be sold to support the university, in the short term there was insufficient cash to pay for construction.

Obtaining immediate funding was a harder political struggle and Davie's motion to obtain a state loan was passed only narrowly in the Commons in December 1791 by 57 votes to 53, and by 28 to 11 in the Senate.[5] The next step was to determine where the university should be sited. Willie Jones

---

[2] Of the fifty-five trustees who would be appointed through to 1795, some thirty-six, possibly more, were freemasons. See appendix three.

[3] *CSRNC*, volume 21, p. 417: 'Resolved, that the thanks of the General Assembly be presented to Col. Benjamin Smith of Brunswick County for his very generous donation of Twenty Thousand Acres of Land to the University of North Carolina, and that this resolution be published in all the Gazettes of this State.' Smith served as grand master of the GLNC from 1808-10.

[4] See appendix three.

[5] The loan - US$10,000 - was later converted into an outright gift.

proposed a campus within fifteen miles of the geographical centre of the state, a compromise agreed by the trustees who approved in-principle the purchase of a 2,000 acre campus on which the university would be built and from which it would be supplied, and delegated the final choice of location to a sub-committee.

Various locations were short-listed and at each the trustees were offered inducements of land and cash, contingent on the university being built there.[6] It was no different at Chapel Hill in Orange County, around twenty-five miles from the new state capital at Raleigh, where local landowners offered some 1,390 acres and a contribution of almost £800. What *was* different was the scale of the prospective donations, which outweighed those elsewhere. The site was advantageous in other respects: equidistant between the Appalachians and the east coast; just west of the Fall Line Road running from Petersburg to Fayetteville; and close to the cross-state trail from New Bern to Salisbury. The combination swayed the committee and Chapel Hill was approved as the location for the university.

In the same manner that George Washington took his oath of office on a bible belonging to New York's St John's Lodge and laid the foundation of the Capitol wearing masonic regalia, North Carolina incorporated masonic ritual into the university's foundation ceremony and embraced masonic symbolism in its construction.

> On the twelfth instant, the Commissioners appointed by the board of Trustees of the University of this State met at Chapel Hill for the purpose of laying the cornerstone of the present building and disposing of the lots in the village. A number of the brethren of the Masonic order from Hillsborough, Chatham, Granville and Warren attended to assist at the ceremonies of placing the corner-stone, and the procession for

---

[6] Minutes of the Board of Trustees, 3-13 December 1792: reports regarding the site of the university.

William R. Davie laying the Cornerstone at the University of North Carolina
Detail from the Mural by Allyn Cox c.1960
Grand Lodge of North Carolina, Raleigh

the purpose moved from Mr Patterson's at 12 o'clock in the following order: the Masonic Brethren in their usual order of procession; the Commissioners; the trustees not Commissioners; the Hon. Judge Macay and other public officers; then followed the gentlemen of the vicinity. On approaching the south end of the building the Masons opened to the right and left, and the Commissioners, etc. passed through and took their places. The Masonic procession then moved on round the foundation of the building and halted with their usual ceremonies opposite to the southeast corner where William Richardson Davie, Grand Master of the fraternity, etc., in this State, assisted by two masters of lodges and four other officers laid the cornerstone, enclosing a plate to commemorate the transaction.[7]

> The Right Worshipful
> William Richardson Davie
> Grand Master
> The Most Ancient and Honorable Fraternity
> of Free Masons, in the State of North Carolina
> One of the Trustees of University
> of the Said State,
> And a Commissioner of the Same
> Assisted By
> The Other Commissioners and the Brethren
> of the Eagle and Independence Lodges
> On the 12th day of October
> In the Year of Masonry 5793
> And in the 18th year of American Independence
> Laid the corner stone
> of this edifice

Planning for the university's construction had begun the prior year with the first building to be completed twelve months after the stone laying. The original plan shows a single building running north to south but this was altered and a decision taken to build three separate blocks perpendicular to one another, albeit that it would take two decades to realise the complete design.

---

[7] *North Carolina Journal*, 30 October 1793. The stone laying took place on 23 October. It was the first public masonic event held under the auspices of the GLNC.

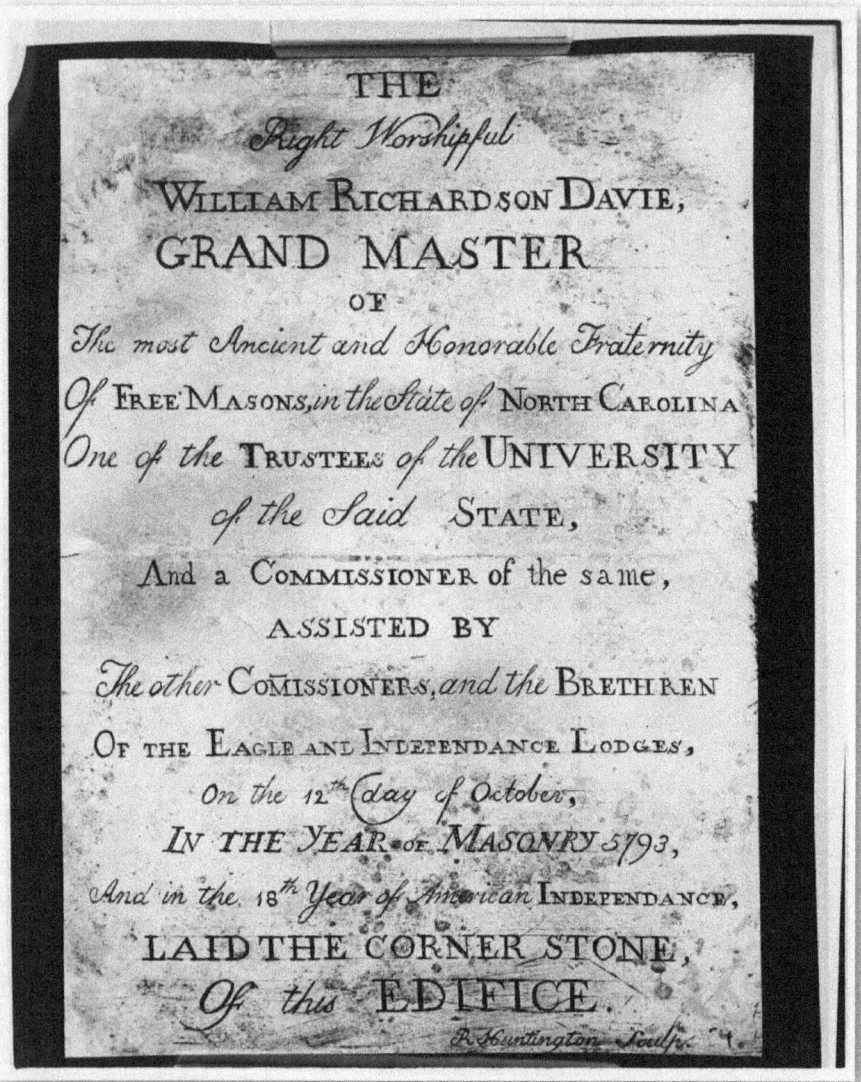

Cornerstone Plate of the University of North Carolina, 1793

The minutes of the trustees are silent on the rationale but the availability of finance would have been one obvious consideration, with construction and the related costs phased over a several years rather than incurred entirely at inception. Another was masonic symbolism.

It has been noted widely that the core of the UNC campus is laid out like a masonic lodge with the three main buildings situated in the east, west and south, and with an open north side. The Old Well in the centre of the open-sided quadrangle takes the place of a masonic alter. In this context the east building represents the master of a lodge; the west, the senior warden; and the south, the junior warden. The open north represents masonic darkness. The masonic associations of the university's founders suggests that such symbolism is unlikely to have been accidental.

Davie ensured that freemasonry's Enlightenment tenets became an integral part of the university's curriculum. His ideas for UNC were not based on the traditional classical education he had received at the College of New Jersey but on the writings of European moral philosophers such as John Locke,[8] Montesquieu,[9] Jean-Jacques Burlamaqui[10] and David Hume.[11] Their ideas introduced UNC's students to new concepts of government, including an understanding of empiricism and utilitarianism, and involved a syllabus that embraced science – physics, chemistry and mathematics.

The curriculum also contained other masonic characteristics. The principal tenets of freemasonry - Moderns and Antients - centred on religious

---

[8] John Locke (1632-1704), an English philosopher regarded as one of the most influential Enlightenment thinkers.

[9] Charles-Louis de Secondat, Baron de La Brède et de Montesquieu (1689-1755), a French moral philosopher (and freemason) known for his concept of the separation of constitutional powers.

[10] Jean-Jacques Burlamaqui (1694-1748), a Swiss theorist whose *Principles of Natural and Politic Law* and work on constitutionalism substantially influenced eighteenth-century American political thought.

[11] David Hume (1711-1776), a Scottish philosopher, empiricist, economist and historian.

toleration, including an embrace of deism and latitudinarianism, as well as moral self-improvement and spiritual self-awareness. Freemasonry also proselytised the concept of constitutional government, with masonic ritual altered in the 1720s to promote the concept of a 'supreme legislature' – a government marked by the separation of powers rather than absolute monarchy.

The overall approach was teleological, with eighteenth-century freemasons encouraged to pursue a belief in a divine being - 'the All-wise and Almighty Architect of the Universe',[12] and at the same time to interpret the world through rational observation:[13] 'Natural Philosophy is that Science which gives the Reasons and Causes of the Effects and Changes which naturally happens in Bodies... We ought to call into question all such things as have an appearance of falsehood, that by a new Examen we may be led to the Truth.'[14]

The latter concept became integral to freemasonry's core beliefs: 'As Masons we only pursue the universal Religion or the Religion of Nature. This is the Cement which unites Men of the most different Principles in one sacred Band and brings together those who were most distant from one another.'[15]

Importantly, freemasonry was supportive of revolution where a king was deemed to be in breach of his Lockean moral contract with those he governed. It was this philosophical argument that had provided the intellectual foundations for the Glorious Revolution and the justification for replacing James II with William and Mary. No longer would it be necessary to be

---

[12] J.T. Desaguliers, *The Newtonian System of the World: The Best Model of Government* (London, 1728), *Dedication*, pp. iii-iv.

[13] Cf., *Foundations*, esp. chapters two and six.

[14] Desaguliers, *Lectures in Mechanical and Experimental Philosophy* (London, 1717), *Foreword*.

[15] William Smith, *A Pocket Companion for Freemasons* (London: E. Rider, 1735), pp. 43-5.

a 'true liegemen to the king of England without any treason or falsehood', as had been the case in freemasonry's *Old Charges*.[16] People would instead be 'guided, not enslaved'.[17]

The same Enlightenment arguments supported the American Revolution and the colonies' quest for independence from Britain.

The trustees' objective was to provide North Carolina's future leaders with a secular rather than a classical religious education. As Davie wrote in his preamble to the curriculum, 'in every free government the law emanates from the people [and] the people should receive an education to enable them to direct the laws, and the political part of this education should be consonant to the constitutions under which they live'.[18] Harry Watson interprets this functionally: 'Davie clearly believed that popular self-government could never succeed unless the people's representatives learned to think as he did. Teaching them to do so was the intended mission of the University of North Carolina.'[19] He may be correct.

When Davie returned on 14 April 1798 to lay the cornerstone for the South Building in what would be his last public engagement as grand master of GLNC, he issued a dispensation to Eagle Lodge No. 19 to meet at the university and initiate Joseph Caldwell, the then presiding professor, together with other faculty members.

The dedication of the building saw the cornerstone 'laid by the Most Worshipful General Davie, Grand Master, assisted by a respectable number of the craft', following which 'an address was delivered by the Rev. Joseph

---

[16] *Watson* MS. Cf., *William Watson* MS in AQC *Antigrapha*, 3.4 (1891). The MS was copied in York in 1687. UGLE Library & Museum of Freemasonry, London: BE 42 WAT.

[17] Desaguliers, *The Newtonian System of the World*.

[18] Harry L. Watson, 'William Richardson Davie and the University of the People: Ironies and Paradoxes', 18 April 2006, Gladys Hall Coates University History Lecture, UNC, Chapel Hill.

[19] Ibid.

Caldwell, professor of mathematics, etc., on the effects of science and literature and their rapid progress in this country.'[20]

The initiation of Caldwell and other faculty members underlines and makes plain the masonic nature of the event, which would have been understood by all who attended:

> The procession was then formed by all the Brothers aforesaid clothed in masonic order, and in solemn form proceeded to the place destined; when a general procession was again formed in company with the Craft by all the above mentioned Gentlemen under the direction and superintendence of the most worshipful William R. Davie, Grand Master and Major General of the Militia in this State, in the following order:
>
> *Architect*
> *Mechanics and peasants*
> *Grand Music*
> *Teachers and Students of Chatham Academy*
> *Students of the University*
> *The Faculty of the University*
> *Gentlemen of the Bar*
> *The Hon. the Judges*
> *The Hon. the Council of State*
> *His Excellency the Governor*
> *The Trustees of the University*
> *The Masonic Craft with*
> *The Grand Master*

---

[20] *North Carolina Journal*, 7 May 1798.

Following the stone laying, 'the procession of the Craft was ... conducted by the Grand Master to the lodge room and after the business of the lodge was finished it was adjourned in due form'.[21]

There were then 166 students at UNC. The first student to be admitted, Hinton James,[22] was a member of St John's Lodge in Wilmington. He was also a member of the first literary club at the university and sequentially of both debating clubs, the Dialectic Society and then the Concord, later the Philanthropic Society, each of which were founded in 1795.

The Dialectic Society adopted the masonic square and compasses as its symbol and both debating clubs used masonic procedures. Secret ballots determined admission; an initiation ritual included a pledge to secrecy and the provision of benevolence for distressed members of each society; and in common with the procedures adopted in America's masonic lodges, the presidents of the Dialectic and Philanthropic societies wore hats as a symbol of their authority.

Each debating society adopted a colour, with the Dialectic Society opting for light blue and the Philanthropic Society white. The combination of the two colours represents the three degrees of Craft freemasonry. Intentionally or otherwise, when UNC's collegiate athletic teams were formed in 1888 they also took Craft blue and white as their colours, and they remain the colours of UNC today.

---

[21] *Proceedings of the Grand Lodge of North Carolina*, 1798.

[22] Hinton James (1776-1847), an engineer and later legislator. Elected to the state legislature in 1807, he served three terms; he was also mayor of Wilmington and a magistrate for New Hanover County.

Afterword

The counterpart to the post-war westward shift in North Carolina's population was the diminution in size and significance of many eastern towns and settlements. Freemasonry followed the same path as it expanded into the Piedmont and crossed the Blue Ridge Mountains into Tennessee. Fourteen predominantly eastern lodges surrendered their warrants or were dissolved prior to 1800, including Crown Point in Pitt County, Dornoch in Warren County, Royal William at Winton, and Unanimity at Edenton. But the counterpart was a broader membership base.

Where in the 1770s North Carolina had around ten lodges whose members were derived from the local elites - even in the Piedmont, at the beginning of the new century the number exceeded thirty with a membership that had been extended to include the aspirational middling and those lower down the social and economic ladder. Over the following two decades, some thirty new lodges would be constituted and ten cease to meet. It was a period of explosive growth for freemasonry, not only in North Carolina and Tennessee, but across America, with lodges chartered in nearly every town of size.

Freemasonry gained considerable appeal following Independence. Differences of religion and politics, between Hamiltonian Federalists and states' rights Jeffersonians, could, in theory, be bridged through freemasonry, with the Craft positioned as a unifying force that combined spirituality, benevolence and self-improvement with morality and equality. There were however also elements of self-interest, given that the lodge provided networking opportunities and political and business contacts, as well as mutual assistance.

But beneath a seemingly benign surface lay less agreeable realities. One of North Carolina's earliest masonic arguments was an internecine disagreement as to whether New Bern's St John's or Halifax's Royal White Hart should have precedence as the second-ranked lodge behind Wilmington.

New Bern's petition was presented as the restoration of its seniority and was delivered by Francois-Xavier Martin,[1] a notable attorney, jurist and publisher, who had given the masonic oration at Richard Caswell's funeral.[2]

The dispute threatened to destroy any sense of harmony at the GLNC meeting in December 1793 when St John's refused to recognise its 1791 charter and made it known that its claim to recover its prior status as 'Lodge No. 2' had the unanimous support of its membership who had resolved to 'retain, the old and established No. 2 and shall from this date be known by no other number'.[3] The lodge also committed to withholding payment of its fees to GLNC until the issue had been determined in its favour.[4]

Davie did not respond positively to what he viewed as a threat and encouraged grand lodge to halt any discussion of the matter until the fee arrears were satisfied.[5] He also instructed the grand secretary to write to St John's to inform the lodge that he viewed their behaviour as inappropriate, and ordered that a delegation appear at GLNC's next meeting to explain the lodge's conduct.[6]

St John's believed nonetheless that it had a valid case. After all, it was self-evident that the lodge pre-dated that at Halifax. Not only did St John's continue to refuse to pay its arrears but it now sought the support of other lodges. However, although St John's established a committee in July 1794 to bolster its case for recognition, no support was forthcoming from the broader North Carolina masonic community and it was forced to give way.

The dispute was resolved the following year with St John's obliged reluctantly to accept the decision of a grand lodge committee that without documentary

---

[1] François-Xavier Martin (1762-1846), originally from France, a newspaper proprietor, publisher, attorney and jurist.

[2] J.W. Bunney, *Freemason's Magazine, Or General and Complete Library*, volume 5 (London, 1796), p. 298.

[3] Minutes, St John's Lodge New Bern, 16 January 1792.

[4] Minutes, St John's Lodge New Bern, 10 October 1793.

[5] *Proceedings*, GLNC, 10 January 1794.

[6] Ibid.

Royal White Hart Lodge, Working Tools c.1770
From the Collection of the Grand Lodge of North Carolina

evidence of a claim to masonic seniority, the decision of grand lodge to issue a charter giving St John's precedence as 'No. 3' rather than 'No. 2' would stand.[7]

Other minor and major crises followed. Several members were censured or expelled for criminal or un-masonic behaviour. And a number of lodges divided into acrimonious factions or split. But arguably the most significant calamity occurred with the suspension of James Glasgow, the deputy grand master, 'until he shall make his innocence appear on a legal investigation'. When Glasgow was convicted of land fraud in 1800 and fined, he was expelled from the Craft and shortly afterwards relocated to Tennessee.

But in the scheme of things these and other similar occurrences were minor obstacles on the road to freemasonry's embrace by the social and political

---

[7] David Witherspoon of New Bern appeared before the GLNC on 20 January 1795 and accepted the decision on behalf of St John's.

establishment. Independence had, in Jefferson's words, brought with it a new sovereign - the American people - and freemasonry became for the next several decades the association of choice for what was seen as America's 'natural aristocracy' of leaders whose authority to rule was vested not in the circumstances of their birth but in their intellectual merit and 'moral virtues'.

The lodge became a destination for the aspirational, including those who wished emulate and associate with the nation's leaders. And freemasonry was positioned as the epitome of post-war Enlightenment virtues, embracing high moral principles, promoting education, and working for the benefit of the community as a whole.

This aspect was made tangible in the role that freemasonry played in the public dedication of new buildings, churches and monuments, from the Capitol in Washington to the UNC at Chapel Hill, where Davie presided not simply as the grand master of freemasons but as a war hero, a patriotic politician who had helped to frame the U.S. Constitution, and a senior figure in the state legislature.

The laying of the cornerstone of the first building at the University of North Carolina, 'Old East', and its consecration, took place in a ceremony that united the civic and masonic spheres and underscored freemasonry's affinity with the university. Davie dressed the cornerstone with corn, the masonic emblem of plenty, then dowsed it with wine to represent joy, and finally anointed it with oil to signify peace. He then tested it symbolically to ensure that it was square, level and plumb – the respective signs of the master, senior and junior wardens of the lodge.

Davie's actions represented an amalgam of operative and speculative freemasonry, after all, 'the Plumb is an instrument used by operative masons to try perpendiculars, the Square to square their work, and the Level to prove horizontals. But we, as Free and Accepted Masons, are taught to use them for more noble and glorious purposes. The Plumb admonishes us to walk uprightly in our several stations before God and man, squaring our actions by the Square of Virtue, ever remembering that we are traveling upon the Level of Time to that undiscovered country from whose bourne no traveller returns'.[8]

---

[8] Second Degree: Explanation of the Working Tools.

The Grand Lodge of North Carolina
Detail from the Mural by Allyn Cox c.1960
Grand Lodge of North Carolina, Raleigh

APPENDICES

Appendix One

'MODERNS' PROVINCIAL GRAND MASTERS IN NORTH AMERICA

Date of Patent	Name	Territory	Death
1730	Daniel Cox	New York, New Jersey & Pennsylvania	1739
1733	Henry Price	New England	1780
1735	Robert Hugh Lacy	Georgia	1738
1736	Robert Tomlinson	New England	1740
1736	John Hammerton	South Carolina	1762
1737	Richard Riggs	New York	1773
1743	Thomas Oxnard	North America	1754
1749	William Allen	Pennsylvania	1780
1751	Francis Goelet	New York	1767
1753	George Harison	New York	1773
1754	Peter Leigh	South Carolina	1759
1755	Jeremy Gridley	North America	1767
1760	Grey Elliott	Georgia	1787
1761	Benjamin Smith	South & North Carolina	1770
1766	Presley Thornton	Virginia	1769
1767	Sir John Johnson	New York	1830
1768	John Rowe	North America	1787
1770	Sir Egerton Leigh	South Carolina	1781

1771	Joseph Montfort	North Carolina[1]	1776
1773	Peyton Randolph	Virginia	1775
1773	Hon. Noble Jones	Georgia	1775

---

[1] The minutes of the Grand Lodge of England for 6 February 1771 record Montfort's deputation as 'Provincial G.M. for North Carolina', his warrant as 'Provincial Grand Master of and for America'.

Appendix Two

ROYAL WHITE HART LODGE, HALIFAX

The minute books between 1772 and 1783 are missing; the names of members of the lodge recorded in the minute books prior to this period are set out below:

Royal White Hart Lodge
Members, 1764-72 [1]

William Alexander[2]	James Auld
Thomas Bell	William Brimage
Nathaniel Brown	Charles Bruce
John Burnside	John Campbell
Benjamin Chapman[3]	Charles Copeland
John Deloach	Joseph Dickinson
Henry Dowse	James Duncan
William Edwards	Robert Frear
John Geddy	Robert Goodloe
Edward Hall	John Haller
Douglas Hamilton	Egbert Haywood
William Johnson	John Linton
David London	Joseph Long
Daniel Lovel	Henry Machen
William Martin	Andrew Miller
James Milner	Joseph Montfort
William Moore	Thomas Mutter

---

[1] John Raymond Shute Papers, #2889, Southern Historical Collection, The Wilson Library, UNC, Chapel Hill.
[2] William Alexander (d.1765).
[3] Also written as 'Chapmen'.

Robert Nelson   Julius Nicholas
William Parke   Charles Pasteur
Ambrose Ramsey   John Rogers
Frederick Schulzer   M. W. Sears
Frederick Simons   Henry Skipwith
David Stokes   Frederick Sumner
Peter Thompson   Peter Troughton
Robert Turnbull   Thomas Wild
  - Wright

Appendix Three

Trustees of the University of North Carolina, 1789-95 [1]

Samuel Johnston	Royal Edwin Lodge, Windsor
James Iredell	*No evidence*
Charles Johnson	Unanimity Lodge, Edenton
Hugh Williamson	St John's Lodge, Wilmington
Stephen Carbarrus	Unanimity Lodge, Edenton
Richard Dobbs Spaight	St John's Lodge, New Bern
William Blount	Johnston-Caswell Lodge, Warrenton[2] [?]
Benjamin Williams	St John's Lodge, New Bern
John Sitgreaves	*No evidence*
Frederick Hargett	St John's Lodge, Kinston
Robert Whitehurst Snead	Possible, but no primary evidence
Archibald MacLaine	St John's Lodge, Wilmington
Samuel Ashe	*No evidence*
Robert Dickson	Possible, but no primary evidence
Benjamin Smith	St John's Lodge, Wilmington
Samuel Spencer	*No evidence*
John Hay	Possible, but no primary evidence
James Hogg	Royal White Hart Lodge, Halifax
Henry William Harrington	*No evidence*
William Barry Grove	Phoenix Lodge, Fayetteville
Samuel Eusebius McCorkle	*No evidence*
Adlai Osborne	Old Cone Lodge, Salisbury
John Stokes	Royal White Hart Lodge, Halifax
John Hamilton	*No evidence*

---

[1] As from the Stephen Fletcher Trustee Plaque
[2] Possibly also Unanimity Lodge, Edenton.

Joseph Graham	Possible, but no primary evidence
John Williams	St John's Lodge, New Bern
Thomas Person	*No evidence*
Alfred Moore	St John's Lodge, Wilmington [?]
Alexander Mebane	*No evidence*
Joel Lane	Possible, but no primary evidence
Willie Jones	Royal White Hart, Halifax
Benjamin Hawkins	*No evidence*
John Haywood Sr.	Royal White Hart, Halifax
John Macon	Johnston-Caswell Lodge, Warrenton [3]
William Richardson Davie	Royal White Hart Lodge, Halifax
Joseph Dixson[4]	American George Lodge, Murfreesboro
William Lenoir	Unanimity Lodge, Surry County, and Liberty Lodge, Wilkes County[5]
Joseph McDowell Sr.	St John's Lodge, New Bern
James Holland	Fellowship Lodge, Rutherford County[6]
William Porter	Lodge unknown[7]
Alexander Martin	Phoenix Lodge, Fayetteville
James Kenan	St John's Lodge, Duplin County
James Glasgow	St John's Lodge, Kinston *et al*.
Charles Pettigrew	*No evidence*
Joseph McDowell Jr.	Rising Son Lodge, Morganton
William Polk	Phalanx Lodge, Charlotte
William Henry Hill	St John's Lodge, Wilmington
David Stone	*No evidence*

---

[3] Also referenced *inter alia* as a member of Dornoch Lodge, Bute County.

[4] 'Joseph Dickson'.

[5] I am grateful for Steven Campbell for this reference.

[6] Ibid.

[7] Named in *GLNC Proceedings*, Fayetteville, 19 November 1788, p. 6.

Thomas Blount	Johnston-Caswell Lodge, Warrenton
John Louis Taylor	Phoenix Lodge, Fayetteville
Thomas Wynns	Unanimity Lodge, Edenton [?]
	Royal William, Winton [?]
Josiah Collins	*No evidence*
John Moore	*No evidence*
John Skinner	*No evidence*
William Person Little	Royal William, Winton

Appendix Four

AMERICAN MILITARY LODGES DURING THE WAR OF INDEPENDENCE

There were relatively few military lodges attached to the Continental Army, partly as a result of the uncertainty surrounding the relationship between American freemasonry and the home grand lodges of England, Ireland and Scotland. J. Hugo Tatsch lists the following:[1]

Lodge	Date of Charter
St John's Regimental Lodge[2]	1775
American Union Lodge[3]	1776
Washington Lodge No. 10, Massachusetts Line[4]	1779
Unity Lodge No. 18, AYM, 17th Regiment of Foot[5]	n.a.
Lodge No. 19, AYM, Pennsylvania Artillery[6]	1779

---

[1] J. Hugo Tatsch, *Freemasonry in the Thirteen Colonies* (New York, NY: Macoy, 1933), pp. 202-22.

[2] St John's Regimental Lodge, chartered 24 July 1775 by the Provincial Grand Lodge of New York; later Lodge No. 18, Warwick, New York. Ceased 1825.

[3] Chartered 15 February 1776 by the St John's Grand Lodge of Massachusetts Authorised to work 'wherever your Body shall remove on the Continent of America, provided it's where no Grand Master is appointed'.

[4] Chartered 11 November 1779 by the Antients Grand Lodge of Massachusetts at West Point, New York.

[5] Chartered as No. 169, 12 November 1771, by the Grand Lodge of Scotland. The charter was captured at the Battle of Princeton on 3 January 1777 and a replacement charter was issued by Pennsylvania. Cf., Julius Sachse, *Old Masonic Lodges of Pennsylvania* (Philadelphia, PA: 1912), volume I, pp. 361-6.

[6] Lodge No. 19, AYM, Pennsylvania Artillery. Charter issued 18 May 1779 [?], probably by the Grand Lodge of Pennsylvania.

Lodge No. 20, AYM, North Carolina Line[7]	1779
Lodge No. 27, AYM, Pennsylvania Line[8]	not known
Lodge No. 28, AYM, Maryland Line[9]	not known
Pennsylvania-Union Lodge No. 29, AYM[10]	1780
Lodge No. 30 AYM, Delaware Regimental Line[11]	1780
Lodge No. 36 AYM, New Jersey Brigade[12]	1782

---

[7] Charter issued 4 October 1779[?] by the Grand Lodge of Pennsylvania.

[8] Lodge No. 27, AYM, Maryland Line [cited by Gould]. Date of warrant unknown. Grand Lodge of Pennsylvania.

[9] Lodge No. 28, AYM, Pennsylvania Line. Date of warrant unknown. Grand Lodge of Pennsylvania.

[10] Pennsylvania Line lodge. Charter issued 27 July 1780 by Grand Lodge of Pennsylvania. A second charter was subsequently issued to a second lodge with the same number.

[11] Charter issued in 1780, probably by the Grand Lodge of Pennsylvania.

[12] Charter issued 2 September 1782, probably by the Grand Lodge of Pennsylvania.

Appendix Five

MEMBERS OF THE ROSE TAVERN LODGE

Members of the Rose Tavern Lodge, London (1730)

John Kemp Esq., Master
John Pollexfen Esq., Senior Warden
[Edward] Lewis Esq., Junior Warden
Nicholas Pollexfen Esq.
Sir Thomas Twisden
The Hon. John Chichester Esq.
Israel Woolaston Esq.[1]
-    Hollings Esq.
Henry Butler Pacey Esq.
James Newman Esq.
William Mead Esq.
William Busby Esq.
John Hopkins Esq.
Mr Edward Lambert
Mr Richard Taylor
Mr Thomas Reason
Mr Thomas Alford
Mr Richard Gowland
Mr Samuel Cowne
Mr James Pringle
Mr John Ladyman
Thomas Moore Esq.

---

[1] Either Sir Isaac Woolaston (d.1750), a wool merchant, or his nephew, a solicitor in Chancery Lane. Cf. *The Gentleman's Magazine* (1806), part 1, p. 188.

Philip Barns Esq.
Mr Thomas Parsons
Sir Richard Everard
Mr Francis Riggs
Mr Thomas Rawlins
Brownlow Sherrard Esq.[2]
Mr Henry Walthoe
Mr John Hepden
Mr Richard Matthews
Mr John Eversman

---

[2] Sir Brownlow Sherrard, either the 3rd (1668-1736) or 4th baronet (1702-1748), a gentleman usher of the Privy Chamber. Cf., Chamberlain, *Magnae Britanniae Notitia* (1728), part 2, p. 56.

Appendix Six

The Will of William Herritage

IN THE NAME OF GOD AMEN. I, William Herritage, of Craven County, in the Province of North Carolina, Gent., Being Weak in Body But of Sound and Disposing Mind and Memory, Do this Eighth Day of March, in the Year of Our Lord, One Thousand, Seven Hundred and Sixty Nine, make and Declare this to be my Last Will and Testament in manner and Form following, that is to say:

Imprimis. I Will and require that my Body be Decently Interred at the Discretion of my Executors hereinafter named; and that my Just Debts and Funeral Charges be first paid and satisfied.

Item. I give and Devise to my Son, Heneage Herritage, the Land and Plantation where on I Dwell, commonly called Springfield, on the East Side of Jemmys Creek; the Land I bought of George Metts, lying on the West side of Jemmys Creek; and Fifty Acres of Land, which I took up in the front of the said Land I bought of George Metts, and Patened in my own name. Also, the Land I had of Adam Moore, Grand Father to my said Son, Heneage, called Jemmys Neck lying on the East side of Jemmys Creek, at and below the Mouth thereof; and Five hundred and twenty Acres of Land joining the above mentioned Land, Called Springfield, and the Lands of Adam Moore & others as per. the Patent for the same will at large appear, And to his Heirs Male Lawfully Begottn; and in default of such Issue, to my right Heirs forever. I also Give and Devise to my said son, Heneage Herritage, one Lott of Land lying in Newbern Town, and known in the plan of the said town by the number (21) to him and his Heirs and Asignes forever.

Item. I Give and Bequeath to my said Son, Heneage Herritage, One Negro Man Named Mingo, One Negro Man Named Sherbro, One Negro Woman Named Tamer, One Negro Man Named Ben, One Negro Man Named Bill son of a Negro Woman named Bettress, One Negro Man Named Sam, one

Negro Woman named Betto, one Negro Woman Named Kate, and all the Children she, the said Negro Woman Named Kate now hath or hereafter shall have, one Negro Woman Named Tortola and one Negro Child named Phebe, And to his Asignes forever.

Item. I Give and Devise to my Son, John Heritage, all that Tract of Land or Plantation Called Harrow, Situate in Dobbs County (but formerly Called Johnson County); and also my other Lands adjoining or lying or being within three miles of my said Plantation called Harrow; and also my Land on the North side of Neuse River called Atkins Banks, containing as per Patent, Six Hundred and Forty Acres: be the same more or less, and whereon the Town of Kingston now is Situate And to his Heirs Male Lawfully Begotten Forever and In Default of such Issue to my Right Heirs forever.

Item. I give and Devise to my said Son, John Heritage, one Lott of Land situate lying & being in New Bern Town, and known in the plan of the said town by the number (79), and to the Heirs Male lawfully begotten of his Body forever; and in Default of such issue then to my Right Heirs forever.

Item. I Give and Bequeath to my said son John Heritage, One Negro Man Named Pompey, one Negro Man Named Joe, one Negro Man Named Peter (a cooper), one Negro Man Named Jack, who once belonged to John Williams, One Negro Woman Named Venus, Daughter of my Negro Woman Named Phillis, one Negro Woman Named Maria, one Negro Boy named Solomon, one Negro Boy Named Jacob, one Negro Girl named Moll, one Negro Woman Named Lucy, and one Negro Boy Ben, her son, and also the Money due me by Bond from Stephen Lee for a Negro Woman Named Venus, which I sold to him, to the said John Heritage and His Asignes forever.

Item. I Give and Devise to my Son, William Martin Heritage, all that Tract of Land or Plantation Situate in Craven County, Commonly Called Fort Barnwell, and also all my lands Contiguous and adjoining thereto, and within three miles of any part thereof, which I now have or hereafter may have take up or purchase; And also, four hundred Acres of Land I Bought of Robert Hays, Situate in Dobbs County (but then called Johnston County), and also, all the Land I have, Or shall take up, or Purchase, adjoining the same, and to his Heirs Male, Lawfully Begotten forever; and in Default of such Issue to my Right Heirs forever. I also Give and Devise to my said son, William Martin Heritage, one Lot of Land Situate In the Town of New Bern, and known in the Plan of The said Town by the Number (22) and also the Front of the said Lot, to hold to him and his Heirs Male Lawfully Begotten, forever, and in Default of such Issue to my Right Heirs forever.

Item. I Give and Bequeath to my said son, William Martin Heritage, one Negro Man Named Scipeo, One Negro Man Named Caesar (a cooper), one Negro Man Named Tom, one Negro Man named London, One Negro Woman Named Jude Daughter of my Negro Woman Named Phillis, one Negro boy named Tom, one Negro Boy named Stephen, one Negro Man Named Balaam, one Negro Girl Named Suse Daughter of my Negro Woman Named Judith (Stephens Wife), one Negro Girl Named Winifred, and one Negro Girl Named Abigaal, two others Daughters of my Negro Woman Named Big Bess, and one Negro Boy Named Virgil son of my Negro Woman Named Priss, and to his Asignes forever.

Item. I Give and Devise to my Son in Law, Richard Caswell, a Piece or Parcell of Land, Situate in Dobbs County near Bear Creek, and above the Land Commonly Called Judge Smiths, on the North side of Neuse River, at or near a place called Herritages's Banks and the Lot or Land Situate in New Bern Town on the North Side, whereon Mary Dupree lived, and is known in the Plan of the said Town, by the Number (190), to him and his Heirs and Asignes forever; and also one Negro Man Named Prince, one Negro Woman Named Big Rose, one Negro Woman Named Phillis, one Mulatto Boy Named Hesketh, one Negro Boy Named Isaac, one Negro Girl Named Sabina and one Negro Man Named Stephen, and to his Asignes forever for the use and subject to the Incumbrances herein mentioned that is to say; That He, the said Richard Caswell, his Executors or Administrators, shall Annually pay to my Daughter, Susanna, and During her Natural life the Sum of Forty Pounds, Proclamation Money, one Fourth part thereof to be paid to her once in every three Months in each Year, during the Time of her life, Which said Forty Pounds to be paid as aforesaid, I Give to my said Daughter for her separate Maintenance and Support, without being subject to the payment of Debt or Debts now due, or which may hereafter become due, to any person or persons from the present Husband of my said Daughter, or to his will or demand in any Respect Whatsoever; And the said Negro Man Named Stephen to be Employed in Tanning and Making of Shoes for my several Children herein mentioned and their Families and Slaves.

Item. I Give and Devise to my Daughter, Elizabeth Heritage, one Lot of Land Lying in New Bern Town whereon Mary Dupree formerly Dwelt, being a Corner Lot and Numbered in the Plan of the Said Town (191), and also one other Lot of Land lying in the said Town of New Bern and Numbered in the Plan of the said Town (84), and to her Heirs Male Lawfully Begotten forever and for Default of such Issue then to my Right Heirs forever.

Item. I Give and Bequeath to my said Daughter, Elizabeth Heritage, one Negro Man Named Jack, which I bought of Mr John Campell, one Negro Woman Named Clarinda, one Negro Woman Named Judith (Stephens wife), one Negro Man named Harry, one Negro Boy Named Carolina, one Negro Man Named Mercury, one Negro Woman Named Big Bess, one Negro Girl named Jenny, Daughter of Big Bess, one Negro Girl Named Moll, Daughter of Clarinda, one Negro Girl Named Amy, and one Negro Boy Named Sam, the Two Children of Tamer, one Negro Boy Named Jupiter, one Negro Girl Named Hannah Daughter of Tortola, and one Negro Woman Named Priss, and to her Asignes forever.

Item. I Give and Devise to my Son in Law, Richard Caswell, Thirty Eight ft. of Land in Front, lying in New Bern Town running Easterly and Westerly and Southerly Down or across near the mouth of Trent River, which said piece of Land I bought of Nicholas Routledge, and is the same whereon my two Stores are situate, opposite the Lot Known in. the Plan of the said Town by the Number (15) with its Appurtenances, to hold to him his Heirs and Asignes forever.

Item. I Give and Bequeath to my Daughter, Anna, now Wife of George Lovick, Esq., One Negro Woman Named Little Rose, one Negro Man Named Cado, son of my Negro Woman Named Clarinda, one Negro Man Named Frank, one Negro Girl Named Sall, Daughter of my Negro Woman Named Judith, and one Negro Man Named Billey, my late Waiting Man, and to her Asignes forever.

Item. I Give and Bequeath to my Daughter Sarah, Now Wife of Richard Caswell, one Negro Man Named George, one Negro Man Named Moses, his Brother, one Negro Man Named Cato son of my Negro Woman Named Phillis, one Negro Boy Named Daniel son of my Negro Woman Named Tamer, one Negro Woman Named Judy Mother of my Negro Woman Named Tamer, and one Negro Woman Named Rachel, And to her Asides forever.

Item. It is my Will and Desire that my Son in Law, Richard Caswell have the Tuition and Guardianship of my Daughter, Elizabeth Heritage, and my Son, William Martin Heritage, and I do appoint the said Richard Caswell Guardian to my said Daughter and Son accordingly during their Minority.

Item. I will and Ordain that the Executor of this my last Will and Testament shall, with all convenient speed for and toward the performance of this my last Will and Testament (after my Decease) Bargain, Sell and Alien all those my Lands I shall be possessed of at my Death, except such as are by this Will Specially Given and Devised, and for the Doing, Executing and perfect finishing whereof I do by these Presents Give, Grant, Will, and Transfer to my said Executors and the Survivors or Survivor of them full power and Authority to Grant, Alien, Bargain, Sell, Convey, and Assure all my said Lands Except as before Excepted, to any Person or Persons and their Heirs forever, by all and every such Lawful Ways and Means in the Law, as to my said Executors or Survivors or Survivor of them, as their Council Learned in Law shall think Necessary.

Item. I Will and Desire That all the rest of my Personal Estate not herein particularly Given, be sold at Public Vendue to the Highest Bidder at twelve months Credit, the Purchaser or Purchasers to Give Bond with Sufficient

Securities, on Interest, before the Delivery of the Article or Articles, he, she or they, may or shall Purchase, and the Monies arising therefrom, together with the Monies arising from the sale of my Lands above directed to be sold, together with my outstanding Debts be Divided Equally among my Children hereafter Named, that is to say: my Son Heneage Heritage, my son John Heritage, my son William Martin Heritage, my Daughter Sarah Caswell, wife of Richard Caswell, my Daughter Anna Lovick, wife of George Phenny Lovick, and my Daughter Elizabeth Heritage, they first paying thereout to the Children my Daughter Susannah may, have Lawfully Begotten before she shall be a Widow if it shall so happen, on the arrival of the Eldest of them to the age of Fourteen Years, the sum of Fifty Pounds Proclamation Money with Interest from the Sale of my said Estate above mentioned until the same shall be paid to the said Children of my said Daughter Susannah, but in case she shall *** arrive to the age of Fourteen, that then and in such case the said Fifty Pounds above mentioned shall be paid to her my said daughter Susannah with the Interest due to the time the same shall be paid her, for her own proper use and behoof forever.

Item. I Will and Direct that my Executors hereafter named, out of the Monies arising by and out of the sale of my Lands and Personal Estate above directed to be sold, pay unto the Servant I may have living with me as a House keeper at the time of my Death, the sum of Ten Pounds Proclamation money Unto whom I give and Bequeath the same forever, to be paid within Six months after my Decease.

And Whereas I, the Said William Heritage, sometime between the Years of our Lord, one thousand seven hundred & forty four, and One thousand seven hundred and forty eight, did by four several Deeds of Gifts Give to four of my Children, to wit: Heneage Heritage, Sarah Heritage, Anna Heritage, and Susannah Heritage, Sundry Pieces or parcels of Land lying in Craven and Johnston Counties; and also sundry Goods and Chattels, Which said Several Deeds I kept in my own Custody not having suffered them or any of them to be proved or acknowledged in order to Alter, Destroy, and Revoke, or other wise to make void the same as I thereafter should or might think proper, Since the Execution of which said Deeds, the same are lost, mislaid or privately taken out of my Custody so that I could not now cannot Alter, Revoke, Destroy and make void the same as my intention is to do could I find and get Possession of them, Wherefore, to prevent any Disputes or Law Suits which may arise Between my Children after my Decease, for or by Reason of, the Gift to them, or any of them of any Lands, Goods or Chattels, contained or mentioned in the above mentioned Deeds, which said Deeds I do hereby Revoke, Disannull, and Make Void, to all intents and purposes as if the same had never been made, Therefore, it is hereby, Provided always, and my further Will is, and I hereby Expressly Declare, that if my Son or Sons, Daughter or Daughters, Legatees, and Divisees herein mentioned or their or either of their Husbands, or their or either of their Heirs, or other Legal Representative or Representatives, shall at any time hereafter Controvert or Oppose any Part of this my Will, or shall Obstruct or hinder the admittance of all or any of the before mentioned Legatees and Devises or their Heirs, or any other Legal Representatives or Representative, of, in, or to, any of the Hereditaments, Lands, Tenements, Goods or Chattels, or other the Premises hereby Respectively given them as aforesaid, or shall at any time after such their, or any of their Admittance and Possession either in Law or Equity or otherwise Molest, Sue, or Trouble any such Legatee or Divisee whereby, to put him, them, or any of them, out of or get, or take possession of the same Premises or any part thereof, for or by Reason of the Deeds of Gifts as aforesaid Made and above mentioned, or for, or upon account of my not having cancelled or otherwise made Void the same * * * but not otherwise, & I hereby Revoke and make Void the Legacy, Estate, Share, and Interest of her, him or them, my above mentioned Son, or Sons, Daughter, or Daughters, Legatees or Devisees aforesaid. or her or their Respective Husbands, and of their Respective Heirs, Executors and Administrators, and other Legal Representative or Representatives, of, in and unto, the before mentioned Legacies and Devises so given to them as aforesaid, and then, and in such case, but not Otherwise, I hereby Give, Devise, and Bequeath all such said Estate & Estates, Legacies, and Bequests hereby given, from such of them, my said Son or Daughter, or their, or either of their, Legal Representative or Representatives as shall so Controvert, Obstruct, oppose or Molest all, or any of the before mentioned Legatees or Divisees in manner aforesaid, unto such Legatee or Legatees, Devisee or Devisees, who by Means thereof shall be Prejudiced or suffer thereby, the same to go and be paid to *** use of, and be paid to such Legatee or Legatees, Devisee or Devisees so Prejudiced, and to their Respective Heirs, Executors and Administrators, or other Legal Representative or Representatives proportionably according to His Her, or their, loss or damage sustained by means thereof. Provided, nevertheless, that if my said Son or Sons, Daughter or Daughters, Legatee or Legatees, aforesaid and all other persons Lawfully Claiming Any Estate, Right or Interest of in or to the Premises by, from or under them,— either of them shall and do as soon as may be, or can be after my Decease Ratify and confirm this my Will, and also Release unto the said other Legatees or Devisees Respectively all their Estate Rights Title and Interest of, in, and to the several Estates, Monies, Legacies, Devises & Premises so by me hereby Respectively Given as aforesaid, then ;—and in that case, the last before mentioned Proviso shall be void and of none effect, anything therein contained to the contrary in any wise Notwithstanding.

And Lastly, I hereby Make, and Ordain, and Appoint, my Son in Law, Richard Caswell, and my Sons, Heneage Heritage and John Heritage, Executors of this my Last Will and Testament, which is comprised in three sheets of paper Wrote on Every side thereof, hereby Revoking all other and former, Wills by me heretofore made, and Ratifying and confirming this to be my Last Will and Testament and none other.

In Witness whereof, I have hereunto put and affixed my Hand and Seal the day and year first above written.

WILLIAM HERRITAGE

Appendix Seven

Phoenix Lodge No. 8[1]

James Porterfield,[2] Worshipful Master
John Winslow,[3] Senior Warden
Duncan McAuslan, Junior Warden
Samuel Murley, Secretary
David Anderson, Treasurer
David McNeill, Senior Deacon
Robert Norriss, Junior Deacon
Lee DeKeyser,[4] Steward
John Burke, Steward

Thomas Branton	James Brenan
Richard Cochran	William Cochran
Roger Cutlar	Dolphin Davis
Thomas Davis[5]	Robert Donaldson
Guilford Dudley	John Earle
Edward Etting	James Etting

---

[1] Membership Roster at the 1788 Installation Meeting. Cf., Edward Lee Winslow, *An Address Containing the History of Phoenix Lodge No. 8 from its Formation: Delivered Before the Officers and Members, at the Public Installation of the Officers, December 24th, 1849, by Edward Lee Winslow, Worshipful Master*: https://www.phoenixlodge8.com/history/historical-documents-we-hold/.

[2] James Porterfield (d.1795), a merchant and member of the North Carolina Commons (1791).

[3] John Winslow (1765-1820), president of the Bank of Cape Fear, Fayetteville, and a member of the North Carolina Commons (1815-19). His son, Warren, was a lawyer, state senator and speaker of the state senate.

[4] Colonel Lehancius DeKeyser, an ensign and adjutant, then 2nd lieutenant 1st NC Regiment, later, captain and lieutenant colonel in the Georgia militia.

[5] Member of the North Carolina Commons (1803, 1809, 1814).

William Barry Grove
Richard Henderson
James Howat
James Leonard
Peter McArther
Walter McNaughton
Robinson Mumford
John Porterfield
John Sibley
Elisha Stedman
Peter Tarbee
James Thorburn
J. Williamson

Richard Hallett
Caleb Dana Howard
David Kerr
Saunders Malborne
Robert McFarlan
William Meng
John Naylor
Isaac Sessions
Oliver Spear
Peter Strong
John Louis Taylor[6]
Daniel Wheaton
Joshua Winslow

---

[6] First chief justice of the North Carolina State Supreme Court; member of the North Carolina Commons (1792-1794).

Selected Bibliography

The raw material for this book has been found largely in primary sources of which key repositories were the *Colonial and State Papers of North Carolina* (online at http://docsouth.unc.edu/csr/); the Special Collections at the Wilson and University Libraries at the University of North Carolina at Chapel Hill; and the UK's National Archives. Among the latter should be mentioned the *Houghton Papers* within the Manuscripts Collection at the University Library, University of Cambridge, and data within the *Calendar of State Papers Colonial, America and West Indies*, the *Calendar of Treasury Books and Papers*, the *Calendar of State Papers*, the *Journals of the Board of Trade and Plantations*, the *House of Lords' Journals*, the *House of Commons' Journals*, and the *House of Commons Parliamentary Papers*. The records of individual lodges and grand lodges on both sides of the Atlantic have also proved invaluable, as has original correspondence within the collections of the Library & Museum of Freemasonry, Great Queen Street, London.

Biographical information has been sourced widely but two of the most valuable repositories are the *Dictionary of North Carolina Biography* (William Powell (ed), (Chapel Hill, NC: UNCP, 1979-1996) and online at https://www.ncpedia.org/category/entry-source/dictionary-no); and the *Oxford Dictionary of National Biography*, available in print and online at http://www.oxforddnb.com/. Data concerning North Carolina land grants are accessible at State Archives of North Carolina, North Carolina Land Grants Images and Data (www.nclandgrants.com). Digitised copies of eighteenth-century British and (some) Irish newspapers are within the British Library's *17th and 18th Century Burney Collection Database*. The collection is available online via Gale Databases. Digitised copies of early American newspapers are located more disparately and relatively few are free to access. Some early English lodge records are accessible via John Lane's Masonic Records, 1717-1894, version 1.0 at www.hrionline.ac.uk/lane, although caution should be used since not all the material is accurate. A useful guide to early eighteenth century London is John Strype's *A Survey of the Cities of London and Westminster*, online at https://www.dhi.ac.uk/strype/. But the most useful repositories are probably British History Online at http://www.british-history.ac.uk/catalogue/primary-sources, and the Victoria County Histories, especially William

Page (ed), *A History of the County of London: Volume 1, London Within the Bars, Westminster and Southwark* (London, 1909) at http://www.british-history.ac.uk/vch/london/vol1.

In addition to the material detailed below, the reader may wish to refer to the bibliographies in *Loyalists & Malcontents* and *Foundations*. The former relates predominantly to eighteenth-century South Carolina and the latter to seventeenth and eighteenth-century England.

SELECTED PRIMARY SOURCES

Charter of Carolina, 24 March 1663, revised 30 June 1665. North Carolina Office of Archives and History, Raleigh, NC. Online at http://avalon.law.yale.edu/17th_century/nc01.asp.

Anderson, James. *The Constitutions of the Freemasons*. London: John Senex & John Hooke, 1723.

- *The Ancient Constitutions of the Free and Accepted Masons*. Enlarged Second Edition. London: B. Creake, 1731.
- *The new book of constitutions of the antient and honourable fraternity of free and accepted masons*. London: Caesar Ward and Richard Chandler for Anderson, 1738.
- *The Constitutions of the Ancient and honourable fraternity of Free and Accepted Masons*. Revised and enlarged by John Entick. London: J. Scott, 1756.

Anonymous [Samuel Spencer]. *A Defence of Freemasonry*. London: published privately, 1765.

Barlowe, Arthur. *The First Voyage to Roanoke, 1584*. Published in Richard Hakluyt, *Principal Navigations, Voyages, Traffiques and Discoveries of the English*. London: 1589.

Dashwood, J.R. *Early Records of the Grand Lodge of England according to the Old Institutions*, Quatuor Coronatum Antigrapha, Volume XI. London: QC, 1958.

- *The Minutes of the Grand Lodge of Freemasons of England 1740-58*, Masonic Reprints, vol. XII. London: QC, 1960.

Dermott, Lawrence. *Ahiman Rezon*. London, 1756. Cf., also later editions published in London, Dublin and Philadelphia.

Dobbs, Arthur. *An Essay on the Trade and Improvement of Ireland.* Dublin, Ireland: J. Smith & W. Bruce, 1729.

Grimes, J. Bryan. *North Carolina Wills and Inventories.* Raleigh, NC: Trustees of the Public Libraries, 1910.

Lane, John. *Masonic Records 1717-1894*: http://www.hrionline.ac.uk/lane/index.php

Richmond, Charles. *A Duke and His Friends: The Life and Letters of the Second duke of Richmond.* London: Hutchinson & Co., 1911. Reprinted Husain Press, 2008.

Songhurst, W.J. *The Minutes of the Grand Lodge of Freemasons of England 1723-1739.* Masonic Reprints, vol. X. London: QC, 1913.

Strype, John. *Survey of London and Westminster.* London, 1720.

SELECTED SECONDARY SOURCES

Barratt, Norris S. & Sachse, Julius S. *Freemasonry in Pennsylvania, 1727-1907.* Philadelphia, PA: Grand Lodge of Philadelphia. Vol's I (1908), II (1909) & III (1919).

Barzilay, Karen Northrop. *Fifty Gentlemen Total Strangers: A Portrait of the First Continental Congress.* PhD Dissertation to the Graduate Faculty of The College of William and Mary, VA: Ann Arbor, 2009.

Berman, Richard. *Foundations of Modern Freemasonry.* Brighton: Sussex Academic Press, 2011.

- *Foundations*, second revised edition, 2014.
- *Schism: the Battle that Forged Freemasonry.* Brighton: Sussex Academic Press, 2012.
- *Espionage, Diplomacy & the Lodge.* Oxfordshire: The Old Stables Press, 2017.

Bullock, Stephen. *Revolutionary Brotherhood: Freemasonry and the Transformation of the American Social Order, 1730-1840.* Chapel Hill, NC: UNC Press, Institute of Early American History and Culture, 1996.

Calder, Jenni. *Scots in the USA.* Edinburgh: Luath Press, 2005.

Carpenter, Audrey T. *John Theophilus Desaguliers. A Natural Philosopher, Engineer and Freemason in Newtonian England.* London: Bloomsbury, 2011.

Chamberlayne, John. *Magnae Britanniae Notitia.* London: various editions.

Clark, Peter. *British Clubs and Societies 1580-1800.* Oxford: OUP, 2000.

Crittenden, Charles C. *The Commerce of North Carolina, 1763- 1789.* New Haven, CN: YUP, 1936.

Dobson, David. *Scottish Emigration to Colonial America, 1607-1785.* Athens, GA: University of Georgia Press, 2004.

Dyer, Colin. *The Grand Stewards and Their Lodge.* London: Grand Steward's Lodge, 1985.

Edgar, Walter B. and Bailey, N. Louise (eds). *Biographical Dictionary of the South Carolina House of Representatives, 1692-1775.* Columbia, SC: USC Press, 1977.

Ekirch, A. Roger. *'Poor Carolina': Politics and Society in Colonial North Carolina, 1729-1776.* Chapel Hill, NC: UNCP, 2011.

Gould, Robert Freke. *History of Freemasonry Throughout the World.* New York, NY: Charles Scribner's Sons, 1936, vol. 5. (reprint)

- *The History of Freemasonry: Its Antiquities, Symbols, Constitutions, Customs, Etc.* London: J. Beacham, 1885.

Gwynn, Robin. *Huguenot Heritage.* Brighton: Sussex Academic Press, 2001.

Harland-Jacobs, Jessica. *Builders of Empire: Freemasonry and British Imperialism, 1717-1927.* Chapel Hill, NC: UNC Press, 2007.

Haywood, Marshall De Lancey. *The Beginnings of Freemasonry in North Carolina and Tennessee.* Raleigh, NC: Hayward, 1906.

Hughan, William J. & Stillson, Henry Leonard. *History of the Ancient and Honorable Fraternity of Free and Accepted Masons, and Concordant Orders.* Boston, MA: Fraternity Publishing Co., 1895.

Kolchin, Peter. *American Slavery: 1619-1877.* New York, NY: Hill & Wang, 2003.

Lee Lawrence. *The Lower Cape Fear in Colonial Days.* Chapel Hill, NC: UNCP, 1965.

Lennon, Donald R. & Kellam, Ida Brooks (eds). *The Wilmington Town Book, 1743-1778.* Raleigh, NC: Division of Archives and History, North Carolina Department of Cultural Resources, 1973.

Library Committee of the Grand Lodge of Pennsylvania. *The History of the Grand Lodge of Pennsylvania.* Philadelphia, PA: Grand Lodge of Pennsylvania, 1877.

Mackey, Albert G. *History of Freemasonry in South Carolina.* Columbia, SC: South Carolinian Steam Press, 1861.

Massey, Gregory D. *John Laurens and the American Revolution.* Columbia, SC: USC Press, 2000.

Merrens, Harry Roy. Colonial North Carolina in the eighteenth Century. Chapel Hill, NC: UNCP, 1984.

Morgan (ed.), Edmund S. *Prologue To Revolution: Sources And Documents On The Stamp Act Crisis, 1764-1766.* Chapel Hill, NC: UNC Press, 1959.

Parramore, Thomas C. *Launching the Craft: The First Half-Century of Freemasonry in North Carolina.* Raleigh, NC: GLNC, 1975.

Powell, William S. *North Carolina Through Four Centuries.* Chapel Hill, NC: UNCP, 1989.

• *North Carolina. A History.* Chapel Hill, NC: UNCP, 1977.

Powell, William S. & Hill, Michael. *The North Carolina Gazetteer*, 2nd edition: *A Dictionary of Tar Heel Places and Their History.* Chapel Hill, NC: UNCP, 2010.

Puckrein, Gary A. *Little England: A Plantation Society and Anglo-Barbadian Politics, 1627-1700.* New York, NY: NYUP, 1984.

Sachse, Julius S. *Old Masonic Lodges of Pennsylvania, Moderns & Ancients, 1730-1800.* Philadelphia, PA: 1912.

Sedgwick, Romney. (ed.). *The History of Parliament: the House of Commons, 1715-1754.* Martlesham: Boydell & Brewer, 1970.

Tatsch, J. Hugo. *Freemasonry in the Thirteen Colonies.* New York, NY: Macoy, 1933.

Taylor, Alan. *Slavery and War in Virginia, 1772-1832, The Internal Enemy.* New York, NY: W.W. Norton, 2013.

JOURNAL ARTICLES

There are multiple relevant journal articles and far more that are complementary to what is discussed in this work. Those cited in the footnotes provide no more than a starting point. Readers are recommended to use *JSTOR* (www.jstor.org), which provides access to an unrivalled collection of academic journal articles; *Academic Search Complete* (www.ebsco.

com/products/research-databases/academic-search-complete); *Early English Books Online - EEBO*; and *Eighteenth-Century Collections Online* – ECCO. I would also recommend reviewing early editions of *NOCALORE* - the *Transactions of the North Carolina Lodge of Research*, No. 666, A.F. & F.M. (Monroe, NC), especially volumes I, II, III, IV, VI, VIII, IX and X; and selected articles from *Ars Quatuor Coronaturum*, the *Transactions* of Quatuor Coronati Lodge, No. 2076, EC.

THE OLD
STABLES
PRESS

• Oxfordshire •

www.ingramcontent.com/pod-product-compliance
Lightning Source LLC
Chambersburg PA
CBHW031134160426
43193CB00008B/133